THE PERSUASIVE EDGE

MYLES MARTEL, Ph.D.

THE PERSUASIVE EDGE

The Executive's Guide to Speaking and Presenting

A REVISED AND EXPANDED
EDITION OF THE FORMERLY TITLED
BEFORE YOU SAY A WORD

Fawcett Columbine ▪ New York

To my wife, Susan, and my son, David.
Their support was total—
and so is my appreciation.

CONTENTS

ACKNOWLEDGMENTS

So many people were enormously supportive in helping to make *The Persuasive Edge* a reality.

I am particularly indebted to:

Betsy Rapoport, my editor, for her keen editorial insights, consummate professionalism, and steady, contagious confidence.

Libby and Bob House for their splendid advice and encouragement.

Irv Rockwood, my literary agent, for his solid guidance.

Bill Anixter, Peter Bloom, Joachin Bowman, Fred Buchstein, Jeff Close, Tom Herskovits, Carolyn Keefe, Landon Parvin, Frank Ryan, Margo Schleman, John Vlandis, and Harold Zullow for their excellent ideas.

Martha Brown, for her fine illustrations.

Jean Reagan, my secretary, for her superb typing assistance and uncommon patience.

Peggy Ruggiero, my assistant, for operating Martel & Associates smoothly as I devoted my energies to writing this book.

Finally, I wish to thank the scores of people who have sought our counsel over the years. Their support is the bedrock for this book.

Part I

THE PREMESSAGE PHASE

Chapter 1

YOUR ROLE AS PERSUADER

Persuasion is a vital part of your leadership ability, management know-how, and communication with the world around you. Not a day goes by when you do not attempt to persuade some individual or group to accept your point of view or when some individual or group does not try to exert its influence on you.

Consider these typical business scenarios involving persuasion:

Persuading your boss to allow you to hire another staff member.

Persuading a committee to approve a budget.

Persuading your banker to give you a loan.

Persuading financial analysts that your firm is an attractive investment.

Persuading your board of directors that you are operating the firm well.

Persuading your sales people to work harder.

Persuading your assembly-line staff not to compromise safety for productivity.

Persuading a key member of your management team to take a new, difficult assignment.

Persuading the media that your firm handled a difficult situation, for example, a layoff, plant closing, or crisis, responsibly.

Persuading a current client or customer to continue to use your firm.

Persuading a prospective client or customer to select your firm.

Persuading a quality candidate to join your firm.

PERSUASION DEFINED

What is persuasion? It is a process of selecting and arranging ideas, words, vocal and body cues, and controlling an environment to modify the audience's attitude(s) or behavior. The following characteristics of the process will help you to understand better the challenges behind capturing the persuasive edge:

Persuasion is complex. As you seek to persuade, you are attempting to bridge an attitudinal gap between yourself and your audience. If no difference existed, persuasion would be superfluous. But when differences do exist and communication bridges need to be built, the construction process involves a host of factors to make the bridges sturdy. These factors include precise goal setting; accurate analysis of the audience, setting, and occasion; the appropriate selection of ideas, support, and words; good organization; plus the ability to transmit your message credibly and convincingly.

Persuasion is often inherently competitive. If your point of view and mine do not match, they are competing. When I seek to persuade you, I create within you a conscious or subconscious feeling of competition between your attitudes, values, or needs (including your priorities) and mine.

Persuasion is frequently difficult. Although the inherent complexity and competitiveness of persuasion make it difficult, the difficulty is compounded manifold by the deep roots of our attitudes plus our natural resistance to change.

Persuasion is incremental. Because persuasion is complex, competitive, and difficult, people's attitudes do not normally change dramatically when someone attempts to persuade them. They "move" in small increments—by degrees. The realistic persuader, therefore, must establish goals and expectations reflecting this fact, knowing full well that one presentation may be but a single step in an overall persuasive campaign.

Persuasion is dynamic. As you attempt to persuade your audience, their conscious and subconscious reactions to you and your message at any given time are in constant flux, vacillating in response to the constellation of stimuli generated by your message, their own mind-sets, and the environment around them. As a persuader, your role is to do everything possible to ensure that the stimuli of your message (including your delivery) dominate any competing stimuli and to sustain your persuasive momentum as effectively as possible.

Persuasion is an art. No exact scientific formula exists for influencing others to believe or act in a predetermined manner.

Although no exact formula or recipe exists for capturing the persuasive edge, a large body of insights does exist to guide us as persuaders. This book, which draws on these insights and relies heavily on my own experience as a communication advisor to America's corporate and political leaders, is designed to serve as your "on-call" advisor for a wide range of communication challenges.

The first major section, "The Premessage Phase," walks you through the major steps necessary to plan a persuasive speech or presentation. In essence, it presents you with an efficient management system to help you eliminate surprises, enhance your confidence level, and hit your target audience dead center. You will learn how to set goals for your audience, perform audience analysis and advance work, assess the needs of your target, plan and outline an effective speech, research your points, and select appropriate visual aids.

The second section, "Delivering Your Message," focuses on the presentational aspects of your message. You will learn, first of all, how to overcome speech anxiety—the number one concern facing so many people I advise—regardless of your present level of expertise or self-confidence. In addition, you will receive practical, to-the-point insights regarding the advantages and disadvantages of using scripted, memorized, and extemporaneous speeches. I will highlight the significance of nonverbal communication and introduce you to the Martel Method, a systematic game plan I've developed for practicing speech delivery—a method that has helped literally hundreds of the people my consulting firm advises. Finally, there is a chapter on how to prepare for question-and-answer sessions, an essential skill which is often undervalued during the preparation process.

The third section, "The Media," provides a solid foundation for dealing with the print and electronic media in a wide variety of settings, e.g., one-on-one interviews, news conferences, and crisis situations.

The fourth section, "Special Challenges," covers a wide range of settings and skills that call for special counsel: ceremonial speaking, meetings and teleconferences, panels and debates, and executive testimony. In addition, this section contains a collection of discussions related to preparing for team presentations, hiring a speechwriter, selecting a guest speaker, choosing a consulting firm, and persuading an executive to work with a communication consultant.

One of my favorite expressions is, "There is no such thing as a perfect communicator." However, we can all learn to improve this skill. The challenge each of us faces is to accept this realization and to make a commitment to become more effective, persuasive communicators. *The Persuasive Edge* will help make that commitment pay off.

Chapter 2

GOAL SETTING

What is the genesis of your speech or presentation? In many cases, you will have been invited by someone else to give it and have little choice but to accept—for example, your boss wants you to make a presentation at an important meeting. In some cases, you'll have more freedom of choice; you may have little or no obligation to the inviting party and will have the option to decide whether or not you want to speak or present.

If you fall into the latter category—if you have greater freedom of choice—consider carefully not only the rewards and risks of making the presentation but also the advantages and disadvantages of the speech or presentation as a medium of communication.

ADVANTAGES OF A
SPEECH OR PRESENTATION

- It is time-efficient. It allows you to reach many people at once rather than communicating with them one at a time.
- It is personal. It allows the strength of your personality and leadership to give you the persuasive edge that written communication cannot capture.

- It is interactive and flexible. The feedback you receive from your audience allows you to adjust your message on the spot, giving you another persuasive advantage not offered by written communication.

DISADVANTAGES OF A SPEECH OR PRESENTATION

- Logistically, it may be difficult to assemble the "right" people at the "right" time.
- Audiences are conditioned to tune out poor speakers.
- The content of your message may be too complex for oral presentation and therefore may be more conducive to written communication.
- Speeches are frequently one-shot opportunities. If your speech doesn't work, your message may have limited potential in another medium.
- People often remember more about the tone or feeling of a speech or presentation than they do its content.

GOAL SETTING

If you decide that the advantages of making a speech or presentation outweigh the risks—or if you have no choice in the matter—you're now ready to take the first major step in the preparation process: defining your goals.

Goal setting allows you to proceed with a sense of purpose and direction. It helps you to set priorities, apportion time, and pinpoint an organizational approach and persuasive strategy for your message. It automatically imposes a strict litmus test for what you should and should not include in your message, thereby increasing the likelihood that your message will not be diluted by superfluous material that can impede your persuasive momentum.

Goal setting helps you to counter the temptation to allow the time allocated for your presentation to unduly influence the preparation process. A typical query from one of my clients is, "I was told that I have a thirty-minute slot on the meeting schedule; how can I fill most of it and have a little time for Q&A?" My response: "Let's forget about the clock until you first define your persuasive goals."

Goal setting should always be the first step of your preparation process, one that you will fine-tune after your more in-depth audience analysis.

Your goals can be defined from three vantage points: net effects, substance, and image.

Net-effects goals have to do with the responses you seek to elicit from your audience. They can be positive (encouraging a desirable result) or preventive (discouraging an undesirable result), overt (conveying your intentions openly), or covert (disguising your intentions). For example:

Positive/Overt
  To persuade my audience to contribute $100,000 more to the Juvenile Diabetes Foundation than it did last year.

Positive/Covert
  To heighten my leadership profile in the community.

Preventive/Overt
  To persuade my audience that they should not approve the proposed convention center.

Preventive/Covert
  To paint a positive picture of the benefits of belonging to our organization *in order to prevent membership erosion.*

To illustrate further, let's say that you plan to announce to your employees a major reorganization that will result in layoffs. Some of your net-effects goals (preventive, overt, and covert) may be:

- To prevent damaging rumors
- To prevent a drop in morale
- To prevent a decline in productivity
- To prevent attrition by key people who will not be laid off
- To prevent unwanted union activity
- To prevent adverse publicity

Substance goals represent the specific major information, arguments, and action you need to convey to help consummate your net-effects goals. They are classified into four categories:

1. *To inform* the audience, for example, "The layoff will begin on August 11th."
2. *To convince* the audience of one or more of the following:
   - A need or lack thereof for a proposed or adopted change ("We need to reorganize.")
   - A cause-and-effect relationship ("Growing competition has resulted in the need for reorganization.")
   - A classification ("This is mainly a reorganization, not mainly a layoff.")
   - A value judgment ("This plan is the best approach for the company and its employees.")
   - The validity or invalidity of a stated fact ("The company is not in financial trouble.")
3. *To inspire* the audience, which involves heightening the level of interest or commitment of those who support your point of view.
4. *To actuate* the audience. This goal, frequently the most formidable, involves inducing your listeners to respond to a specific call to action, for example, signing a pledge, making a donation, writing a political leader, volunteering support, approving a proposal, or avoiding a contemplated action.

Image goals have to do with the specific traits or impressions you wish to generate in order to support your substance and net-effects goals. They are the most neglected type of goal as executives prepare for speeches, presentations, and media appearances. Yet, they can be the most important, for the ultimate feeling you convey and its impact on you or your company's credibility can surpass the importance you place on content. As you define your image goals, ask yourself which impressions you wish to convey regarding one or more of the following channels of persuasion:

- Yourself
- Your ideas
- Your company (especially in external presentations)
- Your division
- Your profession or industry

Image goals can also be classified into positive and preventive. Your positive goals in the example above would be to project yourself as confident, competent, and reasonably caring, your ideas as sensible and fair, and your company as reasonable, fair, and caring. Your preventive goals would be to avoid appearing defensive or insensitive. The accompanying chart should help you to define your image goals.

Image Traits: 57 Varieties

Using a number from the scale below, rate the importance of each of the following traits in meeting your net-effects goals. Then rely on this ranking to prioritize your image goals.

Very important	Important	Somewhat important	Unimportant
1	2	3	4

1. ____ action orientation
2. ____ aggressiveness
3. ____ analytical ability
4. ____ anger
5. ____ anxiety/stress/tension
6. ____ appreciation
7. ____ arrogance/aloofness
8. ____ assertiveness
9. ____ candor
10. ____ charisma
11. ____ compassion
12. ____ competence
13. ____ competitiveness
14. ____ composure

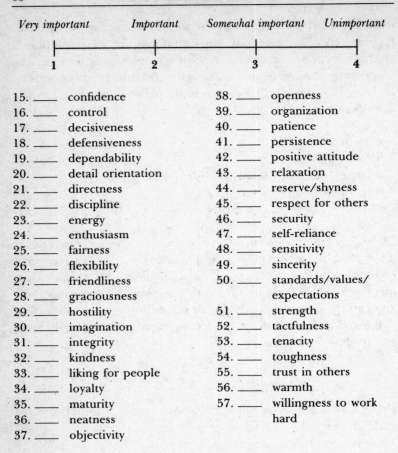

Very important	Important	Somewhat important	Unimportant
1	2	3	4

15. _____ confidence

16. _____ control

17. _____ decisiveness

18. _____ defensiveness

19. _____ dependability

20. _____ detail orientation

21. _____ directness

22. _____ discipline

23. _____ energy

24. _____ enthusiasm

25. _____ fairness

26. _____ flexibility

27. _____ friendliness

28. _____ graciousness

29. _____ hostility

30. _____ imagination

31. _____ integrity

32. _____ kindness

33. _____ liking for people

34. _____ loyalty

35. _____ maturity

36. _____ neatness

37. _____ objectivity

38. _____ openness

39. _____ organization

40. _____ patience

41. _____ persistence

42. _____ positive attitude

43. _____ relaxation

44. _____ reserve/shyness

45. _____ respect for others

46. _____ security

47. _____ self-reliance

48. _____ sensitivity

49. _____ sincerity

50. _____ standards/values/
expectations

51. _____ strength

52. _____ tactfulness

53. _____ tenacity

54. _____ toughness

55. _____ trust in others

56. _____ warmth

57. _____ willingness to work
hard

As you engage in the goal-setting process, keep the following in mind:

- Most of your presentations and speeches should have some persuasive dimension to give you an opportunity to influence your audience's attitudes and/or behavior, most particularly the opportunity to display your expertise, leadership, or management talent.
- Be prepared to modify any of your goals based on additional information you acquire about the audience and the occasion.

- Discuss your net-effects, substance, and image goals with trusted colleagues and advisors. Ask them, Does each goal make sense? Are any important goals being neglected? Are my priorities on target? Collectively, are the goals realistic or too ambitious?

- Most important, as you embark on finding and selecting ideas, evidence, and other amplifying materials for your presentation, keep this "needs test" uppermost in your mind: *"I will use this idea or information only if it clearly reinforces one or more of my goals."*

Chapter 3

AUDIENCE ANALYSIS AND ADVANCE WORK

You are now planning a speech to accomplish important net-effects, image, and substance goals. What's the audience's reason for attending?

- Are they coerced—there because they have to be there? Is it a condition of employment that they attend a session with their supervisor or boss? Are they students forced to attend a lecture? Are members of the audience attending out of social necessity—as much to be seen as to hear?
- Is the audience there because it wants to hear someone other than you?
- Is the audience in voluntary attendance—there of its own free will because of a genuine interest in you and your message?
- Is the audience there more because they want to see you or meet you than to actually hear what you have to say?
- Is the audience there primarily to advance their own agenda, particularly during the question-and-answer session?

Answers to questions such as these can help you tailor your presentation to your audience. For example, if your audience is coerced to attend, you may need to work harder in establishing rapport with them than if they were a voluntary audience genuinely interested in you and your message. In addition, a coerced audience may require a different style of delivery, for example, a more intimate style to build on that rapport or a more energized style to motivate them past their natural resistance.

If you learn that your audience is more interested in advancing their own agenda, you have several tactical options. For example, you may want to demonstrate your understanding of their point of view in your prepared remarks. Or you may decide to shorten or eliminate the question-and-answer session to prevent their agenda from overtaking yours.

Analyzing your audience is one of the most important steps in the preparation process. Ironically it is also one of the most neglected. Here's why:

- Presenters and speakers are often more self-centered or content-centered than audience-centered. They may consciously or subconsciously—and erroneously—conclude that the inherent value of what they have to say—often combined with a sense of their own importance—will generate the reaction they seek.
- In a related vein, too many presenters and speakers do not understand how the selection of ideas, support, and phrasing can influence the outcome of their message. For example, a scientist specializing in genetic engineering may wish to talk about the "competitiveness of the human species," that is, our genetic capacity to fight disease and increase longevity. However, the choice of language may have unpleasant overtones of racial superiority and may offend many in the audience.
- Many presenters and speakers do not know how to conduct an audience analysis, a concern that I will now resolve.

PLANNING YOUR AUDIENCE ANALYSIS

An audience analysis should cover three dimensions: demographics, knowledge level, and attitudes.

Demographics: Relevant census data of the audience: age, sex, marital status, number of children, age of children, educational level, military service, employment record, travel, religion, ethnic identification, political preference, investment practices, memberships, etc.

Knowledge Level: The audience's degree of familiarity with the topic and the issues being presented

Attitudes: The audience's specific feelings regarding the speaker, his or her organization, industry, or profession, and message

A thorough demographic analysis not only cues you into your audience's potential sensitivities, but also alerts you to opportunities to establish common ground with your listeners, for example:

"I, too, am the father of a teenager."

"How many of you remember your first TV set?"

"How many of you still rely on a bank for most of your savings?"

A high-quality analysis of your audience's knowledge level helps you determine how much background information you need to present before accelerating your persuasive advances. Moreover, it guides you in determining how technical your message needs to be.

A careful attitudinal analysis of your audience is crucial in determining how to focus your presentation. If, for example, your analysis reveals that your audience knows little about you but doesn't think highly about your company, you face formidable challenges to your credibility, which you must address skillfully before your audience will concentrate on your message. If you learn in advance that key members of your audience are significantly opposed to your point of view, you will need to learn why and shape your message around their resistance.

You just read the words *key members.* A quality audience analysis involves determining what the "key members" of your audience—that is, your "target audience"—think. Your target audience consists of those persons who, through authority, power, or some other capability, can best help you to achieve your goals. In a sales presentation, they are either the key decision makers or those persons most capable of influencing them. In a political speech, depending on your goals, they are the persons most likely to join your campaign, to donate to it, or to vote for you. During a sermon, they are the people most prone to reflect your theme in their daily living.

CONDUCTING YOUR AUDIENCE ANALYSIS

When conducting your audience analysis, try to quantify your audience's predisposition toward any of the relevant channels of persuasion, which include you, your company or division, your message, and your industry. Simply categorizing your audience on a pro/con basis is too superficial and provides you with little direction in refining your persuasive strategy. I would recommend that you quantify your audience's predisposition toward your message by using a scale from 1 to 10, with *1* defined as "overtly opposed to your message" and *10* defined as "actively supportive of your message." Our clients find the following scale especially helpful when conducting their analyses:

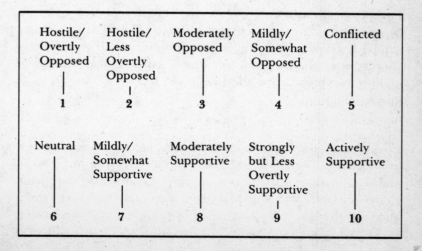

Hostile/ Overtly Opposed	Hostile/ Less Overtly Opposed	Moderately Opposed	Mildly/ Somewhat Opposed	Conflicted
1	2	3	4	5
Neutral	Mildly/ Somewhat Supportive	Moderately Supportive	Strongly but Less Overtly Supportive	Actively Supportive
6	7	8	9	10

Once you've quantified your audience's attitude toward your presentation, keep the following principles in mind as you develop your approach:

- Those key audience members whose attitudes regarding your message are closest to your own (8–10) normally require less of your attention. However, be careful not to make them feel neglected or allow them to perceive you as pandering to the opposition.
- Those key audience members whose attitudes are closest to the fence (5–7) are the ones *most open* to your persuasive advances.
- Those to the left of the fence (1–4) are less susceptible to persuasion. Therefore, if key audience members fall in this range, you will probably need to devise an overall communication strategy in addition to your speech to influence them.

You can conduct a high-quality audience analysis with the following four approaches, used separately or in combination: the telephone, private meetings, informal contacts, and the formal survey.

The Telephone

For an outside speaking engagement or presentation before a prospective or current client, a telephone call to reliable sources can be a terrific investment in preparation time. If your time is short, you can prepare your secretary, assistant, or public-information staff member to ask the questions.

Private Meetings

Private meetings can be most helpful for major outside, as well as internal, presentations. Meeting with informed sources or key audience members in advance can help you discern where your audience stands and why. Moreover, a meeting with a key audience member can also provide an opening for your persuasive advances. Therefore, your audience analysis will double as a lobbying effort.

Informal Contacts

Valuable intelligence regarding your audience can be gleaned deliberately or occur spontaneously in the most informal settings—over coffee, lunch, in the hallway, or on the way to work. In fact, the company grapevine can provide the latest information regarding who will attend your presentation and what the current "pulse" is regarding it. However, don't accept any of this information as gospel; do your best to verify it!

The Formal Survey

Although the formal survey may seem a bit unorthodox, my clients and I have used it most successfully for several of our speaking engagements. Our company drafts the survey, and the host organization distributes and returns it for our tabulation and interpretation. Then the message is based around it, with specific references to the data during both the speech and the question-and-answer session to give the presentation a more personalized approach.

Specificity and accuracy are the main advantages of the survey. You need not rely merely on the input of a few audience members or representatives of the host organization; rather, you can secure data from most, if not all, of your audience.

ADVANCING YOUR PRESENTATION

One of the more critical elements of any operation—political, military, social, business, or otherwise—is to gather intelligence before the event occurs in order to eliminate the element of surprise and to capture the persuasive edge by taking the fullest advantage of opportunities learned through the process of gathering information. Advancing your presentation is as important a step as analyzing your audience.

In the political world, the person who performs this task is the "advance man." His or her job is to travel ahead of the politician or candidate, choose desirable locations for speeches, make hotel reservations, get a feel for the public's pulse, arrange for any special needs of the speaker, drum up interest among the media, put out brushfires among the locals, and prepare a meticulous schedule of the politician's movements; minute by minute, step by step.

Regardless of whether your speech or presentation is internal or external, you, too, need advance work, even if you do the work yourself. The more you are aware of what to expect, the more confident you should be—and the less you should be preoccupied with a fear of the unknown. Moreover, this awareness can help determine your range of control over your speaking environment; *the greater your range of control, the greater your potential to capture the persuasive edge.*

You are about to be introduced to a comprehensive set of questions to guide your advance work. The importance of the audience and occasion will dictate how much effort you or your team should devote to advancing the event by telephone or in person. Whatever effort you exert, abandon any concern that your inquiries will pose an imposition to your hosts. Chances are that your careful planning will signal the value you attach to your host's invitation to speak.

The Occasion and the Schedule

1. What do you need to know about the host organization and the event? Is this a major event? How often does it occur? What is its purpose? Does the organization represent values, or does the event carry a theme that you should key into?
2. Should you be accompanied by staff or family members?
3. When should you arrive? Have you made sure that a delayed flight or train or traffic jam won't prevent you from speaking on time?

4. Who will greet you?

5. Are you committed to any special events (e.g., receptions) before or after your presentation?

6. Are you the only speaker? If not, who will precede and follow you? Do you—or can you—have a say in your placement in the program?

7. Will you come onto the stage from the wings or from the floor?

8. Where will you be seated before you speak? At the head table?

9. Who will be seated next to you? What are their backgrounds?

10. Do you need to seek out anyone expected to attend or refer to him or her in your speech?

11. Will a meal be served before you speak? When will the dishes be cleared?

12. What type of attire should you wear?

13. How long are you expected to speak? Is this realistic vis-à-vis your goals?

14. Who will introduce you? What will he or she say? Have you provided current information about you and your company, including a "suggested" introduction?

15. Will a question-and-answer period follow your speech? If so, how long will it be? If other speakers will also be fielding questions, how active a role will the moderator assume?

16. How will you get off stage? Can you arrange for the host or moderator to assist you in ending your presentation if you have a particular schedule to follow?

Knowing answers to these questions can be enormously beneficial. For example:

- Acknowledging the organization's values in your remarks (item 1) can help strengthen your persuasive bond with your audience and signal them that your message has been tailored for them, not merely a "canned" speech identical to the one you deliver to numerous other audiences.
- Being accompanied by staff can create "the entourage ef-

fect," thereby projecting your importance or prestige. Being accompanied by your family can project your family values as well as your fuller support of the event.

■ If you are not the only speaker and you can choose your place in the speaking order, you need to decide whether being the "lead-off batter" or "cleanup hitter" will best position you and your message. This decision depends heavily on what you expect the other speakers to say and how well you expect them to say it. For example, you do not want to follow a superior speaker who may be covering ground similar to yours.

The Facilities

1. Do you need overnight accommodations?
2. What arrangements have been made for parking?
3. Does the building or room have historic significance?
4. What are the dimensions of the room? The best advance men try to arrange for a room that is just slightly too small for the occasion. They figure it looks better to have 500 persons in a room seating 475 than 500 in a room seating 1,000. Don't go overboard, though; you run the risk of alienating your audience if you can't seat them comfortably.
5. What will be the seating arrangements? Rows? Round tables? U-shaped tables? How will they be spaced in relation to the room's dimensions?
6. How will the room be decorated?
7. Will you be speaking from a platform or riser? How close will the first row of your audience be?
8. Will there be a podium? How high is it? Is it adjustable? Does it have a lip to prevent your notes from falling to the floor? (If not, you may want to use your navel as a temporary lip.) Can it accommodate your notes? A Scriptmaster (see page 131)? Does it have a light? Controls for audiovisual equipment?
9. Will you need a microphone? Will the microphone be mounted or attached to you via cord or tie clip? Will it be wireless?

10. What kind of lighting will be used? How controllable is it? Will you be well illuminated when you speak?

11. Will you need water? (Arrange for a few filled stemless glasses on an adjacent stand rather than having to pour the water during the speech or question-and-answer session.)

12. Will you also be seen on a large screen or on monitors as you speak? How large? Where will it or they be placed?

13. Does the room accommodate projectors? Do you need to bring your own projector, flip chart, easel, screen, audiotape or videotape recorder? If you use the host's equipment, is it compatible with your films, slides, or tapes? Will you have a chance to check out the host's equipment in advance for proper operation? Will you need a projectionist? Is a stock of extension cords, projector lamps, and fuses available?

14. Will you need a pointer? Metal, light, or laser?

15. Should you arrange for an on-site rehearsal before you speak?

16. Should you arrange for your presentation to be taped (audio or video)?

17. Do you need an office before or after your presentation? Should you obtain a telephone number in advance to leave with your office for emergencies?

The Publicity

1. Should the media be notified of your appearance? By the host organization? By your organization?

2. How aggressively should you seek media coverage?

3. Should you offer to assist the host organization in arranging for media coverage?

4. Should you prepare a media kit with a press release and/or text of your speech?

5. Should you reprint the speech for wider distribution?

6. Should you submit it for publication (e.g., to *Vital Speeches*)?

Chapter 4

YOUR PERSUASIVE STRATEGY

The effectiveness of your speech or presentation depends entirely on your ability to establish perceptual linkages between yourself, your message, and your audience. Without such linkages, there is no bonding between you and your audience. With strong linkages, your persuasive potential can be virtually boundless.

Thorough audience analysis and advance work provide the foundation for establishing the linkages. Using these data, you can create an overall strategy to meet your persuasive goals and select specific tactics to reinforce your strategy.

Your strategy should reflect a blending of the three classical modes of proof—ethical, emotional, and logical. Ethical proof refers to your credibility or believability; emotional proof relies on the appeal to your audience's sympathies or emotions, and logical proof involves the intrinsic logic of the case being made, including its specific arguments.

Your audience analysis will help you determine the appropriate blend of proof. For example, let's say that, as a legislator, you advocate stiffer penalties for driving under the influence of alcohol or illegal drugs. When addressing fellow legislators who know you well, you will probably need to focus less on ethical proof and more on emotional and logical proof. If most of your colleagues are lawyers, you may need to emphasize the logical over the emotional. However, if you are addressing a group from MADD (Mothers Against Drunk Driving) for the first time, you will probably need to emphasize ethical and emotional proof over logical proof. The following discussion further clarifies these three forms of proof and provides practical advice regarding how they should be folded into your strategy.

ETHICAL PROOF: ESTABLISHING CREDIBILITY WITH YOUR AUDIENCE

Credibility is the major pillar to any persuasive strategy. If you or your organization's credibility is in question, the persuasive impact of your message will be compromised, regardless of how well it is researched, styled, or delivered.

Scores of studies have addressed the fundamental question, What are the major components of credibility? Despite some variation in their conclusions, most reveal that credibility consists of three principal components: perceived trustworthiness, perceived competence, and perceived dynamism or conviction. The word *perceived* is repeated deliberately, for regardless of whether the persuader is or is not *actually* trustworthy, competent, or dynamic, what matters in persuasion is how he or she is perceived. *Perceptions are realities.*

If your audience analysis reveals any need to shore up your own or your organization's credibility, your first strategic challenge is to address it. If the issue is trustworthiness—the most challenging credibility issue of all—how do you address it? Can the person introducing you help "sell" your trustworthiness? Should you deal directly in the beginning of your speech with your own or your company's trustworthiness? Or would that be too defensive? Will a well-conceived "common ground" strategy help? As you will see, simple answers to these questions do not exist.

The audience's perception of your competence can be cultivated by your prior reputation, by how you are introduced during a speaking engagement, by what you say, and, yes, by how you say it. The introducer can help to establish your competency by acknowledging the related attributes and accomplishments you may be reluctant to mention for fear of being perceived as egotistical. However, you alone are mainly responsible for selling your competence. Therefore, as you plan your remarks, select ideas, examples, and illustrations that reflect your wealth of experience—including the more impressive results you have achieved. Then find a way of expressing them that is neither too egotistical nor too understated.

You convey your perceived dynamism or conviction by both the language you use and your vocal delivery. Practice delivering the following lines, noting the natural escalation of intensity produced by the word change in each succeeding line:

1. The situation facing the homeless people *is most unfortunate.*
2. The situation facing the homeless people *is sad.*
3. The *pathetic* situation facing the homeless people *deeply concerns me.*

The first line reveals the speaker's distance and lack of involvement. The second line demonstrates a greater sympathy, but the final line is the most empathetic expression of the speaker's involvement with the subject matter.

Common Ground

Common ground is one of the most classical approaches to building rapport or trust with your audience. Basically it involves highlighting demographic, experiential, or attitudinal similarities between you and your audience.

Demographic
- Since you and I are both parents of teenagers . . .
- Since you and I both belong to the (Republican or Democratic) party . . .

Experiential
- How many of you remember the scene in *Crocodile Dundee II* when . . . ?
- Since most of you travel, I'm sure you share with me the frustration of pulling out of the jetway only to wait an hour or more until takeoff.

Attitudinal
- You and I both agree that the only way to negotiate is from a position of strength.
- As educators, you understand well my position that the only way America can be competitive is for the American people to be well educated.

As you develop a common-ground strategy, keep the following principles in mind:

1. Choose common-ground linkages that are important to your audience and relevant to your message. Using material that is unimportant or irrelevant is not only ineffective, but could make you appear crassly manipulative or pandering.
2. Be sure to create common-ground linkages with *each* important segment of your audience.
3. Make the linkages noticeable but not too transparent.

Enhancing Credibility and Common Ground: A Checklist

The following checklist will help you plan your credibility and common-ground strategy more systematically:

Premessage Phase
1. Have you taken advantage of all opportunities to publicize your engagement?
2. Have you made sure that key decision makers or opinion leaders will be present? Do you need to "prime the persuasion pump" by lobbying before your engagement?

3. What has been the nature of your prior contact with the people whom you will be addressing? How do they perceive you?
4. Have you made sure that you will be well introduced? Does the linkage between the elements of the introduction and the audience's values or motives facilitate a common ground between you and your audience?

Message Phase
1. Are you projecting sufficient confidence?
2. Are you projecting sufficient conviction?
3. Are you weaving into your message enough references to your experience—including results you have achieved—that the audience can sense your competence or expertise?
4. Does the audience sense the goodwill in your message toward them as individuals or toward their organization? Or does your message appear too self-centered?
5. Is your overall presentation sufficiently professional, reflecting careful preparation and signaling respect for the audience and occasion?
6. Have you chosen language, concepts, examples, and visual aids suited to the audience's knowledge and educational levels?
7. Is your overall vocal, visual, and verbal image compatible with your goals and the audience's expectations? (See page 132.)

Postmessage Phase
1. Should your engagement be publicized?
2. Should you distribute a manuscript, videotape, or audiotape to key people who attended or missed your speech?
3. Should you plan to give the speech again?
4. Should you or your colleagues follow up with the key audience members in person, by phone, or in writing to enhance the potential impact of your message?

EMOTIONAL PROOF: ESTABLISHING SYMPATHY WITH YOUR AUDIENCE

Motivational psychology provides the foundation for understanding the use of emotion in persuasion. At its heart is the premise that our behavior is motivated by our attempts to satisfy our wants, desires, needs, or drives. To capture the persuasive edge, you need to understand what motivates your audience.

For example, to motivate your sales representatives to try harder, you may appeal to their desire for financial gain; to convince an audience to donate money to the SPCA, you may appeal to their sense of sympathy or pity; to persuade a top-notch candidate to join your firm, you may appeal to his or her sense of opportunity (including self-esteem).

Of the vast amount of research conducted in motivational psychology, the study that remains the most dominant and practical is psychologist Abraham Maslow's hierarchy of needs. Maslow postulated that all human beings are motivated by the following needs, from the most basic to the most advanced. He contended further that fulfillment of a more advanced need is not attainable without satisfaction of the less advanced needs:

1. Physiological, including survival and self-preservation
2. Safety, including security (freedom from fear), stability, and order
3. Love, including a sense of belonging, approval, and acceptance
4. Esteem, including self-respect, recognition
5. Self-actualization, including self-fulfillment and mastery

Relying on Maslow, your goal as a persuader is to define precisely how your argument or proposal can create within your audience the perception that one or more of their needs can be satisfied.

A Carrot or a Stick?

As you plan your persuasive advances, you must decide whether you should use a carrot—a positive appeal—or a stick—a negative appeal. A positive appeal promises the listener some reward, either material or psychological, if he or she behaves in accordance with the speaker's recommendation (e.g., "Implementing this plan will increase your revenues by 25 percent."). A negative appeal is generally used to relate the speaker's subject to a situation that directly affects the listener or his or her loved ones (e.g., "If we don't receive the necessary funding for the new auditorium, our children won't be able to participate in the after-school special activities we've all planned."). Several studies underscore the effectiveness of a negative appeal when its use is not perceived as unduly manipulative or alarmist and the basis for it appears reasonably probable, for example, selling flood insurance in the Mississippi Delta region versus in the Sahara desert.

Values

Your audience's values represent a major reservoir for building and reinforcing your emotional proof. Their values are, in essence, the attitudinal guideposts or compass points that influence how they respond to an idea or object. Sociologists James Christianson and Choon Yang rank-ordered Americans' dominant personal and social values based on people's expressed preferences:

1. Moral integrity (honesty)
2. Personal freedom
3. Patriotism
4. Work
5. Being practical and efficient
6. Political democracy
7. Helping others
8. Achievement (getting ahead)
9. National progress

10. Material comfort
11. Leisure (recreation)
12. Racial equality
13. Individualism (nonconformity)
14. Sexual equality

References to several of these values are reflected in the following two speech excerpts.

From the conclusion of Chief Justice William H. Rehnquist's address delivered at the Boston University commencement, May 17, 1987:

> And so, as you go forth from your University studies to conquer new worlds, bear in mind this nigh universal message from the older generation to the younger generation. The most priceless asset that can be accumulated in the course of any life is time well spent. (value 5)

From Ronald Reagan's address to the American people on June 15, 1987, following the European economic summit meeting:

> I know that over the years many of you have seen the pictures and news clips of the wall that divides Berlin.
> But, believe me, no American who sees firsthand—the concrete and mortar, the guard posts and machine gun towers, the dog runs, and the barbed wire—can ever again take for granted his or her freedom or the precious gift that is America. (values 2, 3, 6, and 10)

When you establish the values you or your company shares with your audience, keep the following advice in mind:

- Emphasize a value that is or can be well appreciated by the audience.
- Consider describing the value graphically, as in the Reagan example, to maximize its impact.
- Avoid appearing preachy or pandering.

LOGICAL PROOF:
REASONING WITH YOUR AUDIENCE

Logical proof is intended to appeal to a listener's sense of reason. Four types of reasoning dominate our thinking: from *example, signs, cause,* and *analogy.*

Reasoning From Example

As you attempt to persuade a customer to purchase a faster and more powerful computer, a key decision maker asks you to prove that your computer is faster than theirs. Relying on reasoning by example, you provide a comparative demonstration, the statistical results of a research report, or an authoritative quotation. Reasoning by example, then, helps satisfy the "show me" tendency in all of us.

Reasoning From Signs

During your sales presentation one of the key decision makers takes copious notes and asks you several pertinent—and positive—questions. You reason (correctly or incorrectly) that his or her behavior is a sign of serious interest in your computer system.

Reasoning From Cause

One of the major points of your presentation is that the frequency of repair of the customer's current system was due to its being designed for much lighter use. This argument relates cause (demand) to effect (frequency of repair). The implication of the argument also relates cause to effect: "Buy our computer (cause) and your servicing headaches will diminish" (effect).

Reasoning From Analogy

Reasoning from analogy is an extension of reasoning by example. Let's say that you want to convince your customer that your computer system is working well in similar firms. You provide specific names, description of the application, and customer-satisfaction information. You are, in essence, helping your customer to reason by analogy.

I have separated logic and emotion in this discussion only for purposes of clarity; in reality, they are inextricably intertwined. For example, as you attempt to persuade a firm to purchase a computer that is clearly faster and more powerful than their current one, don't overlook the emotional implications of your argument: a new computer can result in cost savings (logically demonstrated) that can make the buyer's boss perceive her as a better manager, thereby enhancing her security and self-esteem needs.

ATTENTION AUDIT
AND ATTENTION PLAN

You may have concocted a presentation containing the perfect blend of ethical, emotional, and logical proof, but unless you present it in a manner that gains and maintains the audience's attention and interest, it may fall on deaf ears.

The possibility of a "deaf ears" reaction suggests the importance of an attention audit, a careful review of your overall message to determine the attention-getting potential of your arguments or ideas, support, and language, plus the vocal and visual dimensions of your delivery. This audit should be based on your audience analysis—specifically their level of interest in you—your overall message, and its arguments. For example, a less-educated audience is generally less attentive to technical explanations than a more-educated one. A group of youngsters tends to be more distractible than a group of middle-aged people. A group of elderly people may not hear as well as a younger group—or be as alert. A group of busy big-city executives may be more impatient than a group of small-town business people.

Once you complete your attention audit, you should develop

an attention plan, a deliberate effort to generate, build, and maintain your audience's attention.

What factors help draw our attention? Persuasion theorists divide them into two categories, external and internal. The external factors have the capacity to command our attention. The internal factors influence our innate tendency to respond attentively to external stimuli.

External Factors

- *Concreteness.* We tend to focus our attention more readily on something we can easily visualize than on something requiring mental activity. For example:

  The Gettysburg battlefield poses a striking contrast between the bloody three-day battle fought there in July, 1863, and its current quiet, expansive beauty. The imagination must strain to visualize the deafening sound of gunfire, the countless Union and Confederate soldiers locked in hand-to-hand combat, and the thousands of blood-soaked dead—mostly young men—strewn across the formerly innocent farmland now dedicated to their memory.

  Knowing our attraction to the concrete, you should seek opportunities to create "word pictures" in the audience's minds by appealing to one or more of their five senses.
- *Intensity.* Normally a bright color or a loud sound will be more attention getting than a less intense color or sound.
- *Contrast.* A behavior or object that defies expectations or norms grabs our attention, for example, an executive speaking with uncharacteristic force to stress a point.
- *Novelty.* We are drawn to the unusual. Do you remember your first reaction to a hand-held miniature TV? Does the Goodyear blimp still capture your attention?
- *Movement and energized activity.* Watching the Goodyear blimp for more than a few minutes is probably less exciting than watching a jet fighter perform combat maneuvers.

Internal Factors

- *Proximity.* The near at hand, especially if it threatens our sense of personal safety, health, or financial security, automatically seizes our attention. For example, our concern for drought in another part of the nation heightens as it becomes a more serious probability in our area.
- *Conflict.* Human beings are attracted to conflict. A debate between two candidates will probably draw a larger crowd than the combined attendance of individual appearances by each candidate. The seemingly endless conflict between George Steinbrenner, owner of the Yankees, and Billy Martin, the manager he repeatedly fires, continues to feed the media's interest and, as a result, our own.
- *Curiosity.* Cats may be curious, but we must not underestimate our own curiosity—our natural tendency to ask who, what, when, where, and how. The effective persuader usually has numerous opportunities to play to the audience's curiosity through skillful use of both rhetorical questions and pauses.
- *Adventure/Escape.* We are attracted to messages that help us relax and enjoy—that take us to another place and perhaps another time. Humor, especially humorous anecdotes, can be an effective attention getter. Detailed illustrations, real and hypothetical, can also aid the persuader greatly.

As you develop an attention plan for your message, keep in mind the relationship between delivery and attention. As you deliver the speech, your vocal and physical cues—especially the external factors of intensity (volume, emphasis), contrast (varying volume and tone), and movement (gestures, facial expression, and overall movement)—can significantly influence how much your audience pays attention to you. Yes, in addition to your message, you are an attention-getting vehicle. Plan accordingly!

THE NEXT STEP

Your strategy is now well defined. You have decided on the proper blend of ethical, emotional, and logical proof. And you have planned to gain and maintain the audience's attention and interest. Your next step is to decide on specific tactical approaches that may not have surfaced as you were formulating your strategy.

You can receive valuable guidance regarding tactics from the wealth of experiments conducted by researchers in communication, speech, and psychology. Understanding the following research issues can be especially helpful:

One-sided Versus Two-sided Arguments

When preparing a persuasive speech, the speaker must decide whether to present both sides of an argument or only the side he or she is advocating. Which is better? According to the research:

- A two-sided argument is more effective when the audience is opposed to the speaker's argument, when the audience is well educated, or when they are expected to be exposed to opposing arguments in the future.
- A one-sided argument is more effective if the audience is predisposed to the speaker's position.
- Fair-minded refutation of the opposing position (with an emphasis on logical versus emotional proof) is generally advisable when offering the two-sided argument.

Disclosing Persuasive Intent

Does informing your audience in the beginning of your speech that you "intend to convince them that . . ." have any positive or negative effect?

One study tells us that forewarning the audience may either reduce the persuasiveness of a message or prevent persuasion altogether. In some instances the audience is aware of the speaker's intent in advance. Here the speaker should not attempt to hide his or her intent. However, neither should he or she be too direct, for example, "I will definitely convince you that . . ." or "What I am about to show you will surely change your minds." Such expressions tend to promote the audience's defensiveness.

Primacy Versus Recency

When you have total freedom of choice, where in your speech should you place your major arguments, first or last? Primacy occurs when the major argument that has the greatest effect in creating attitude change is placed first. Recency occurs when the major argument is placed last in the speech for the strongest effect. Although no conclusive findings exist regarding which position is preferable, the following general guidelines should be helpful:

- Even if you cannot decide whether your strongest argument would be more effective first or last, either is better than "burying" it in the body of your speech.
- Consider beginning and ending a series of arguments with your two strongest arguments; this allows you to take the fullest advantage of both the primacy and the recency phenomenon.
- When you and your audience differ greatly on an argument, consider dealing with it early in your speech—possibly first. This may help prevent the audience from becoming preoccupied with their position on one issue while you are presenting others.
- If you use a one-sided persuasive speech, building your case to a climax at the end (recency) may be stronger than presenting your strongest argument first.
- If an argument is weak and its absence will not be conspicuous or unethical, consider omitting it.

Optimism Versus Pessimism

University of Pennsylvania psychologist Harold Zullow designed a path-breaking research study to predict the persuasiveness of presidential candidates based on their levels of expressed optimism versus pessimism. His insights are also especially valuable to the business executive or manager who must set an appropriate leadership tone.

Zullow focuses specifically on the issue of pessimism versus optimism expressed in one's explanation of the cause of a problem. The pessimistic approach is characterized by one or more of the following characteristics:

- A *stable* explanation (e.g., "It's going to last forever.")
- A *global* explanation (e.g., "It's going to affect everything I do.")
- An *internal* explanation (e.g., "It's my fault.")

In contrast, the three optimistic ways of explaining the cause of a problem are

- *Unstable* (e.g., "It's only temporary.")
- *Specific* (e.g., "It's only affecting this one situation.")
- *External* (e.g., "It's the fault of the situation I'm [we're] in.")

Zullow stresses the greater effectiveness of the optimistic approach and offers the following specific advice:

- Don't ruminate about your pessimism; stress instead what you're going to do about the problem.
- Try to speak optimistically by targeting specific, temporary causes in a blame-free way.
- If you must accept blame or responsibility, do so in a *specific* and *unstable* way.

Chapter 5

THE GOOD MAP: ORGANIZE BY OUTLINING

Once you have analyzed your audience, you need to plan the organization of your message—regardless of whether you're going to read from a manuscript or speak extemporaneously.

Any message receives a better hearing when it is presented in an organized and logical manner. In fact, no matter how vivid, persuasive, and well supported your message is, it will probably be lost if your listeners cannot easily process the information you are presenting. Moreover, the stronger your own sense of organization, the more confident you will be in your overall presentation, and the more energized you may become while delivering it.

To illustrate this point, think of this hypothetical situation: A friend invites you for the first time to his house for a dinner party. He gives you a loose set of oral directions, which you're pretty sure will suffice. However, as you are within minutes of your destination, the directions become less and less helpful—and you become anxious that you'll arrive late.

A good map would have prevented your anxiety. Similarly, a good outline provides a speaker with a clear sense of direction and prevents unnecessary and potentially risky detours and side excursions.

One of the best ways to prepare for your speech is to make an outline. Don't worry about following some rule book's description of the perfect form; use whatever format works best for you.

The structure you build should not be too evident to your audience; you are constructing an internal skeleton, not an external scaffolding.

PATTERNS OF ORGANIZATION

You may choose from several general blueprints or patterns of organization for almost any presentation or speech you'll be making. Study and select the pattern or combination of patterns that best meets your goals.

Time Pattern

The time pattern organizes your presentation or speech by chronology. It is particularly helpful in discussing processes and historical trends. However, when you use this pattern, avoid the potentially boring use of too many time-related subcategories; instead, focus more on trends than on the calendar or clock.

> Potentially boring: "In 1970 we . . . In 1972 we . . . In 1973 we . . . In 1975 we . . ."

> Preferable: "The period between 1970 and 1975 can be called our early maturation phase. During this phase we . . ."

Topical Pattern

The topical pattern is governed neither by space nor by time. Rather, it involves selecting and sequencing ideas in a manner that best achieves your goals.

Let's say my goal is to persuade you to vote for candidate X. In very general terms, my approach may look like this:

A. She's experienced.
B. She understands the people of our district.
C. Her ideas for improving education and creating jobs make sense.
D. She's a hard worker.

Notice that each point is a separate topic. Also notice that I have considerable freedom regarding the ordering of any of my points. If, for instance, most of my audience has already acknowledged my candidate's experience but is less aware of her positions on the issues, I might want C to replace A as my first point. To capture the persuasive edge, you need to assess carefully which sequence within a topical order works best for you. As you do, keep the following questions and advice in mind, which apply also to other speech formats:

Q. *Should I begin with the topic of foremost concern to my audience?*
A. This is often a good idea, particularly if your point or case is strong. However, if your audience's viewpoint varies significantly from yours, be sure your approach is not too blunt; it should reflect your respect for their viewpoint as you refute it.

Q. *Or should I cover one or more other topics first, building up to the one that interests them the most?*
A. This may be a good idea as you seek to broaden your audience's perspective on an issue. However, too long a delay in covering a topic of major concern to them could make them feel bypassed (unless you signal them earlier that you will address their concern).

Q. *Should I end my sequence of topics with a strong point?*
A. Generally you should. Years of research indicate that we tend to remember best what comes first and last (called the "primacy-recency" principle*). Ending on a weak note can compromise the overall persuasiveness of your case.

*Refer to page 37 for a fuller discussion.

Q. *How should I handle points that are relevant but have less persuasive potential?*

A. If possible, omit your weaker points, unless their absence would be too conspicuous to your target audience. If you need to include them, devote less time to them than to your stronger points and, unless logic dictates otherwise, place the weaker points toward the middle of your series of arguments.

Spatial Pattern

This pattern organizes ideas according to space or geography. For example, to review your company's sales performance, you may choose to discuss each region separately. In essence, your organization pattern merely mirrors an existing structure within your company.

Sometimes you can use space and time patterns together, for example, in explaining a manufacturing process. Note the implied chronology of A through C, although the actual topics apply to the specific geographical area of each phase of the process.

II. The Body
  A. The Machine Shop
    1. Machining of parts to specifications
    2. Random inspection of parts
  B. The Assembly Line
    1. Assembly of parts
    2. Random inspection of assembly
  C. The Shipping Area
    1. Packaging
    2. Loading
    3. Delivery

Causal Pattern

Causal patterns focus on why an event has occurred or is occurring. Why did the stock market crash on October 19, 1987? Why is Gorbachev more reform minded?

Four types of causal patterns help explain why events occur: problem-cause-solution, comparative-advantages, cause-to-effect, and effect-to-cause.

PROBLEM-CAUSE-SOLUTION PATTERN   The problem-cause-solution (P-C-S) pattern follows an organizational scheme that answers the following questions:

1. What is the *problem*?
   a. Who is being affected by it?
   b. How seriously?
2. What is *causing* (or has caused) the problem?
3. What is the proposed *solution*?
   a. How will it resolve the problem?
   b. Will it produce any negative side effects?
   c. Will it produce any additional benefits or advantages?

This pattern is especially helpful in advocating an internal or public policy change. For example:

Internal
We should centralize our computer operation.
We should modernize our molding equipment.
We should close our plant in East Kaiotz.

Public Policy
We should raise taxes.
We should build a larger prison.
We should strengthen our laws against drug dealers.

A few pieces of advice in using the P-C-S approach:

- Don't reveal your solution too prematurely. First convince the audience of the problem and the need for a change; then they will be more receptive to listening to your solution.
- If your audience essentially accepts the existence of a problem, you won't need to spend as much time developing it in their minds. But make sure that you and they are on the same wavelength regarding what the problem is *and* how serious it is.
- Many presenters tend to skip over the causal-analysis step. This may be advisable or inadvisable: It is advisable if you and your audience already have a shared view of the causes or if your causal analysis might result in politically sensitive finger pointing. It is inadvisable if your audience is not sufficiently informed. In this case they may not appreciate the full import of your solution.

COMPARATIVE-ADVANTAGES PATTERN   The presenter who chooses this pattern contends that adopting a certain course of action will result in a situation or condition that is comparatively advantageous to the status quo. Therefore, when using this pattern, the presenter does not need to convince the audience of a need or problem. The pattern has three basic elements:

1. Shared Goal or Value: *"We are all committed to increasing sales."*
2. Solution: *"Let's make two more targeted sales calls a day."*
3. Advantages:
   a. *"Doing so can increase sales by at least 3 to 5 percent."*
   b. *"It will help us maintain our position as one of the firm's leading sales offices."*

Note, in the example above, that the speaker did not identify an existing sales problem, but focused instead on two clear advantages for the proposed action.

One important caveat:

Since resistance to change is such a fundamental aspect of the human condition, your audience must want to increase sales and be convinced of your logic. They must be convinced that the two extra calls can truly make a difference and not lead to one or more significant disadvantages, for example, sloppy preparation or fatigue.

CAUSE-TO-EFFECT PATTERN   This pattern can be helpful for presentations in which the audience is aware of a cause but wants to learn more about the effects:

Cause
The company has just announced a reorganization plan, which is expected to have a significant impact on the organization.

Effects (short-term and long-term)
A. Morale
B. Financial conditions
C. Competitive positioning
D. Customer perception

EFFECT-TO-CAUSE PATTERN   This pattern, the opposite of cause-to-effect, should be used for presentations in which the audience wants more information about the causes of a situation.

Effects
Executive retreats have suddenly become increasingly popular.

Causes
A. Business books and periodicals are placing increasing emphasis on high-quality teamwork.
B. Executive retreats are being well reviewed in business publications.
C. Executives who have had positive retreat experiences are promoting them.

OUTLINING ADVICE

Once you've selected an appropriate pattern of organization, you're ready to outline your message. Your outline should be your map—a visual representation of the road you will take in presenting your message. In its early stages, it can alert you if you have not adequately prepared yourself and point the way to areas requiring further thought or research.

1. Since outlining is often the most difficult phase of the preparation process, before you begin, summon all the patience—and flexibility—at your command.
2. Any presentation, long or short, internal or external, needs an introduction, body, and conclusion.
3. Don't prepare the introduction and conclusion until you have outlined the body of your presentation. The content of the body should influence the content and tone of the introduction and conclusion, not vice versa.
4. Focus first on getting your main ideas and support down on paper, keeping in mind your audience's attitudes and levels of knowledge and interest. Don't labor unduly in the early outlining stages on style or sequence; this can impede your flow of thoughts. Mind mapping (see page 176) can be especially helpful in facilitating the flow.
5. Apportion the time you devote to each idea to its importance in fulfilling your goals. It is all too easy to get carried away making a point that interests you but diverts the persuasive momentum you need.
6. When you have a series of arguments or a series of support for them with the flexibility to arrange them any way you wish, always begin and end each series strongly—with the arguments or evidence that can most likely generate your audience's interest and belief.
7. Phrase your lead sentences for maximum persuasive impact. For example, which of the following leads is the strongest?
   a. "The results I just described are largely due to our fine sales team."
   b. "These terrific sales results reflect the superior performance of our dedicated, talented, and aggressive sales team."
   c. "These results are due to our dedicated, talented, and aggressive sales team."

You and I probably agree that *b* is the strongest lead. But the real question is, will it be the strongest for your target audience? Or is it too strong? Your audience analysis will help you to make decisions such as these.

8. When you make your outline, write down each idea on a separate line. Note the main point you need to make, the evidence you'll have to present to support it, and the subpoints you'll use to reinforce your main point. This will help you to grasp the point quickly at each stage of the outline.

9. Check over your work to make sure that the order is logical, with subpoints subordinate to main points. For example:

MAIN POINT: "Drug-related crime in our suburbs has increased alarmingly over the past three years."
EVIDENCE: "According to the FBI crime reports, this increase amounts to _____ percent over the preceding three years."
SUBPOINT: "Violent drug-related crime in the suburbs has increased at an even faster pace."
SUB-SUBPOINTS: "Murder . . ." "Armed robbery . . ." "Assault and battery . . ."

Note that the main point is general and serves as an umbrella for the subpoints and sub-subpoints. Also notice that the evidence is factually specific while the points, subpoints, and sub-subpoints are assertions that, depending on the audience's attitudes, knowledge level, and confidence in you, may or may not need to be supported.

10. Remember again, whatever is included in your outline—no matter how you prepare it—should be virtually indispensable to accomplishing your net, image, and substance goals. Beware of including an idea simply because you enjoy talking about it.

11. Make sure that each and every idea clearly supports your net effects, substance, and image goals and reinforces your persuasive strategy.

You may want to develop two or more separate drafts for your outline: a complete-sentence outline to use in the earliest stages of preparation and a key-word or key-phrase outline to use for rehearsals and for the presentation itself.

If you choose the complete-sentence outline as your final outline, check over your main points to be sure that they're as concise and vivid as possible. Write out your subpoints as complete sentences, making sure they support the logic of your main points. Finally, develop fully all the evidence you'll need to reinforce your argument. Do a final check of this outline to be certain it achieves your net, substance, and image goals.

Here is a sample outline of my recent discussions in this book, with the major points stated first—and simply—in complete-sentence form:

I.   Plan your initial preparation.
    A. Define your goals.
        1. Net Effects
        2. Substance
        3. Image
    B. Analyze your audience.
        1. Demographics
        2. Knowledge Level
        3. Attitudes
    C. Analyze the occasion.
    D. Analyze the setting.
    E. Refine your goals vis-à-vis your analysis of the audience, occasion, and setting.
    F. Formulate a persuasive strategy.

II. Develop a rough draft of your outline.
    A. List, in rough form, the main points you want to cover, *making sure that they support your net effects, substance, and image goals.*
    B. Rearrange these main points in a logical sequence.
    C. Insert and arrange subpoints under each main point.
    D. Make a general note of the supporting material (evidence) required for each main point.

E. Check over your rough draft to see that it meets your goals.

III. Recast the outline into final form
    A. Rephrase main points to make them concise, vivid, and easy to deliver.
    B. Write out the subpoints as full sentences.
        1. Make sure they contribute to your overall message.
        2. Make sure they are logically subordinate to the main point.
    C. Fully develop supporting materials (see chapter 6).
        1. Check for relevance.
        2. Check for inherent persuasiveness, including authority, recency, and sufficiency (see page 54).
    D. Recheck the entire outline to make sure that you
        1. Are comfortable with the form
        2. Have covered the subject
        3. Have met your goals
    E. (Optional) Develop a key-phrase outline to use in rehearsal.

Here is the third section of the same outline in a key-phrase form.

I. Recast for final form
    A. Rephrase main points
    B. Write out subpoints
        1. Contribute to message
        2. Subordinate to main points
    C. Develop support
        1. Relevance
        2. Persuasiveness
    D. Recheck outline
        1. Comfort with form
        2. Subject covered
        3. Goals met

TIES AND POLISH

Once your outline passes muster, review it to plan how you intend to smooth out the flow from one idea to the next. Two major tools to help you here are the transition and the internal summary:

Transitions

The transitional sentence bridges the succeeding and the preceding idea. It can be phrased as a question (see *A*, below) or as a declarative sentence (*B*):

A. "In addition to transitions, what other factors contribute to flow?"
B. "Now that we have discussed transitions, let's examine the internal summary."

The Internal Summary

Presentations and speeches are frequently collections of mini-speeches—well developed, self-contained ideas. Occasionally a transition may not adequately bridge two major sections of the message, especially if the preceding section is lengthy or complex.

Enter the internal summary, an elongated transition that recaps the major points in the preceding idea and creates a bridge to the next one. The summary can be a basic review (see *A*, below) or it can be more developed and pointed (*B*).

A. "We have discussed the benefits of sound organization, the various organization patterns from which you may choose methods of outlining, and specific techniques to make your speech flow more smoothly. Let's now turn our attention to the remaining components of your message, the introduction and conclusion."

B. "Before we move on to the next part of my presentation, let me briefly reiterate a few major points related to organization:

    1. Organization is key to the audience's comprehension and to the professionalism of your overall approach.

    2. Several basic patterns can provide the skeleton for your presentation.

    3. An outline, no matter how simple or complex, can be most helpful.

    4. Devote careful attention to smoothness by using transitional sentences and internal summaries."

Chapter 6

CLARIFYING AND PROVING YOUR POINT WITH EVIDENCE

You have analyzed your audience, the occasion, and the setting; you have defined your goals, formulated a strategy, selected at least most of your ideas, and chosen a pattern of organization. What comes next? Answer: making sure your ideas are developed to generate maximum clarity and persuasiveness. To gain the persuasive edge as you develop your ideas, keep these questions uppermost in mind: What type of information, and how much of it, lends itself best to increasing my audience's potential to both understand and be convinced of what I am saying? And if I need more information that is not immediately accessible, where do I find it? This chapter will help you better understand the functions of support or evidence and direct you to several valuable resources to reinforce your message.

Assessing when and how to reinforce your arguments depends significantly on your audience analysis. Their *knowledge level* should influence your use of examples and illustrations to *clarify* your points. Their *attitudes* should influence your use of evidence to *prove* them.

As you seek to prove your point, your audience consciously or subconsciously assesses the believability of your assertions. These assessments are based on your personal and/or institutional credibility coupled with their knowledge level and attitudes regarding the argument per se. The following example puts these dynamics in perspective:

Unsupported Arguments

Argument: Crime in our larger cities has increased significantly in the past two years.

Subargument: Drug-related crime has been the major contributor to this increase.

Unless your audience analysis reveals that your audience regards you as an authority on urban crime, the two arguments above will probably have limited persuasive appeal. Moreover, you would still bear the burden of proof if your audience regards you as an authority but differs with your argument or subargument.

Supported Arguments

Argument: Crime in our larger cities has increased significantly in the past two years.

Evidence A: According to the FBI, crime in our major cities has increased 15 percent in our twenty largest cities in the past two years.
Evidence B: Furthermore, according to the same study, crime in our five larger cities has increased at an even greater rate, 25 percent.

Subargument: Drug-related crime has been the major contributor to this increase.

Definition A: Dr. X, professor of sociology and criminology at Bayou University, defines drug-related crime as . . .
Evidence B: According to her study, the percentage of drug-related crime in our major cities has increased 50 percent—five times faster than other types of crime.

Referring to the example above, please note the following:

- The distinction between argument and evidence: an argument is a general statement characterizing a past, present, or future condition or relationship; evidence is specific data or testimony used to enhance the audience's understanding and perception of the probability of that condition or relationship.
- The distinction between an argument and a subargument, and their relationship: both are general statements, but the argument is more general than the subargument.
- The types of support used: statistics, an FBI report, and university research; expert testimony for the definition of drug-related crime.
- The intrinsic credibility of the support used: the FBI, a professor at Bayou University. Your audience analysis can help you determine whether your audience would probably accept these sources as credible.

In addition to these types of support, you may also use examples, photographs, and real objects. In fact, real objects can be enormously persuasive. Let's say that you are planning to testify before the United States Senate on the hazards of dumping used medical laboratory specimens and syringes into the Atlantic Ocean. Which is bound to be more compelling, a photograph of these items or a carton full of them dumped onto the hearing-room table? Yes, the real thing often has its own persuasive edge, especially if it can be easily seen by those present and is not too offensive.

GUIDELINES FOR
SELECTING AND USING SUPPORT

The following guidelines should prove helpful in selecting and using support:

1. Select the most credible support available, making sure that your answer to each of these questions is a confident yes.
   a. Will my audience regard the support as sufficiently relevant to my argument or subargument?
   b. Will my audience regard the source (person, institution, publication) as sufficiently credible and free from bias?
   c. Will my audience accept the methodology behind the support?
   d. Will my audience regard the support as sufficiently recent?
   e. Do I expect the support to be sufficient in potency and in quantity to convince my audience of my argument?
2. If you are using several pieces of support to reinforce an argument, be sure that the first and last pieces are stronger, for again, we tend to remember best what is presented first and last.
3. Be careful not to provide too much support for an idea your audience essentially accepts. Otherwise, you could appear defensive, cultivating the "methinks the maid doth protest too much" reaction.
4. Try not to rely too heavily on any specific type of support in making your overall case or in presenting any single argument, for example, statistics or testimony.
5. Recognize that certain audience characteristics, as inferred from your audience analysis, may influence the type of evidence you select. For example, scientists, engineers, bankers, and accountants may be more disposed to accepting quantitative information as proof than "softer" or more inferential forms of proof, for example, testimony and examples.
6. When choosing examples to support your ideas, make sure they represent more the rule than the exception.
7. When selecting statistics, be ready to defend the way they were gleaned, remembering the famous line "There are three types of lies—lies, damn lies, and statistics."

"(YOUR NAME), PRIVATE INVESTIGATOR"

Once you have a reasonable idea of what type of support you need, do you know where to find it? A wide array of resources awaits you as you begin your detective work.

The Library

Several types of libraries are available to you. Your job is to select the ones most suited to your subject.

Your local library. Often good for general background research, but of limited use for in-depth research unless it is a main branch in a large city.

A college or university library. Generally far better for in-depth research than a local library. Reference librarians are also accustomed to processing more challenging research requests.

Specialized libraries. Various graduate institutions, companies, and organizations house libraries specializing in a certain subject, for example, law, medicine, dentistry, and veterinary medicine, pharmaceutical research, engineering, energy exploration, and so on. Contact the Special Libraries Association, 1700 18th Street NW, Washington, D.C. 20009 (202) 234-4700. One of their information specialists will try to identify a special library related to your subject.

Indexes, Your First Line of Support

If you are not used to conducting research on a topic, you may be picturing yourself poring through stacks of periodicals or books until you find the various pieces of support you need. You needn't worry any longer, for several easy-to-use indexes are available to you:

Reader's Guide to Periodical Literature
- Indexes articles published in about two hundred popular magazines, including *Time, Newsweek, U.S. News and World Report.*

- Available in most libraries.
- Supplements issued monthly.
- Can be most helpful in gaining a more general understanding of a highly technical subject.

The Magazine Index
- Covers about four hundred magazines of general interest.
- Contained on a special microfilm terminal.
- Very easy to use.

Business Periodicals Index
- Covers articles published in nearly three hundred business-oriented periodicals, including trade periodicals.
- Supplements issued monthly.
- Most libraries have it.

Subject Guide to Books in Print
- Lists *all* new and old books currently in print, by subject.
- Available in most libraries and bookstores.

Forthcoming Books
- Lists books just released or projected to be released within five months.
- Supplements issued bimonthly.
- Available in larger libraries and most bookstores.

National Newspaper Index
- A comprehensive microfilm index of the *New York Times, Wall Street Journal, Los Angeles Times, Christian Science Monitor,* and *Washington Post.*
- Easy to use.
- Available in most larger and academic libraries.

The Wall Street Journal Index
- Covers all articles covered in the *Wall Street Journal* and in *Barron's.*
- Contains both a subject index and a company-name index.

- Supplements issued monthly.
- Available in most libraries.

Funk & Scott Index
- Covers articles about industries and company activities and developments published in leading and more specialized business periodicals.
- Supplements issued weekly and monthly.
- Available in most libraries and nearly all business libraries.

Standard & Poor's Register of Corporations (3 vols.)
- Alphabetical listing of approximately forty-five thousand corporations. Separate volume lists directors and executives.
- Available in larger libraries and in business libraries.

Dun & Bradstreet's Million Dollar Directory (5 vols.)
- Covers over 160,000 companies with a net worth above $500,000.
- Provides alphabetical listing of company names, subsidiary relationships, headquarters, addresses, phone numbers, and so on.
- Available in larger libraries and in business libraries.

Thomas Register of American Manufacturers (3 sets of vols.)
- Explains who manufactures what product and where.
- Third set contains actual catalog data from about twelve hundred companies.
- Available in most larger libraries.

Findex: The Directory of Market Research Reports, Studies, and Surveys
- Guide to published, commercially available market and business research.
- Found most often in corporate libraries; not usually found in public or university libraries.
- Most studies and surveys listed are for sale, some costing thousands of dollars.

Directory of Directories
- Describes nearly eight thousand types of specialized directories.
- Published annually.
- Available in most large public libraries.

Encyclopedia of Geographic Information Services
- Lists of resources available on various geographic entities worldwide.
- Available in many large public and university libraries.

Research Centers Directory
- Annual directory of seventy-five hundred university, government, and nonprofit research entities.
- Identifies who is conducting research on which subjects (U.S.A. only).
- Available in university libraries.

Congressional Information Service Indexes
- a. *American Statistical Index:* for sources of government statistics.
- b. *Index to International Statistics:* for foreign statistics.
- c. *Statistical Reference Index:* for nongovernment statistics.

Researching People

Let's say you've found a very helpful article written by someone you've never heard of. Since you want to use this article to reinforce one or more of your key points, you want to make sure that the author's credentials meet your own standards and will be well received by your audience. Where do you turn? Here are five possible sources:

Marquis Who's Who Series
- *Who's Who in America* and several more specialized *Who's Who* volumes, including *Who's Who in Finance and Industry, Who's Who in the East, Who's Who of American Women.*

- Most libraries have *Who's Who in America;* other volumes are available in larger and more specialized libraries.

Current Biography
- Features articles about people prominent in the news; also includes obituaries.
- Articles printed in a single volume at end of the year.
- Indexed.
- Available in most medium-size and large libraries.

Biography Index
- Scans over 2,600 periodicals, books, and so forth, to identify and index various sources of information on prominent people.
- Available in large libraries.

Biography and Genealogy Master Index
- Index to biographical directories providing information on over 2 million current and historical figures referred to in 565 publications (including all volumes of *Who's Who*).
- Available in larger libraries.

New York Times Obituaries Index
- Index to all obituaries published in the *New York Times* from 1858 to 1978.
- Available in most libraries.

Going to the Experts

As helpful as your library research may or may not be, perhaps you feel that your detective work impels you to go directly to the source—the author, researcher, or interest group most likely to answer your questions.

This may be an excellent idea. In fact, you may find the experts more available to you and even more cooperative than you had expected. However, keep these caveats in mind to get the most out of your personal or telephone interview:

1. Don't rely on the expert to help you do your basic homework. To establish your own credibility with the expert and to gain the most from the interview, do a reasonable amount of background reading on your own.
2. Before you get too far into the interview, let the expert know why you are calling and approximately how much of his or her time you will probably need.
3. Devote the lion's share of your interview to questioning—not discussing or debating.
4. Realize that experts also have biases. Decide whether or not his or her bias disqualifies this expert as a source for your speech or presentation.
5. Follow through with a thank-you note and, if advisable, with a copy of your speech.

If you have difficulty locating a specific expert, you can contact the publisher of the book or periodical in which his or her work appeared. Or you can consult *Who's Who*.

If you are more interested in contacting an interest group rather than an expert per se, call or write:

American Society of Association Executives
1575 Eye Street, NW
Washington, D.C. 20005
(202) 626-2723

Most organizations will send you ready-made kits consisting of background information, publicity, position papers regarding various issues, and a bibliography.

You may also want to consult the *Encyclopedia of Associations*. Most major libraries have it.

Mining the U.S. Government

When I think about all the research tasks the various people I've advised have had to undertake, I estimate that more than half have relied on information available from the U.S. government.

The U.S. government is a virtual gold mine for gleaning support for your speech, but like the bureaucracy itself, finding this information can be extremely complicated. The following resources can help you to identify the bureau, division, or person that can best assist you:

United States Government Manual
- Comprehensive guide to the agencies and offices that make up the federal government.
- Available in many libraries.
- Can be ordered from:

> Superintendent of Documents
> Government Printing Office
> Washington, D.C. 20402

Federal Information Centers (FIC)
- Clearinghouses established by the government for persons who want to obtain information about the federal government.
- The FIC will either answer your question or identify the expert who can.
- The national headquarters number is (202) 566-1937.

Washington Information Directory
- Breaks down various departments and agencies into their particular divisions and briefly describes each.
- Provides contact person and phone number for each division.
- Also lists important nonfederal private and public organizations based in Washington, D.C.
- Available in most larger libraries.

Federal Executive Directory
- Very detailed listing of federal personnel, including names, titles, and phone numbers.
- Available in most large libraries.

Information U.S.A.
- Published by Penguin Books, it offers over a thousand pages of government information sources.
- Easy to use because of a detailed subject index.
- Available in many bookstores or directly through the publisher.

The Library of Congress
- Can also direct you to a specific agency or expert.
- Maintains telephone information services for determining the status of a specific piece of legislation.

For further information regarding the wide range of assistance the library can provide, write:

Library of Congress
1st Street between E. Capitol and Independence Avenue SE
Washington, D.C. 20540
(202) 287-6500

The Electronic Researcher

Computers are gaining an increasingly dominant position on the research landscape as they demonstrate four major assets:

1. The capacity to store huge amounts of information.
2. Speed.
3. Accuracy (due to instantaneous updating and correcting capabilities).
4. Precise retrievability via key-word searches.

To retrieve information from a computer, you must access the appropriate data bases available at your library for a fee based on usage or from an "on-line vendor." These data bases sort through a vast number of references for books, journal articles, dissertations, published reports, newspaper articles, government documents, statistics, and so on. In fact, over four hundred data bases are now available, and new ones are being added regularly.

A data base search is recommended when

- The subject is complex, involving two or more concepts, time spans, or subject areas. The computer combines terms, making references more accessible and searching more efficient.
- You need the most recent citations.
- No printed equivalent to the data base exists.
- Time is of the essence. The computer can search several years or volumes at once.

The main criterion in selecting an on-line vendor is that it have data bases that store the types of information you need. Here are a few of the most established vendors:

Dow Jones News/Retrieval
P.O. Box 300
Princeton, New Jersey 08543

Specializes in economic and business information.

Compu Serve
P.O. Box 20212
Columbus, Ohio 43220

Geared more toward consumer and home information.

VU/Text
1211 Chestnut Street
Philadelphia, Pennsylvania 19107

Strong in regional news coverage.

Dialog
3460 Hillview Avenue
Palo Alto, California 94304

Good for hard-to-find information.

For more information regarding computerized research opportunities, consult the *Directory of Online Databases; Computer Read-*

able Databases or the *Data Base Directory.* Your library will probably contain one or more of these or a similar guide.

The Ultimate Research Tools

No better guides to the myriad research opportunities available to you exist than Robert Berkman's *Find It Fast: How to Uncover Expert Information on Any Subject* (Harper and Row, 1987) and Mona McCormick's *The New York Times Guide to Reference Materials,* revised edition (Dorset, 1985). They are eminently readable, to-the-point, and have proven to be my most valuable companions in relating to this frequently perplexing period we live in—the information age.

Chapter 7

INTRODUCTIONS AND CONCLUSIONS

W e have all heard repeatedly the tiresome but apt phrase, don't judge a book by its cover. Fortunately or not, speeches are often judged by their covers—by the first and last impressions cultivated by their introductions and conclusions.

In my practice, the number-one creative challenge facing my clients is to produce an impactful introduction and conclusion—one that helps the speaker project a confident, commanding presence. The advice found in this chapter will help you to meet this challenge.

THE INTRODUCTION

Your introduction should accomplish the following objectives:

- To gain the audience's attention and ward off their indifference, skepticism, fatigue, distractibility, or whatever other negative traits your audience analysis reveals.
- To give your listeners a sense of your personality and credibility—and to address their reservations about you or your topic.

- To orient them to your topic, including the reasons why they should focus on it.
- To provide them with a sense of direction regarding your overall approach to the topic.

The Attention Getter

Gaining the audience's attention is your first challenge. Therefore, the following lines hardly qualify as quality attention getters, unless your goal is to produce yawns or impede your credibility.

"My topic today is . . ."
"I learned only yesterday that I was to address you."
"I'm not very good at speech making, but . . ."

The eight major types of attention getters available to you are illustrated in your speech to the annual gathering of the National Widget Manufacturer's Society.

1. An attention-grabbing rhetorical question (or series of questions) or statement: "What would you do with a solid-gold million-dollar widget?" Or, "Every one of you could own a solid-gold million-dollar widget within the next ten years."
2. An appropriate quote from a well-known person: "Benjamin Franklin once said, 'You can tell the quality of a man by the type of widget he uses.'"
3. A startling or interesting statistic appropriate to your subject: "In the forty-five minutes since this meeting began, American widget makers have produced 1,356 jumbos and 156,341 midgets—if laid end to end, enough to circle the globe four times."
4. A personal story or an anecdote of relevance and interest: "You all know my company's famous Tom Thumb widgets—at least I hope you all know them, since we spend an awful lot of money on advertising. Well, let me tell you the real story of how they came to be invented."

5. An appropriate and related reference to a current event: "I'm sure you've all heard the news from Washington today about the widget that can withstand ten times greater pressure than the ones we've relied on for the past decade."

6. Unusual or unexpected biographical information: "I've been asked to speak to you today because of my position as chief executive officer of Amalgamated Industries, and I appreciate the honor. But did you know that I'm also a former widget designer and, before that, a stockboy in a widget warehouse?" (Be careful not to sound too egotistical.)

7. The challenge to your audience: "Ladies and gentlemen, we have no one to blame but ourselves for the sorry state of the widget industry! It is my hope, though, that we can come out of this meeting tonight with goals and an understanding that will put us all back on the road to prosperity." A note of caution here: Be careful not to set an impossible assignment—your audience may recognize it as such and tune you out, or they may blame you for failure if the challenge is unmet.

8. The use of common ground, including shared values, coupled with an appeal for a fair hearing. This combination of tactics is particularly appropriate for a hostile audience, especially one that values directness and candor. For example:

> "You and I have one major goal in common—to do everything possible to ensure the survival of the widget industry. However, our survival is imperiled by the escalating dumping of foreign widgets into our markets. Our efforts to erect strong trade barriers have been useless. Our last resort—and I say this following a lot of agonizing thought and discussion with our industry leaders—is to work harder on quality while pricing our widgets more competitively. Please hear me out, because we need to understand the full picture before we make any decision or take any action."

Although example 8 gets to the heart of the speaker's case quickly and directly, it is devoid of jokes, illustrations, and other more creative types of attention getters that might appear too manipulative under the circumstances. However, a statistic accentuating the dumping or its economic impact might appropriately precede the common-ground reference and therefore make the introduction more attention getting.

Make sure your attention getter is credible. If you are quoting someone, make sure that he or she is known and respected by the audience. If you are using a statistic or number, be prepared to increase the audience's sense of its credibility by citing an authoritative source, for example, "According to the U.S. Bureau of the Census . . ."

Also be prepared to walk the fine line between being appropriately dramatic and too dramatic. Seek feedback from trusted colleagues and advisors.

Finally, make sure you are *completely comfortable* with your attention getter. If you think it's too flashy or risky or foreign to your usual style, your discomfort may be reflected in your delivery.

The Need-to-Know Step

Once you have gained the audience's attention, you may need to devote a separate step to explaining why they should listen to your message—to answering their question What's in it for me? Here you will need to produce a "motivational carrot" related to an individual or group value or need. As you search the carrot patches, select a carrot that credibly—and not too crassly—links your topic with your audience's needs. Among the more popular "carrot patches" are

- Profits, sales, financial gain
- Personal pleasure (e.g., travel, personal possessions, opportunities for social contact)
- Competency or control
- Opportunity for health and safety

The Preview

When P. T. Barnum exhorted, "Tell them what you're going to tell them; tell them; then tell them what you told them," he provided timeless advice that applies to most speeches and presentations. The first advice, "Tell them what you're going to tell them," refers to the preview portion of your introduction. It is a brief series of statements that orient your audience to your game plan for the body of your speech.

Previews can be either statements or questions. Consider these two versions based on the same topic, "The Promise of Biotechnology."

Version 1: "Today I shall discuss the advances made in biotechnology, our research agenda into the twenty-first century, and the role of the federal government in creating a climate hospitable to biotechnology."

Version 2: "How has biotechnology demonstrated its promise? What are our research priorities as we approach the twenty-first century? How can the federal government advance the promise of biotechnology?"

I generally prepare the approach reflected in version 2 because it tends to be more attention getting. Regardless of which version you prefer, the following advice should be helpful as you prepare a preview and complete your introduction.

- Make each phrase concise and interesting.
- Try not to raise more than three or four points. If you do, you will probably be taxing your audience's attention span and memory.
- Do not "overdisclose" your point of view or your solution in the preview. Doing so before the audience is properly primed can cause them either to tune you out altogether or to begin preparing counterarguments.
- If your program provides a question-and-answer session, consider making your final preview point ". . . and I will be pleased to respond to your questions following my remarks."

Once you have completed your preview—and therefore your introduction—you are ready to bridge to the body of your speech. A few possible bridges:

"Now I will address the first question . . ."

"A situation I recently faced explains why I regard the first question [repeated] as so important." (Speaker then proceeds with illustration.)

AND IN CONCLUSION...

Throughout the introduction and body of your remarks, you've seized and maintained your audience's attention, you've presented your ideas in a clear and interesting manner. One major step awaits you—your conclusion. Although few absolutes apply to presenting and speech making, one of them is that you must always have a conclusion.

A conclusion is *not*
- The solution to a problem you've been discussing.
- The last idea in your speech.
- A simple line, such as "That's all I have to say."

A conclusion *is*
- A separate section of your remarks devoted to
  a. Recapping your main points in a concise, interesting, and confident manner.
  b. Reinforcing the value of your remarks to your audience and, when appropriate.
  c. Appealing for their support.

In essence, a conclusion gives a sense of wholeness or unity to your presentation, reminds your audience of your key messages, and cultivates or reinforces the residual feeling you wish to stimulate within your audience, for example, sympathy, fear, urgency, the desire to take action.

Let me offer some practical advice for preparing and delivering your conclusion.

Preparation

1. Prepare your conclusion last, after you have prepared the introduction and body.
2. Plan what you want to accomplish from a substance-and-image standpoint. What key messages do you want to reinforce? What feelings do you wish to cultivate or reinforce regarding you and your message?
3. Make sure that your speech contains *only one conclusion*. We've all been victimized by the speaker who seems to be concluding and then goes on and on.
4. Try to avoid worn signposts to announce your conclusion: "in conclusion," "in summary," and so on.
   a. You can signal your audience that you're concluding by pausing briefly before you close, followed by the asking of a question ("What major conclusions can we draw from the state of our industry?"). Or you can reaffirm your major premise(s) ("Yes, our industry faces greater challenges than ever before—challenges based on . . .").
   b. You can walk in front of the lectern or, if already in front of it, take a few steps closer to your audience to signal your conclusion and to create a somewhat more intimate feeling with your audience. (But remember to take your microphone with you.)
5. Keep the sentences of your conclusion relatively short and crisp. In fact, I frequently advise a version of what I have dubbed the Julius Caesar conclusion:

JULIUS CAESAR	*YOU*
I came	We are talented
I saw	We are committed
I conquered	We will meet the challenge

You can change the words any way you wish; just make sure the phrases are concise and build to a confident climax. (You can reinforce that climax by delivering each line with escalating intensity, enhanced with appropriate gestures.)

6. As you recap your main ideas, don't get caught in the trap of simply giving an abstract of your speech, choosing the same language used in the body. The phrasing of the conclusion should be imbued with an element of freshness.

7. Consider tying your conclusion back to an illustration, example, or quote used in your introduction. This approach can reinforce the overall unity of your remarks:

> "I began my remarks by sharing with you the story of the little girl who used to stand outside the airport in Montego Bay begging for money for her family. Today, twenty years later, that little girl is a very popular schoolteacher—a symbol of hope for those striving to break loose from the shackles of poverty."

8. End with a strong closing line ("Hope is the sustenance for mankind's spirit; it, too, must always be nurtured.").

Delivery

1. Practice your conclusion separately—over and over again—until you barely need to refer to your notes.

2. As you practice, focus on smoothness, confidence, strong eye contact, and strength, making sure that your vocal projection doesn't taper off right before you finish (a highly typical phenomenon).

3. If you want to say "thank you" at the end, don't let it "step on" your closing line. Pause for a few seconds, then say, "Thank you."

CHECKING THE CLOCK

How much time should you devote to your introduction and conclusion? There are no absolutes. Generally your introduction and conclusion should consume no more than a total of 20 percent of your presentation, 12 to 14 percent for your introduction, the balance for the conclusion. Alternatively, you might make your conclusion two-thirds the length of the introduction.

While these estimates may give you a general feel regarding length, the best way to gauge it is to ask for feedback during a planning or practice session. However, do keep these principles in mind:

- If the audience is hostile to you, your company, or your message, you may need to devote additional time in the introduction to building rapport.
- Avoid anything in the introduction or conclusion that seems too lengthy, such as drawn-out jokes, shaggy-dog stories, rambling examples, long lists, and so on. At the beginning of your speech, your audience will generally be eager for you to "get to the meat"—the body—of your discussion. The audience's patience is normally thinner toward the end of the speech than toward the beginning. Why test it?

Chapter 8

HOW TO SAY WHAT YOU MEAN— AND BE HEARD

One of the first things I remember being told as I entered graduate school nearly twenty-five years ago was that "a speech is not an essay on its hind legs." This statement should be kept uppermost in your mind as you plan to impart a sense of style to your speech or presentation. In far too many instances, especially in the business world, speeches and presentations are prepared as orally presented memos—devoid of feeling, lacking in the requisite energy to make an immediate and significant impact on the audience.

The writer who prepares a speech or presentation as an essay or memo on its hind legs has not taken into account the major differences between written and oral communication:

- The reader can reread a written communication if he or she does not understand it upon the first reading. In oral communication the listener must understand the point the first time, possibly aided by the speaker's natural or deliberate redundancy.
- A reader can drop whatever he or she is reading to clarify a difficult word or concept and consult a dictionary or reference work. Oral communication does not afford this luxury.
- For written communication to be effective, the writer must anticipate his or her audience's understanding and reaction

as much as possible. Although this also applies to oral communication, the speaker has the added luxury of adjusting immediately to audience feedback.

TOWARD A MORE ORAL STYLE

The fundamental differences between written and oral communication are reflected in a wide range of stylistic distinctions between the two. The more you understand the following constituent ingredients of an oral style, the greater your opportunity to avert the "hind legs" accusation and make instead a direct connection with your audience:

Repetition reinforces your key messages, facilitates recall, and infuses your style with cadence to convey added strength, authority, and conviction:

Reorganizing our business will enhance our efficiency.
Reorganizing our business will enhance our financial position.
Reorganizing our business will help give us the competitive edge.

Restatement reinforces your key messages and facilitates recall.

Reorganizing is a must proposition. We can't progress as a company without it. Maintaining the status quo—not adapting to change—will relegate us to the fate of the dinosaur.

Personalized communication (via personal pronouns and references) makes your message more engaging:

I realize that reorganization will be a challenge for all of us. Most of the challenge, I feel, is in dealing with change itself—especially since we have not experienced a change of this magnitude for nearly twenty years.

Contractions help maintain the informality of the communication:

We've done everything possible to take your personal needs into account in our reorganization plan. When you review the plan, you're going to see that we truly regard you as our most important asset.

Simple language ensures clarity and maintains attention and interest:

> *The "unsimple":* The rationales for reorganization are based on a multiplicity of indisputable exigencies impacting our industry in general and our company in particular.

> *The simple:* The reorganization is based on clear needs affecting both our industry and our company.

Signposts (e.g., previews, transitions, and internal summaries) remind the listener of the organizational flow of the message:

> Now that we have discussed the reasons behind reorganization, let's focus on the plan itself, including its major planks and a specific timetable for its implementation.

Varied sentence length aids your audience's understanding and attention and infuses your style with added energy to convey conviction and to generate added interest:

> Reorganization will virtually eliminate duplication. No more wondering whether an order is to be processed in the consumer or commercial order department. The two will be combined.

Rhetorical questions stimulate your audience's thinking and attention.

> How much market share have we lost over the past year? More important, how much can we expect to regain through reorganization?

DEVELOPING YOUR STYLE

It is probably safe to say that if something can be defined as "having style," chances are it doesn't. Style is that elusive element that lifts a phrase or thought from background noise to sudden piercing clarity, vitality, and memorability.

Style is a personal matter. You are unique, and your words will be unlike anyone else's if you let them be. The key is to combine that uniqueness with effectiveness.

As you impart the essential features of an oral style to your message, five principal standards should guide you: accuracy, clarity, conciseness, appropriateness, and vividness.

Accuracy

Words are merely symbolic representations for objects or ideas. They have limited meaning outside the context of our experience with them and the personal meaning or connotations we impart to them as a result. When I communicate with you, I need to stimulate within you a connotation that is reasonably representative of mine, despite our varied experiences. Hence, my word choice must both *accurately capture* my thoughts and *accurately stimulate* yours.

Take, for example, the word *reorganization*. A speaker choosing this word must understand that the audience's response to the term will not be a neutral dictionary definition. Rather, *reorganization* can register a host of connotations rooted in each audience member's experience.

To the task-oriented executive, *reorganization* means efficiency, productivity, profits.

To the general employee, *reorganization* means job transfers, plant closings, confusion, uncertainty, turf battles, and so on.

To the less senior employee, *reorganization* means layoffs.

Accuracy is not only a practical consideration, it is also an ethical one. In choosing words we must take pains to avoid allowing our desire for effect to dominate our obligation to communicate accurately and truthfully.

Clarity

Clarity enables you to eliminate any confusion on the part of your audience as a result of your message. This confusion is most frequently rooted in the following factors:

Poor word choice. Avoid words that are either too abstract or not sufficiently familiar to your audience. Users of jargon are among the most serious offenders.

Euphemisms. Euphemisms are a frequent enemy of clarity. *Advancing toward the rear* may sound less like a defeat than the word *retreat,* but *retreat* is the most direct and appropriate term. Leave the propagandizing to others.

Long, complex sentences containing numerous concepts. This is a standard form in written communication. However, in oral communication, such sentences may not afford your listeners enough "processing time" to understand and reflect on the point you're making.

The passive voice. A favorite of the bureaucrat, it takes both the clarity and the energy out of a statement. The passive voice may be a good defensive move, but it is a poor method of communication: "Coinciding with the implementation of rationing was the appearance of an extensive unofficial private market" versus "The black market arrived soon after rationing began."

Confusing syntax. The following examples highlight how awkward syntax can confuse meaning:

- "John told Harry that he had been fired." Who was fired? John or Harry?
- Groucho Marx: "When I was on safari in Africa, I shot an elephant in my pajamas. How he got in my pajamas I'll never know."

Insufficient expressiveness. Business memos are characteristically devoid of feeling. Although this written practice may or may not be appropriate, the business presentation or speech is likely to fall flat if it follows suit. Its main ideas need to be garnished with adjectives and adverbs to help the audience sense your conviction and visualize your ideas.

Let's say that last year's sales were exceptional. How might you communicate this?

1. Our sales growth last year was strong.
2. Our sales growth last year was impressive.
3. Our sales growth last year was explosive.

Clearly, statement 3 is the most expressive. However, before choosing it, make sure it accurately captures your sense of last year's performance. In addition, make sure the term *explosive* would be viewed as appropriate language—and not "hype"—by your audience.

Unstated assumptions. Often speakers improperly assume that they perceive or share the same assumptions with their audience. If speakers do not state the assumptions that are central to their point, the audience may have difficulty tracking their logic. For example, I am assuming that you will relate "tracking logic" to clarity. If you don't, I have failed to be clear.

Insufficient use of support to make the communication concrete. The more abstract the concept, the greater the potential for confusion. Examples, illustrations, statistics, and other forms of proof and amplification will help your audience visualize your message.

Rushed delivery and absence of pauses. If your message is a Niagara of words without sufficient opportunity for the audience to digest and reflect upon it, your clarity and ultimately your persuasive impact will be compromised.

Conciseness

If you make your point too wordy, you may be inviting confusion, lack of attention, and possibly, a total tune-out. Conciseness, on the other hand, facilitates attention, clarity, and can convey strength, authority, and conviction.

What, then, prevents us from being sufficiently concise? There are three principal reasons:

1. *Absence of sufficient preparation.* As we compose on our feet, we may become too wordy or repetitious, frequently compromising clarity in the process.
2. *Insecurity about the audience's understanding or acceptance.* We have a tendency to ramble when we are not sure whether or not our audience understands or agrees with us. They may be sending us limited feedback, or we may be having difficulty interpreting it.
3. *The need to fill the allocated time.* Often we allow our sense of obligation to speak for a given length of time to take precedence over conciseness. To prevent this from happening, try to reduce the time allocation when you are invited to speak and focus mainly on accomplishing net effects, substance, and image goals.

Appropriateness

Your style needs to be tailored to the audience and to the occasion. How formal should you be? How forceful should you be? What tone should you project? The difference in style or tone between a coach trying to stimulate his dispirited team during halftime and a clergyman delivering a eulogy is as wide a stylistic gap as you could find. Good audience analysis and advance work are the keys to gauging the appropriateness of your style.

Vividness

"What did you have for lunch?"
"A hamburger on a bun."
"Oh, that's nice."

"What did you have for lunch?"
"A charcoal-broiled, medium-rare ground beef patty, bubbling with flavor, on a toasted sesame roll with a perfect slice of red Bermuda onion, a dollop of ketchup, and a kosher dill pickle on the side."
"You're making me hungry just hearing you talk about it!"

Oral language offers you the opportunity to use words in their most vivid, evocative forms. And if you have any remaining doubt about the effectiveness of picturesque language in a persuasive presentation, consider this:

Researchers E.F. Loftus and J.C. Palmer showed a fascinating link between language and mental imagery in their studies of a group of subjects who were asked questions about an automobile collision.* Different persons were given different stories about the accident: some were told the cars had "smashed"; others heard that the vehicles had "collided," "bumped," "hit," or "contacted."

The subjects all saw the same film of an accident and were then asked to estimate the speed of the cars. The difference between those told of a "smash" and those told of "contact" was nine miles per hour—no matter that they saw the same accident in the film. The results with average speed:

"Smashed"	40.8 mph
"Collided"	39.3 mph
"Bumped"	38.1 mph
"Hit"	34.0 mph
"Contacted"	31.8 mph

Although there was no broken glass evident in the film shown to the subjects, 32 percent of those who were told of a "smash" reported seeing broken glass, while only 14 percent of those who were told the cars "hit" had the same memory.

All this for the selection of a single verb!

THE GARNISH

Once you have conformed to the basic standards of style, you may be able to generate added impact by relying on any of the

---

*E.F. Loftus and J.C. Palmer, "Reconstruction of Automobile Destruction: An Example of the Interaction between Language and Memory," *Journal of Verbal Learning and Verbal Behavior 13* (1974): 585–589.

following rhetorical devices frequently used in speeches and presentations:

Repetition

As stated earlier, repeating a word, phrase, or sound can add emphasis and elevate the overall energy of a message.
At beginning of phrase:

Now is the time for us to increase our sales.
Now is the time for us to seize a greater market share.
Now is the time for us to achieve true leadership in our industry.

Note the escalation of feeling fed by the repetition and the expanding focus of the phrases—from sales to industry leadership.
Repetition is also effective at the end of a phrase:

Our plan is ready. Our team is ready. Our people are ready.

Or in succession:

Reorganization—reorganization will help us capture our potential. (Note: This device is called an epizeuxis. Try pronouncing *that* and eating spaghetti at the same time.)

Alliteration is the repetition of consonant sounds:

Three *k*eys to *c*redibility are *c*haracter, *c*ompetence, and *c*ompassion.

Assonance is the repetition of vowel sounds:

*E*very *e*ffort must be *e*xerted to *e*ducate our *e*mployees about the *e*xpected benefits of reorganization.

Note: Both alliteration and assonance can be especially effective if they do not draw too much attention to themselves. When they do, they convey the speaker's self-indulgence with style, rather than his or her intent to communicate.

Antithesis

Aristotle said that we tend to understand something best in terms of its opposite (e.g., to understand wealth, we must understand poverty). Antithesis, the use of contrasting words for clarity, emphasis, and a sense of rhythmic balance, can be a most arresting rhetorical device:

> Reorganization will not confuse; it will clarify.
> Reorganization will not tie our hands; it will increase our freedom.
> Reorganization will not impede our pace; it will accelerate it.
> (Note: This is an example of antithesis plus multiple repetitive patterns.)

A more challenging form of antithesis is the antimetabole, a device involving the juxtaposition of key terms for persuasive effect. The most famous example is John F. Kennedy's "Ask not what your country can do for you; ask what you can do for your country." One of my favorite antimetaboles was crafted by the late English philosopher and clergyman L. P. Jacks: "The pessimist sees the difficulty in every opportunity; the optimist, the opportunity in every difficulty."

Personification

"Opportunity knocks only once" and "love is blind" are examples of personification.

This device imputes human qualities to an object or idea, thereby imparting added concreteness and vividness to the idea being conveyed.

Hyperbole

This is intentional exaggeration or overstatement (e.g., "The whole world is watching.").

Understatement

The opposite of hyperbole, understatement can be even more effective, assuming that the audience understands the fact that you are using the device. "Babe Ruth was known to make contact with the ball every now and then," or, to a good-natured and sodden audience after a week of steady rain, "I understand it's been a little damp here lately."

Rhetorical questions

Asking yourself a question is often a good way of introducing a new subject. Asking the question of the audience is often a good way of involving them in your presentation. The danger, though, is that someone might respond to your question aloud with an answer unsuited to your purpose in posing the question.

Parallelism

Parallelism is the use of words in a pattern or rhythm suggestive of music or poetry. "We are fully prepared; we are fully committed; we await the signal to begin." There is an added benefit here: By interspersing short sentences with longer ones and allowing for dramatic pause, you will buy breathing spaces for yourself, thereby aiding your delivery.

Metaphors and Similes

Metaphors and similes evoke graphic images that conjure up the idea being described. They can be found everywhere:*

The Zoo and the Aquarium
  "Writing that report was a bear."
  "He's a sly old fox."

*A handy reference item is *The Dictionary of Similes* by Frank J. Wilstach, reprinted by Gale Research Company (Detroit, 1981).

"She's a barracuda."
"He's a shark."
"That's a whale of an idea."

The Food Market
"She's a sharp cookie."
"He's as smooth as butter."
"That's the icing on the cake."

The General Store
"She's as smooth as silk."
"He's as tough as nails."
"The news hit me like a ton of bricks."
"That opens a new can of worms."

The Stadium
"Our reorganization plan is at the five-yard line."
"He dropped the ball."
"Keep your eye on the ball."
"We have no choice but to punt."

The History Books
"You hit my Achilles heel."
"I feel like General Custer right before the Indians attacked."

Metaphors are effective because they stimulate word pictures, support conciseness, and are frequently clever. However, they should neither be labored to excess nor mixed: "Our new sales program is *sailing along* smoothly. In fact, we dealt our competitor a major *knockout punch* yesterday. All we have to do now is to keep our *eye on the ball.*"

COMPLEMENTING
YOUR STYLE WITH HUMOR

A good sense of humor can be a terrific way of rounding off your style, and a dash of effective humor can be just what your audience needs in your introduction or at any other point throughout your speech. While tickling the audience's funny bone, humor can relieve their tension and yours, convey your friendliness and approachability, make a point, and ultimately enhance your credibility. In short, effective humor can put your audience in a frame of mind conducive to meeting your substance and image goals— to your capturing the persuasive edge.

But the key word in discussing humor is *effective,* for we all know the risks of the proverbial lead balloon and the skunk at a garden party.

The Basics of Humor

Speakers who are good humorists are good risk assessors and regularly reflect the following advice in their use of humor:

- If you are not by nature a good joke teller, chances are you will have difficulty telling one well during a speech. Don't attempt to do so until you feel completely at ease with your ability. Nothing kills a joke like an uncomfortable delivery.
- If you have a good sense of humor but are not a terrific joke teller, one-liners may be your preferred suit.
- Your humor must be relevant. If it is not relevant to the audience, setting, or occasion, it should be relevant to the content of your message.
- Guard carefully against humor that may be overtly or subtly sexist, ethnic, racist, risqué, or overly critical of a person or group. Although you may normally want your words to be memorable, such jokes may make your words too memorable.
- If you have any doubt about whether your joke or line is funny, try it out on your reliable critics, making sure they understand the context in which it is to be presented. If any doubt exists after this pilot test, forget the joke—and hope that your advisors do too.
- Humor is not only a good ice breaker for your introduction. An occasional sprinkling within the body of your speech can

break the tension nicely, especially a one-liner slipped in by surprise.

- Plan how you will introduce the humor. If you begin by saying, "I heard this really funny story," you may cause some audience members to say to themselves defiantly, "Prove to me that it is so funny." Therefore, surprising them with your humor is generally the best approach.
- Don't laugh too hard at your own joke; this can draw attention away from your joke to you. Let the audience know the story is funny, not by your own laughter but by your animation and your enjoyment in the telling.
- Allow the audience's reaction to dissipate before moving on to your more serious content.
- If the joke falls flat, try to be funny about not being funny (e.g., "That's the last time I'll ask my accountant to help me with my speech.").

Memo on Humor From the White House

Ronald Reagan was a superb humorist throughout his presidency. A fair share of the credit for some of his funnier lines and stories goes to Landon Parvin, his personal speech writer. Here is a brief Parvin sampler:

"I heard one presidential candidate say that what this country needed was a president for the nineties. I was set to run again. I thought he said a president *in* his nineties."

At a tribute to Bob Hope: "And, of course, Bob's great love is golf. When we met tonight, the first thing he said was, "By the way, what's your handicap?" I said, "The Congress.""

During the height of the Iran-Contra controversy, the president got a great response at the Gridiron Dinner with this one—"With the Iran thing occupying everyone's attention, I was thinking, Do you remember the flap when I said, 'The bombing begins in five minutes?' Remember when I fell asleep during my audience with the pope? Remember Bitburg . . . boy, those were the good old days."

Part of Parvin's talent is rooted in his keen sensitivity to audience reaction. This is reflected in the following additional advice he gives regarding the use of humor:

- Laugh at other people's jokes before you even get up to speak. Notice during Hollywood roasts that the people at the head table laugh harder than anyone else. They are setting the tone and giving cues.
- Deliver your punch line in one breath.
- One way to overcome a lack of self-confidence in using humor is to use a funny quote by someone else. This puts the burden on the person being quoted, not on the speaker.
- Be careful about using humor with small audiences. You may not have the critical mass needed to get a good, solid laugh. Weak, individual chuckles may be awkward.
- A major reason to use humor is to enhance your likability and credibility with an audience. Any humor that works against this is self-defeating. Speakers are often told to personalize a joke, for example, "On the way over here today a man dressed as a parrot came up to me and said . . ." I believe this hurts your credibility because the audience is already thinking, "Well, that didn't really happen to him." You don't want an audience to have any doubts about you, period. Also, avoid humor that has a sharp edge, unless you're at a roast. You can't go wrong with light, self-deprecating humor. There's a reason politicians love such humor—it works. You can't lose by being gracious and good-natured.
- Avoid puns or plays on words. You're more likely to get a groan than a laugh, and who needs that? And don't tell long, drawn-out jokes. Unless you're a professional speaker, the chances are that the payoff is not going to be worth the buildup.

Self-deprecating Humor

President Reagan was also a virtual trendsetter in the use of self-deprecating humor. Throughout his two terms he was the victim of attacks regarding his age (he was almost seventy-nine when he left office), his tendency to fall asleep during cabinet meetings, and a host of controversial decisions and actions. The following examples reflect his mastery of the self-deprecating quip:

> With so many hot spots around the world, I've told my aides that whenever they hear of trouble, they should wake me up immediately—even if I'm in a cabinet meeting.

During the 1984 presidential campaign, when Walter Mondale accused Reagan of conducting "government by amnesia," Reagan said, "I thought that remark accusing me of having amnesia was uncalled for. I just wish I could remember who said it."

Self-deprecating humor gives the audience permission to laugh at the speaker's foibles, thereby removing an ego barrier between speaker and audience and signaling the audience that the speaker has a certain inner confidence that makes him secure enough to poke fun at himself.

In using self-deprecating humor, the main caveat is not to sound self-abusive. You don't want the audience to think you don't like yourself.

Finding the Right Line

Coming up with a good line can sometimes be more difficult than researching how many babies were born in Pocatello, Idaho, in 1943. In fact, too many executives become so focused on finding the "right" line or joke that they neglect other aspects of their preparation. What, then, should you do?

- Keep a speaker's "funny file" of cartoons and amusing quotes that you come across while reading, watching television, listening to the radio, or conversing with colleagues and friends.
- Consult humor anthologies. Although a joke lifted verbatim from an anthology can be as appetizing as rewarmed corn— and many of them are corn—the anthologies can sometimes

stimulate a thinking pattern that results in a good joke or one-liner.

- If you have a good sense of humor, the event itself—the audience, setting, and occasion—can often generate the humor you seek. Ask yourself whether you have something appropriately humorous to say about

  Your introducer's remarks

  Remarks by a preceding speaker

  One or more persons in attendance

  What happened to you as you parked your car or entered the building

  The building or room in which you are speaking

- Consider hiring a writer experienced in lacing speeches with humor. Thoroughly explain the nature of the audience, occasion, and setting.

As I was putting the finishing touches on this discussion, one of my business advisors called me. During our conversation he told me that he would be turning fifty the following week. I asked, "Is this causing you any pain?" Without skipping a beat, he replied, "No . . . only mentally and physically": A quick, relevant, appropriate, amusing one-liner in which the speaker was the "victim." That's an example of effective humor—and a reflection of an effective style.

Chapter 9

VISUAL AIDS— SIGHTS TO BEHOLD

The old adage, "A picture is worth a thousand words," can apply to presentations and speeches as long as the following criteria are met:

1. The visual aid communicates *more or better* than the words alone would.
2. The visual aid can be well seen by everyone in the audience.

Two seemingly simple criteria. Yet nearly everything that can go wrong with visuals involves one or both of these criteria not being satisfied.

How many times have you witnessed a presentation in which visual aids were actually highly magnified note cards, used more to remind and guide the presenter than to aid the audience? *The principal use of visuals, then, is not to jog the presenter's memory; it is to enhance the audience's understanding.*

How many times have you witnessed a presentation in which one or more of the following conditions prevailed?

- The lettering in the visual aid was too small, or a detail in a drawing or photograph was not sufficiently distinct.
- The visual contained excessive wording, columns of numbers, or drawings that made it difficult for you to focus on the key message it was supposed to support.

- A clear view of the visual was blocked by the speaker, a member of the audience, the projector, or the positioning of the screen.

Before you even begin to select visual aids for a speech or presentation, ask yourself two basic questions:

1. Why do I need them?
2. How might they affect my speaking style?

The answer to the first question should be, "The aids graphically capture concepts related to my main points that are difficult to describe in words alone." Therefore, as you apply the "needs test" to your visuals, make sure that they will help your audience conceptualize an idea related to one of your key messages.

The second question involves a more subtle assessment. Over the years I have seen the styles of scores of speakers compromised by the use of visuals. Specifically, the mechanics of using them preoccupies the speaker and undermines his or her natural spontaneity. He or she is, in essence, overly controlled or too programmed by them. Put another way, when the presentation could be described as "visuals plus speaker," not "speaker plus visuals," your own speaking style and communicative potential are competing with and being overshadowed by your visuals.

Being too programmed by visuals does not automatically mean you should not use them. Rather, you should return to the "needs test" and decide how many visuals you definitely need.

SELECTING THE TYPE OF VISUAL

Different situations call for different media. As you initially determine whether you should use 35-mm slides, overhead transparencies, flip charts, videotapes, and so on, decide which of the criteria implied in each of the following questions applies to you:

1. How do the corporate or meeting norms influence the type of visual chosen?
   - Is one type of visual preferred?
   - Would choosing another type be perceived as a negative? What sources are available to you to answer this question?
2. Do financial constraints affect the type of visual chosen?
   - Are 35-mm slides really too expensive? Could a perception that they are too expensive undermine your presentation? Can this perception be preempted? How?
   - Are actual models reasonably affordable?
   - Are blown-up photographs?
   - Are videotapes?
3. Do room lighting conditions influence the type of medium chosen?
   - If the lighting conditions are not suited to your preferred medium, can they be changed?
4. Does the size of the room or seating arrangement influence the type of visual chosen?
5. Does "transportability" influence the type of medium chosen?
   - Should a bulky item, for example, a model, be shipped to where the presentation is to be made?
6. Does production time influence the type of medium chosen?
   - Are you choosing overheads or flip charts because they are quicker to produce despite your preference for 35-mm slides? Have you double-checked to determine if you might still have time for slides to be prepared?
7. Regardless of the type of medium chosen, will your visuals reflect the proper degree of professionalism?

Major Media Options: Advantages, Disadvantages, and Advice

FLIP CHARTS

Advantages:
- Good for small, informal groups.
- Can be placed close to the group, allowing you to be closer to them.

- Free from the technical problems associated with a projector and screen.
- Easy to handle.
- Usually inexpensive.
- Can be added to easily during the presentation.

Disadvantages:
- Not generally easy to see for audiences larger than forty to fifty. (A dais or amphitheater may permit the exception.)
- Preparation with high-quality lettering can be time-consuming.
- Can be somewhat cumbersome to transport.

Advice:
- Prepare at least most of the chart in advance; too much writing while speaking can be time-consuming, it may cause you to turn away from your audience, and the chart will not appear as professional as one prepared in advance.
- Consider entering your speaking notes lightly on the left margin of the visual so that only you can see them.
- Leave a blank sheet between each visual to prevent the next one from showing.
- Tape the bottom corners of each visual and blank sheet to allow you to unveil each chart with one fluid motion.
- Generally, a pointer is not necessary when using a flip chart.

OBJECTS

Advantages:
- Add great realism to your presentation.

Disadvantages:
- Often they or their most relevant parts are too small to be seen.

Advice:
- Using a blown-up diagram of the object in tandem with the object can be most helpful.
- After showing the object, remove it from view if you feel it might be a distraction.

- Do not pass the object around during the presentation; this can be an enormous distraction.

HANDOUTS

Advantages:
- Adds audience interest and focus.
- Facilitates note taking.
- Allows the audience to take an important part of your message home with them.

Disadvantages:
- Handouts can divert the audience's attention from you. As you proceed through your presentation, portions of your audience could be examining handouts you've already covered or ones you will be covering.
- They can generate such scrutiny that your audience will ask more probing questions than you anticipated—or wanted.

Advice:
- Generally, you should avoid handouts. However, one technique that may work well for you is to hand out an outline of your presentation with ample space for note taking. This will focus your audience on your message and its organization without requiring them to read too much.

OVERHEAD PROJECTOR

Advantages:
- Overhead transparencies can be quickly prepared using a photocopy machine or a special personal computer system during the presentation.
- The overhead projector allows use of newspaper clippings, drawings, cartoons, and other types of art.
- Since the projector is in front of the room, the speaker can operate it while facing the audience.
- The room can remain lit.
- The speaker can write on the transparency to add details.
- The transparencies can be laid on top of one another to produce a "build" effect.

Disadvantages:

- Transparencies usually have limited visual appeal.
- Placing and removing slides, especially if several are used, can be a cumbersome process.
- It is sometimes difficult for the audience to have a full view of both the speaker and the screen.

Advice:

- Place all transparencies in cardboard frames to facilitate ease of handling. (Note: These can be ordered from any stationer.)
- Number transparencies sequentially.
- If you plan to use several transparencies without an on-site computerized setup, consider asking someone to manipulate them for you. Practice with this person ahead of time so that you can make your cues more impressive than repeatedly saying, "Next slide."
- Designate separate locations on the projector table or on an adjacent table for to-be-used versus used transparencies.
- Place your first transparency on the projector before you speak.
- Whenever feasible, stand next to the screen instead of the projector. This prevents you from blocking the audience's view and allows you to project a more commanding presence than by bending over the projector to point to the transparency.
- If you are not familiar with creating and accessing transparencies by computer during the presentation itself, consult an audiovisual specialist. This increasingly popular approach may help you gain the persuasive edge.

35-MM SLIDE PROJECTOR

Advantages:

- Allows for a wide range of color choices, which makes slides visually appealing.
- Easy to manipulate—one push of a forward or reverse button on a wired or wireless remote switch.

- Helps keep a large audience that can't see the speaker well focused on the message.
- Because of computerized graphic programs, slides have become quicker and far less expensive to produce.

Disadvantages:
- Room lights usually need to be dimmed or turned off entirely, leaving the audience in the dark.
- Once your slides are organized in the carousel tray, your flexibility in adjusting your presentation to audience feedback or unexpected time constraints can be limited.

Advice:
- Check your slide carousel before you speak. A missing, extra, upside-down, or backwards slide can instantly signal an inadequate preparation.
- Have paper copies of your slides in front of you as you speak. A reduced photocopy inserted into your notes is a handy reference.
- Place a collection of slides "on reserve" to assist you in answering key anticipated questions. Keep handy an index of their location in the carousel.
- Mount slides consistently; different mounts can cause the projector to focus and refocus repeatedly.
- Prepare two sets of slides for a major presentation. One damaged or lost slide can spell d-i-s-a-s-t-e-r.
- If your slides are being controlled from an electronic console built into the lectern, learn ahead of time how to operate it.
- Certain types of projectors and bulbs "throw" sharper images. Before you assume that the room lighting is not adequate, consult with an audiovisual specialist.
- While using slides during a major presentation, you should never be in the dark. Arrange for a shaft of light to appear on you without washing out the slide.

CHOOSING THE
RIGHT TYPE OF CHART

Charts can be a particularly persuasive visual aid if you choose the right one. The type of chart you choose should depend primarily on the inherent nature of the idea to be conveyed and on your audience's capacity to interpret data rendered visually in various forms.

Circle or "pie" charts are best suited to show proportions, as in dividing up a budget into slices of a pie.

Line graphs help show trends or variations over a period of time, but line graphs with three or more lines are generally inadvisable unless your audience is accustomed to relating to such complexity.

Bar graphs and pictographs highlight comparisons. Two caveats:

1. Do not use long columns of numbers to communicate a trend. For example, the following columns should be converted to a line or bar graph with figures inserted within the bar or above the line:

SALES (IN MILLIONS)

	1984	1985	1986	1987
Commercial	84.2	97.8	114.3	131.1
Domestic	16.3	22.4	28.9	32.2
Overseas	7.1	7.3	7.8	8.4

2. Don't lose the persuasive edge by simply copying charts that appear in books or reports. Many of these are meant to be studied; they are not designed to be quickly digested during a presentation.

UNIVERSAL ADVICE
FOR DESIGNING YOUR VISUAL

- Choose the right amount of detail. Too much detail often appears in two major forms: sentences and clauses when key words would suffice, or columns of data when one or more columns could be eliminated or the "bottom line" could be explained with or without a visual aid.
- Avoid presenting too many concepts on one visual. Keep the visual reasonably simple.
- Make sure the technical information depicted is central to your persuasive goal(s).
- Use the available space wisely. Often the presenter does not adequately consider the amount of space needed between lines or columns or the positioning of a line along the horizontal or vertical axis of the visual.
- Make sure that letters and numbers are legible from the back of the room.
- Take advantage of colors. One of the strongest advantages visuals have over the spoken word is their inherent capacity to stimulate via color. Transparencies, which are normally dull, can be more attractive if they are on colored sheets or, even more desirably, if they are prepared professionally with the attributes of 35-mm slides. Your audiovisual specialist can advise you here.

UNIVERSAL ADVICE FOR
PRESENTING YOUR VISUAL

- Remember the "needs test." Normally the presentation should be you-plus-visuals, not visuals-plus-you.
- The screen should always be placed to the *speaker's left*. This allows you to point in the direction in which people read. The lectern, therefore, should always be placed to the *audience's left*.

- Check out electrical outlets ahead of time. Do you need an extension cord? Do you need to tape any wires to the floor?
- Always check out the operation of projectors ahead of time. And always have a spare bulb handy.
- Position the screen for maximum visibility.
- Choreograph in advance all movements related to your use of visual aids.
- Become sufficiently familiar with your visual aid to prevent yourself from relating more to it than to the audience.
- Use a metal telescopic, light, or laser pointer only if you need to refer to a detail within the aid. Otherwise, merely motion toward the aid.
- Since so many speakers tend to play with their pointers, designate a place for it when you don't need it.
- Prepare verbal leads for your visuals, e.g., "Now I will show you our results for the first quarter" (short pause while presenting visual). This allows you—not your visuals—to control the flow. It also allows your audience to anticipate the slide, thereby adding an element of curiosity or suspense.
- Give the audience time to digest the gist of the visual. You may need to time how long each visual should be shown and indicate the time in your notes.
- Avoid slides that don't coordinate with your message.
- Make sure the aid is shown *only* when you are referring to it. Otherwise, it might be a distraction.
- If a fairly long span of time exists between one slide and the next, you should either turn the machine off, or use a blank slide to block the light projected onto the screen (unless your projector automatically prevents "white light" when a space is left in the carousel).
- At certain points in your presentation you may want the audience to read the slide without your narration. A moment of silence on your part can be most welcome, especially since presenters often "overread" their slides.
- If you're planning to use a videotape cassette, check the cabling to television sets or video projectors and whether the tape cassette is compatible with the player you will use. Also, determine in advance whether television sets have been ad-

justed for proper color and sound. Is the screen or monitor large enough to be seen by the audience?

If you've taken each piece of advice given here to heart and done everything possible to defy Murphy's Law ("If something can possibly go wrong, it will"), then a power failure is about all you can expect to go wrong, and you shouldn't worry too much about that—unless your name is Murphy.

Part II

DELIVERING YOUR MESSAGE

Chapter 10

OVERCOMING SPEECH ANXIETY

We've all seen the comedian's old reliable skit:

The speaker crosses the stage on the wobbliest of knees, grabs onto the podium as if it were a life preserver, and then throws a quick, glassy-eyed stare at the audience. He screws up the courage to say something, but all that comes out at first is a high-pitched squeak. Finally underway, he is three sentences into an obviously memorized recitation of a moribund speech when suddenly his mind goes blank. His mouth moves noiselessly for a few moments and then he proceeds to riffle madly through a stack of papers until they slip from his hands and fly across the stage. And then . . .

Why do we laugh? Mostly out of a sense of shared panic. Many of us have felt that way or feared it would happen to us if we were ever called upon to make a presentation.

Speech anxiety is a common concern for most people called upon to speak, present, or appear before the media. Moreover, it does not discriminate; it affects experienced, articulate, talented, intelligent, well-respected, and thoughtful communicators as well as those who are less endowed. In fact, no less a personality than Sir Winston Churchill remarked that when he began to speak, he felt as if a nine-inch block of ice were resting in the pit of his stomach. And Cicero, considered one of the greatest orators in the history of mankind, said, "I turn pale at the outset of a speech and quake in every limb and in all my soul."

To give you another sense of the magnitude of this malady, *The Book of Lists* cites a poll conducted in the United States in which 41 percent of those asked to name their greatest fear listed fear of speaking in public as number one. The percentages fell dramatically after that—all the way down to number seven— death.

Don't let this information discourage you. In fact, it is a way of telling you that if speech anxiety concerns you, you are not alone. So remember, *speech anxiety is very common; far more people experience it than don't.*

Here's more good news that you should keep uppermost in mind whenever you learn that you have a speaking engagement or a media appearance:

- *Speech anxiety can be helpful.* It can motivate you to channel your tension into a more dynamic performance that can give you the persuasive edge. Remember, if you are too calm, your presentation may lack conviction, a factor that could undermine your credibility.
- *Speech anxiety is often more obvious to you than to your audience.* Time and time again my clients are amazed that the anxiety they experienced during their speech or media appearance is not evident at all—or as evident as they feared—during videotape replay.
- *Speech anxiety is controllable.* It does not normally require therapy, hypnosis, or tranquilizers. Rather, it requires self-understanding and a good management system for controlling and channeling it purposefully.

UNDERSTANDING THE CAUSES

Before I present you with a management system for controlling and channeling your anxiety, you need to understand some of the major reasons why it occurs.

Fear of Embarrassment

The paramount fear behind speech anxiety is the fear of embarrassment. For the past six years my consulting firm has administered hundreds of communication-anxiety surveys to determine which specific fears concern speakers the most. The five most common are:

1. Forgetting or drawing a blank.
2. Making one's fear obvious to the audience (via a quaking voice, perspiration, stilted delivery, and so on).
3. Not being interesting.
4. Being unable to answer a question posed by a key decision maker.
5. Making a misstatement or gaffe.

Each one of these fears is a highly specific form of the fear of failure. The first step in addressing this potentially self-defeating fear is awareness. The next step is practical preparation. For example, to combat the fear of forgetting, you must painstakingly prepare and then practice your speech with a set of high-quality notes.

Your "Control Mentality"

So much of our conscious and subconscious behavior is directed at controlling ourselves and the environment around us. Alarm clocks control when we wake up; dress, cosmetics, diets, and exercise control how we look and feel about ourselves; curfews placed on our teenage children help control their behavior and our worry about them; salaries, reviews, reprimands, and promotions help control the people we rely upon. And the list goes on—almost endlessly. Our lives are, in essence, a cocoon of control.

Being called upon to speak, present, or appear on television or radio strips away from many of us the sense of control that typifies our daily lives. If you are a senior executive of a corporation, you are not only accustomed to exercising effective control, you are also accustomed to communicating power, an essential ingredient of your sense of control. However, when you stand before a large audience or appear in front of a TV camera or microphone, your sense of power can quickly diminish. With a large audience, the factors that help convey your power in the boardroom—authority, command, decisiveness, and intimacy—quickly diminish.

Your sense of control can be compromised even further when you are being interviewed by a reporter. Seldom can you significantly control the slant, accuracy, or fairness of what ends up being printed or broadcast.

The key message in this discussion of control is not that large audiences or media interviews cause you to lose it; rather, that you must *have an attitude of control about your sense of control. When you feel that your sense of control may be compromised, you must do all you can to prevent this from happening.*

Performance Consciousness

How many times have you seen a person who expresses himself impressively while seated at a conference table have difficulty presenting on his feet? It happens all the time. But why? As soon as you stand up, *five* major things occur that differ from your pattern of communication while seated:

1. *You feel more exposed.* You are separated from the group with more of your body showing. An imaginary—or real—spotlight is on you. This brings out a conscious or subconscious need to perform—to somehow be *different* from the person you were when you were merely seated at the table.

2. *Your communication needs to be more structured and stylized than in normal conversation.* Normal conversation usually tolerates a more stream-of-consciousness style of expression. A scheduled presentation or speech requires a sense of thematic unity and coherence, replete with introduction, body, conclusion, internal summaries, transitions, and lead sentences, plus an overall standard of clarity greater than that usually expected from normal conversation.

3. *Your communication needs to be more sustained than in normal conversation.* In normal conversation, depending on the study you rely on, our average utterance ranges between six and twenty seconds. The average length of the presentation my consulting firm works on with our clients is eighteen minutes—fifty-four times the length of the upper limit of the average utterance. This can be very anxiety-producing, especially when considering the following factor:

4. *Your feedback system is altered.* In normal conversation you are used to people sending verbal and nonverbal feedback on a very frequent and readable basis. You make a comment and before you've even finished or right after you've finished, you generally know whether your audience's reaction is positive, negative, or neutral. However, when you speak or present, audiences—especially large ones—tend to be less expressive and even stoic. Why?

- The norms of the setting prevent overt comments while you are speaking.
- The audience's need to concentrate on and comprehend your analysis can cause their behavior to be more inwardly reflective than outwardly supportive.
- The seating arrangements, room conditions, or sheer vastness of your audience may make your audience uncomfortable.
- You may not be doing enough to stimulate the audience's attention, interest, and sense of involvement in your message. *This is where your greatest latitude for controlling their feedback resides.* (see chapter 8)

5. *Your normal communicative style is altered.* One way of classifying our communicative styles is by asking ourselves whether we tend to be more reactive or proactive. If we initiate more, we are proactive; if we tend to speak more when we are spoken to, we are more reactive. Most of my clients regard themselves as principally reactive; to them, initiating communication is more difficult than responding. Therefore, many of them may, to an extent, find a speech or presentation an alien form of communication, because it is inherently proactive. In contrast, when these same

people are called upon to respond, especially in a challenging situation, their competitive juices are stimulated and their performance is optimized. This is one reason why speakers often do better during the question-and-answer period than during their prepared remarks.

False Expectations

Not long ago I worked with a corporate lawyer who told me that his anxiety was exacerbated in part by his sense that he believed his audience expected him to be an excellent speaker because he is a lawyer. I said to him, "Since lawyers are supposed to prove their case, where is your proof for this assumption regarding your audience?" He demurred, "I have none." I then explained that a sophisticated business audience probably expects a lawyer to be clear, logical, and prepared, but they do not necessarily expect him to be a Clarence Darrow or a Melvin Belli.

"Insufficient Ownership"

Regardless of experience, a large percentage of speakers in the business and political worlds are anxious while speaking because they must read a manuscript written by someone else. In effect, they have consciously or subconsciously relinquished control of their message, a reality that often breeds inner conflict, frustration, anxiety, and poor performance.

Fears of the Unknown

Whenever we visit someplace for the first time, our feelings are often a blend of anxiety and adventure. We feel anxious about the unknown—finding our way around, choosing the right sites and restaurants, or perhaps relating to a foreign language. But we also feel a spirit of adventure surrounding the opportunity to explore, including the opportunity to conquer our fear of the unknown.

Speaking engagements and media appearances also stimulate our fear of the unknown. Frequently we are anxious because we are unfamiliar with the audience, occasion, and setting. Who will be present? How will they feel about me, my subject, my company? Who else is speaking? When? What will the room be like? Will there be a lectern? Microphone? And so on. Your anxiety regarding any of these concerns can be effectively resolved via audience analysis and advance work (see chapter 3). As you learn more in advance about your audience, the occasion, and the setting, your anxiety will diminish, your sense of control will increase, and your sense of adventure will emerge.

CONTROLLING PERSPIRATION

Perspiring excessively can make you appear nervous and out of control. One of the questions most frequently asked of me by clients preparing to appear on television is, "How can I control my perspiring on camera?" (Many of us recall the impression created by Richard Nixon's tendency to perspire in his first debate with John F. Kennedy during the 1960 presidential campaign.) Although no surefire approach exists, consider the following advice:

- Avoid wearing wools and clothing that fits too tightly.
- Do not stand under the hot camera lights until you absolutely have to. If they are too hot, tell someone; he or she may be willing to adjust them.
- Avoid heavy liquid intake shortly before you appear. The heat on the set tends to pull the water out of your pores.
- Consider exercising a few hours before your appearance. This can help rid you of excess perspiration.
- Use a quality antiperspirant.
- Keep a handkerchief with you. If your perspiration problem is especially pronounced, you may need to use it during a commercial break or when you are *positive* that the camera is not on you.
- Makeup—particularly powdered foundation—can retard perspiration. Accept makeup if it's offered by a competent

makeup artist or lightly apply a recommended makeup base yourself.

- If the problem persists, consult your physician. He or she may recommend salt tablets or another approach.

A PLAN TO
ALLEVIATE YOUR ANXIETY

The following plan can help you alleviate your anxiety systematically and significantly.

Early Preparation Phase

- Break the ice early. As soon as you know you have an engagement, begin the process of advance work, audience analysis, and goal setting (see chapters 2 and 3). Delaying the preparation process will only feed your anxiety and prevent you from having sufficient time to become thoroughly familiar and comfortable with your message.

Message-Development Phase

- Take a goal-oriented approach to all speeches, presentations, and media appearances. This will give you a sense of focus—a mental agenda that will accentuate your sense of control (see chapter 2).
- Base your speech presentation or media appearance as much as possible on your audience analysis. By doing this you will be responding directly to concerns uppermost in their minds.
- To overcome a feeling of "insufficient ownership," try to prepare the entire speech yourself. If this is not possible, spend more time with the writer before the speech is composed or, at the very least, spend more time editing the

speech and preparing personal segments to insert into the basic text.

- Recognize the relationship between organization and your speech anxiety. The clearer your sense of focus and direction, the more comfortable you will be.

- Find ways of involving your audience. Consider asking them questions, using vital illustrations and examples, and cultivating genuine common ground (see chapter 4). Since speeches, presentations, and media appearances tend to be less involving than normal conversation, the more interactive you can make your communication, the more you will generate positive feedback to allay your anxiety.

- Use visual aids—judiciously. Visual aids help alleviate your fear of forgetting. They also take the spotlight off you, thereby suppressing your performance consciousness. However, don't rely on them too much or they will distract the audience from your message (see chapter 9).

- Plan and practice your introduction carefully. Most speakers are especially anxious during the first two or three minutes. However, several techniques are available to help you control this anxiety (see chapter 10).

- Limit your reliance on memorization. Although memorizing a passage or two may be a good idea, attempting to memorize your entire speech will generally feed your fear of forgetting and encourage stilted delivery and inflexibility (see chapter 11).

- Anticipate the questions that will be uppermost in your audience's minds and imagine yourself answering them. This will help bring out your more spontaneous, less self-conscious, reactive style.

- Use notes without guilt. If you use neat, well-laid-out, easily readable notes, you will increase your confidence without looking awkward as you refer to them, losing your place, or omitting an important point (see chapter 5).

- Time your message. Many persons called upon to speak, appear before the media, or debate, worry needlessly about going overtime or falling too far short of the allocated time.

Again, you can control this form of anxiety. During your practice sessions, time both your overall message and how much time should be appropriated to each segment or major idea.

Practice and Predelivery Phase

- Systematize your practice sessions; practice in segments (see chapter 13).
- Consider exercising or engaging in deep-breathing exercises the day of a major speech, presentation, or media appearance. You might also choose meditation or private time to relax or gather your thoughts.
- Keep your schedule "hassle-free." You don't want last-minute distractions to interfere with your sense of control and concentration.
- Arrive early. Check out the setting, inspect the lectern, and test the microphone. Mingle with your audience to enhance your level of familiarity with them.
- Avoid heavy eating and drinking before your speech. Limit your alcoholic intake. Yes, a glass of wine can relax you—too much.
- Before a television or radio appearance, have someone with whom you're comfortable ask you a few predictable warm-up questions.
- Avoid too many last-minute changes, which can alter your overall familiarity with the speech.
- Make sure you are well introduced. This prevents you from wondering anxiously whether the audience is sufficiently aware of why you are qualified to speak on this subject.
- Don't begin until you are ready (see chapter 13).

Delivery Phase

- Think expert! You deserve to be speaking about this topic.
- Think flexible! Be prepared to respond to audience feedback (see chapter 15)

- Think opportunity! Replace your negative thoughts about fear of failure and risk with the attitude that this speech or media interview is an opportunity for you to achieve your specified goals—for you to capture the persuasive edge.
- Think enlarged conversation! Don't try to sound or behave differently simply because you are standing. Focus on communication—reaching your audience—not on orating or on trying to impress them.
- Think message, not anxiety!
- Think strong, using your vocal strength, gestures, and bodily movement to release your anxiety purposefully.
- Think target audience! Your audience will frequently be composed of supporters, neutrals, and opponents. Don't be too anxious about those you are least likely to influence. Focus instead on those who are most susceptible to your persuasive advances. And when you need a shot of encouragement, turn to a friendly face (I hope you will find more than one).
- Think success! Visualize as graphically as possible a positive reaction by your audience to you and your message, thereby banishing with all the determination you can muster any negative "self-talk" that can sabotage your performance.

Postdelivery Phase

It is not uncommon for a person to get through a speech, presentation, or media interview with minimum discomfort, only to be struck by a sudden wave of anxiety as soon as it is over. Whether you fall into this category or not, the following advice can be helpful to you.

- Analyze an audiotape or videotape of your performance. Therefore, take control in advance of your engagement by arranging for a taping.
- Collect reliable feedback (see chapter 13).

HYPNOSIS AND BETA-BLOCKERS

Increasingly, people with speech anxiety, especially those with acute cases, are turning to professionals for either hypnosis or a form of drug therapy called beta-blockers. Such treatments are no substitute for adequate preparation and practice, which is the focus of the counsel offered by my firm. Although few of our clients have chosen these treatment modes, you should be aware of them, because they have been helpful to · ersons whose speech anxiety does not respond to the methods I recommend above. However, I cannot emphasize strongly enough the need to seek a qualified professional when investigating hypnosis or the use of beta-blockers.

Hypnosis

"Hypnosis is often very successful in alleviating moderate to extreme cases of speech anxiety," according to Peter Bloom, M.D., clinical associate professor of psychiatry, School of Medicine, University of Pennsylvania, and fellow, Society of Clinical and Experimental Hypnosis. He further contends that "additional benefits reward the person who alleviates speech anxiety through hypnosis":

> I have seen unexpected release of energy and enthusiasm, and have witnessed creative ideas emerge from speakers who began to interact with the audience with feeling and, yes, sometimes passion. When freed from energy-draining anxiety, these speakers began to "work" the audience to create shared experiences that became unforgettable. These unexpected benefits are not magic, nor are they due to hypnosis. Rather, they are the result of releasing those special skills and talents that are in all of us—talents and skills that when *unreleased* make speech anxiety a very real crippler of our self-expression.

Bloom advises that hypnosis for speech anxiety be sought from a licensed professional in health care, for example, a physician in medicine or psychiatry, a dentist, clinical psychologist, or social worker. He does not recommend the use of commercial audiotapes, claiming that they do not address the person's own particular concerns.

To obtain the names of qualified professionals in hypnosis contact:

> The American Society of Clinical Hypnosis
> 2250 East Dever Avenue
> Suite 336
> Des Plaines, Illinois 60018
> (312) 297-3317

> The Society for Clinical and Experimental Hypnosis
> 128-A Kings Park Drive
> Liverpool, New York 13090
> (315) 652-7299

Beta-blockers

"Beta-blockers can play an important role in eliminating some of the most uncomfortable and conspicuous symptoms of adrenaline-based panic anxiety," according to William Anixter, M.D., director of the Panic, Anxiety, and Phobia Treatment Program at Highland Hospital, Asheville, North Carolina. The adrenaline response is marked by an increased pulse rate, dry mouth, tremor of the hands, shortness of breath, and a shaking, tight quality to the voice. Beta-blockers reduce heart rate and eliminate tremor, both in the voice and in the hands. Although the person may feel some nervousness after taking beta-blockers, Anixter states that he or she "will not broadcast this discomfort to others."

Anixter considers beta-blockers preferable to tranquilizers for dealing with the physical aspects of the fear, because they cause neither sedation nor mental impairment.

He advises people with asthma, obstructive pulmonary disease, hypoglycemia, or certain cardiac problems not to use beta-blockers. However, he claims that the side effects commonly associated with beta-blockers—light-headedness, fatigue, depression, and gastrointestinal disorders—"rarely occur with the sporadic, low-dose strategies used to alleviate speech anxiety."

It is absolutely essential that anyone considering beta-blockers discuss their use with his or her personal physician before proceeding. Despite Dr. Anixter's extensive private practice, no controlled research findings are yet available regarding the efficacy of beta-blockers for controlling speech anxiety. This is due largely to the fact that prescribing beta-blockers for this purpose is not a "medically indicated use"; that is, speech anxiety is not a medical condition for which the drug was developed. Taking any drug can be a serious matter, and I personally recommend that you first try to overcome your speech anxiety with careful, systematic planning, preparation, and practice. If your physician recommends you use beta-blockers, Anixter recommends that they "be tested well before the speaking engagement—particularly during the practice session—to ensure tolerability."

ON TO THE PERSUASIVE EDGE

Controlling speech anxiety is mainly an exercise of mind over matter. Once you have exercised the wide range of control options available to you, you are far better prepared to capture the persuasive edge.

───────────── Chapter 11 ─────────────

MODES OF DELIVERY

Joseph Montoya made it all the way from the tiny town of Pena Blanca, New Mexico, to the U.S. Senate, but apparently not on the basis of his speaking ability.

At the 1974 National Legislative Conference in Albuquerque, for example, Montoya was scheduled to give a major address. It had been a difficult day, and he had not had a chance to review the speech written for him. As he climbed the steps to the podium, a member of his staff handed him the speech and a copy of the press release that accompanied it.

Oblivious of the horror of his aides and the amusement of his audience, Montoya began to read the press release instead of the speech.

"For immediate release," he began. "Senator Joseph M. Montoya, Democrat of New Mexico, last night told the National Legislative Conference at Albuquerque . . ."

The senator, in fact, read the entire six-page release, including the final paragraph, which noted that he had been "repeatedly interrupted by applause."

We've all been the victim of at least one of these persons:

- The deadly reader, who plows on, oblivious of all around him, reading lifeless prose from a sheaf of papers he has carried to the podium.

- The blank starer, who begins his presentation reasonably well as he delivers a memorized speech, but suddenly loses his mental place and with it all he has to say.
- The rambler, who has neither a written speech nor any predefined thoughts.

You're presumably reading this book because you recognize that none of these speakers, or their equally confused and confusing cousins, is communicating anything but incompetence. How, then, should you prepare to deliver your message?

There are four basic modes of delivery for speeches: memorization, reading verbatim, impromptu speaking, and extemporaneous speaking. Let's examine the advantages and disadvantages of each mode:

MEMORIZATION

Memorization is advisable when addressing ceremonial occasions, such as award ceremonies, or when reading might cause you to appear less than genuine in expressing your feelings, and when speaking extemporaneously might not reflect the eloquence called for by the occasion.

Memorized speaking is also advisable when making remarks to be televised without the aid of a TelePrompTer, for in this medium smoothness and eye contact are essential.

Advantages:

By allowing the speaker to keep precisely to the message and to the words chosen, memorization:

- Encourages full eye contact with the audience.
- Results in a message that is more stylized—and usually more eloquent—than an extemporaneous or impromptu presentation.
- Reduces the risk of misspeaking, since all the ideas and words are planned in advance.

- Helps ensure time control, especially when the overall program is tightly scheduled or if the speaker tends to ramble when using another mode of delivery.

Disadvantages:
- The process of memorizing a lengthy presentation can be very time-consuming.
- Unless you're an accomplished actor, your delivery of memorized speeches may sound stilted and unnatural.
- Memorization creates speech anxiety related to the fear of forgetting.
- Memorization prevents the speaker from being flexible, from adjusting his or her message or delivery to audience feedback.

SPEAKING FROM A
PREPARED MANUSCRIPT

Speaking from a prepared manuscript is advisable when the risk of being misquoted or of running overtime must be very carefully controlled. It is also appropriate for events that require audiovisual aids, such as annual conventions and sales conferences, because it encourages precise coordination. I also recommend this method if you are speaking about an unfamiliar subject or taking an unfamiliar approach to a familiar topic tailored especially for a particular audience and occasion.

Advantages:
- Allows the message to be more stylized.
- Reduces the risk of misspeaking.
- Helps ensure time control.
- Can be helpful for the speaker required to take an unusual approach to a subject or to discuss a matter about which he or she is not especially familiar.
- Does not generate the anxiety associated with memorization.

- Allows the speaker to release a full text to the media, thereby reducing the risk of being misquoted.
- Works well for a major presentation in which slides need to be advanced by a third party.

Disadvantages:
- Few speakers can read a manuscript and still project the feeling that the overall communication is sufficiently audience-centered versus message- or speaker-centered. Most speakers' eye contact, language, and cadence are not natural enough with this method to establish the desired directness with the audience—to bring the speaker and the audience together.
- Manuscript speaking limits the speaker's opportunity to adjust his or her message or delivery to audience feedback, another factor that limits the potential to strike a chord with the audience.

Many executives and political leaders I've advised justify the use of a manuscript by saying, "I must use one; the media expect a copy of my remarks." My response: Don't let the media's expected request for your text force you into a delivery mode that prevents you from looking your best. Because the media want a text doesn't mean that you have to read one. You can hand them your original text or a press release with the major quotes you want reported. Meanwhile, you can speak from an outline or a combination of outline and manuscript, whichever works best for you.

The TelePrompTer

An increasingly popular variation of speaking from a prepared manuscript, especially for major addresses before large audiences (usually over 250), is the TelePrompTer. This device, made especially popular by President Reagan, who mastered it, allows the manuscript to be televised from backstage to a monitor and then reflected onto special optical glass. While the speaker reads the manuscript from the glass located three or four feet in front of him or her, the audience sees only clear glass. This advanced technology allows the speaker to read the manuscript with what appears to be full eye contact.

The TelePrompTer

Although the overall effect of TelePrompTer speaking can be most impressive, it is still manuscript speaking and therefore usually lacks the authenticity of direct interaction.

My choice of the word *usually* above is deliberate, for I have developed a technique that allows the speaker to be more interactive with the audience when using a TelePrompTer. Specifically, I recommend that a portion of the address with which the speaker is familiar and about which he or she has strong feelings be reduced to a key word or short-sentence outline on the Tele-PrompTer. When the speaker sees these cues, he or she can then muster the communicative energy to deliver this portion of the speech more naturally and with greater directness to the audience.

For this approach to be effective, however, the speaker must avoid too dramatic a shift from the delivery of the verbatim segment to that of the outlined segment lest the verbatim segment suffer by comparison. With careful practice, this can be prevented.

IMPROMPTU SPEAKING

The impromptu approach, speaking without specific advance notice or preparation, is best suited for short, informal talks. It requires you to decide on the spot which material to include and exclude. Which of the many things that pop into your mind are worth saying and how best should they be phrased?

Advantages:
- Remarks are spontaneous, conversational, and natural—all desirable elements of communication.

Disadvantages:
- The order of elements is unplanned and often muddled.
- Phrasing can be cumbersome and unduly repetitious.
- The amount of focus given to an idea is not necessarily related to its importance.
- The risk of making a misstatement or gaffe is greater here than with other modes of delivery.

EXTEMPORANEOUS SPEAKING

Contrary to popular misconception, extemporaneous speaking is not to be confused with impromptu or off-the-cuff speaking. Rather, it involves the speaker's selection and organization of his or her ideas in advance and reliance on a written or mental full-sentence or key-word outline. It is the most popular form of presenting in internal business situations, although executives often prefer a text for outside engagements.

Advantages:

- The language and delivery are natural, allowing for maximum directness with the audience.
- It encourages eye contact, especially when the speaker uses a good set of notes.
- The speaker has greater freedom to leave the lectern and move closer to the audience, thereby establishing a sense of rapport with them.
- The speaker can respond to audience feedback with both major message adjustments (e.g., restatement, repetition, elaboration, definition, and the providing of additional support) and major delivery adjustments (e.g., slowing down or picking up the pace, speaking more loudly or softly, or speaking more or less forcefully).

Disadvantages:

- Extemporaneous speaking frequently sacrifices the precise language of a manuscript or memorized presentation. However, such precision often sounds stilted and, therefore, unnatural. A carefully prepared extemporaneous presentation can capture sufficient precision without compromising the naturalness so essential to making a true connection with your audience.
- Extemporaneous speaking increases the risk of misspeaking. However, careful preparation can prevent this.
- It is difficult to control the precise timing of an extemporaneous speech. Some speakers can "get on a roll" while speak-

ing and add several minutes to their remarks—with or without adding quality.

AND THE WINNER IS...

If you've surmised that I am partial to the extemporaneous approach, you're correct. I do place a premium on genuine interaction with the audience and on natural delivery. However, please realize that memorized and manuscript speaking are appropriate for certain circumstances. In fact, in some circumstances you may be best served by a hybrid approach—a combination of an extemporaneous, memorized, and manuscript presentation. For instance, you may choose to memorize the introduction and conclusion of your speech or portions of it; use a manuscript for sensitive material (to avoid being misquoted) or for reading a quotation, illustration, definition, or technical explanation; and rely on the extemporaneous mode for the overall flow of your remarks.

Here are some recommendations for enhancing the effectiveness of an extemporaneous speech while minimizing its disadvantages:

- Create a detailed (but not too detailed) extemporaneous outline so that you will stick to it.
- Focus on the goals of your presentation so that you will be less likely to spend too much time on a single idea or be taken off track.
- To control the timing of your speech, allocate a certain amount of time for each major idea, place notations to that effect in the margin of your outline, keep track of time as you speak with a watch or small clock, and make a commitment to abide by the allocations.

NOTES VERSUS NO NOTES

Should you use notes? This is one of the more gnawing questions facing so many presenters. Unfortunately, there is no hard-and-fast answer to it. A speaker's total freedom from notes can pay significant dividends in the image department; it can project him or her as brighter and more articulate than speakers who rely on them. However, in most instances, the use of notes is not the sin that so many speakers believe it to be.

The major issue regarding notes should not be *whether* or not you use them, but, rather, *how* you use them. In short, overreliance on notes is closer to sin than merely using them.

If you are determined not to use notes because you feel they may lower your audience's estimation of you, consider two important questions: First, are the notes the problem or is the problem the way in which you use them? Second, if you were to avoid using notes, how likely is it that you might forget something crucial to your goals, be sidetracked, feel nervous, devote too much time to an idea, lose smoothness, and so on? If any of these pitfalls concerns you, you need good notes, not no notes.

LECTERN VERSUS NO LECTERN

Should you use a lectern? A lectern normally presents both a physical and a psychological barrier between the speaker and the audience, especially if it is far removed from the first row of audience members. That barrier is accentuated by the speaker who is unable to appear spontaneous and natural behind a piece of furniture because it increases his or her performance consciousness and spells d-i-s-t-a-n-c-e and f-o-r-m-a-l-i-t-y.

For these reasons, I often recommend that you avoid the use of a lectern. There are, however, six exceptions:

1. When a microphone requires you to remain at the lectern
2. When you need to control your slide program from the lectern
3. When you are speaking from behind a dais
4. When you need to read from a manuscript
5. When others on the program are using the lectern and you don't want to upstage them
6. When the formality of the occasion dictates the use of the lectern, for example, a sermon or the annual meeting of a large corporation (although some CEOs leave the lectern for the question-and-answer session).

Whether or not you prefer a lectern for any of these reasons, you should act as if it exists for one solitary reason: to hold your notes or manuscript. Therefore, you should communicate with your audience as if the lectern didn't even exist.

Some speakers prefer to leave the lectern during portions of their remarks and then return to it for security or to consult their notes. This can be reasonably effective if the return visits are smooth and not too frequent.

IF READ YOU MUST...

You can make it *easier* on yourself, but not necessarily *better* for yourself, if you have to read some or all of a written manuscript.

Traditional advice over the years suggests that your manuscripts should be typed in all capital letters or using one of several special small-capital- and large-capital-letter typefaces such as Orator.

Graphic-arts experts, however, contend that all-capital printing is more difficult to read. A reader scanning a line of type recognizes words by their top silhouette. In theory, if you were to cover the lower half of a line of lowercase print, you should still be able to read the words as readily as if you were seeing the whole letters. But the top half of a line of all capitals is difficult if not impossible to decipher, since its top silhouette is often a straight line across.

YOU'LL HAVE TO DECIDE FOR YOURSELF WHETHER THIS PARAGRAPH, SET IN ALL CAPITALS, IS EASIER TO READ THAN A PARAGRAPH SUCH AS THE THE ONE ABOVE, WHICH IS SET IN UPPER-CASE AND LOWER-CASE LETTERS. AGAIN, WHATEVER WORKS FOR YOU IS JUST FINE.

By the way, did you spot the typo in the preceding paragraph? If you didn't see THE THE, your eye got lost in the maze of capital letters.

ADVICE FOR TYPING
AN OUTLINE OR A MANUSCRIPT

The way you type your manuscript or outline can have an enormous impact on your delivery. The following advice, and the accompanying example, should be particularly helpful.

1. Decide on a lettering style and size. Take advantage of the capacity of photocopying machines to make the letters as large as you want. (Many of my clients prefer one-half- to three-quarter-inch.)
2. Number every page clearly at both the top and the bottom.
3. Begin typing as close to the top of the page as possible. This allows you to establish smoother and stronger eye contact with your audience.
4. Begin each sentence in the left-hand margin. Otherwise, if the sentences are set in paragraph style, you will have to search for the end of one sentence and the beginning of the next, a major source of eye contact, vocal delivery, and anxiety problems for the speaker. Example:

Fourscore and seven years ago our fathers brought forth on this continent a new nation, conceived in liberty and dedicated to the proposition that all men are created equal.

Now we are engaged in a great civil war, testing whether that nation or any nation so conceived and so dedicated can long endure.

We are met on a great battlefield of that war.

We have come to dedicate a portion of that field, as a final resting place of those who here gave their lives that that nation might live.

5. _____

Double- or triple-space between lines. Triple-space between paragraphs and place a one-inch line within that space (as above) to indicate the new paragraph.

6. Don't break a sentence, paragraph, or main idea between two pages.

7. Create a balance between long, medium, and short sentences. This allows you to vary your speaking diet between chunks, bites, and morsels. It also helps your breathing pattern.

8. Don't type too far down the page; leave a four- or five-inch margin at the bottom so that your eyes are not drawn to your navel and your voice is not drawn to your feet.

9. Insert delivery advice in the margin: "Use right hand," "Point to screen," "Pick up pace," "Slow down." Also enter time notations.

10. When using a full manuscript, place key words in the margins that can help reinforce your sense both of direction and of movement through the speech. (See the example to the left.)

Key Words in Margins

11. If, like many speakers, you tend to overlook ideas contained in your notes, no matter how well laid out they may be, experiment with this simple technique I developed: Lay out each major idea of your speech in a large rectangle bordered in a different color. Thus, as you treat each idea, your eyes will cover just the materials included in the rectangle.

12. Don't staple or clip the pages of your speech together. Leave

them in a sheaf so that you can easily slide (not turn) them silently after you've finished reading a page.

13. Consider using a Scriptmaster,* a special container for your notes or manuscript. The Scriptmaster is designed with two boxed sections, one for the pages being read, the other for those already read. It helps you to handle your notes more smoothly and casts a more professional look than a manila folder.

*A Scriptmaster can be ordered from Brewer-Cantelmo, Inc., 116 E. 27th St., New York, New York 10016.

Chapter 12

NONVERBAL COMMUNICATION: I SEE WHAT YOU'RE SAYING

"I see what you're saying," someone tells you after a conversation. Truer words may never have been spoken.

How much attention do you pay to the way you stand, sit, use your hands, or configure your face? If you're like most people, you devote considerably more energy to *what* you say than to *how* you say it. But consider this:

> In ordinary conversation between two persons, words convey less than 35 percent of meaning. The remaining 65 percent of meaning is transmitted through nonverbal communication.*

No matter how carefully we research, prepare, choose our words, and select our audience, two-thirds of what we communicate is derived from what we *do* rather than what we *say*. How do we hold our body? What gestures do we make? How are we dressed? What do we do to modify the tone of our voices? Where do we focus our eyes?

*Ray L. Birdwhistell, cited by Mark L. Knapp, *Essentials of Nonverbal Communication* (New York, Holt, Rinehart & Winston, 1980), page 15.

TYPES OF
NONVERBAL BEHAVIOR

The various categories of nonverbal communication encompass a wide range of human action and behavior.*

Body motion or kinesic behavior: These include gestures, movements of the body, facial expressions, eye behavior (blinking, direction of gaze, and size and liveliness of pupils), and posture.

Emblems: These are nonverbal acts with a culturally recognized meaning; in our society these can range from circling of the ear with an outstretched finger ("He's nuts," the message reads), to fingers pinching off the nose ("It stinks"), to the coarser, derogatory communication of an outstretched middle finger.

Illustrators: These connote a picture of a word or image drawn with the hands or otherwise demonstrated by the speaker.

Regulators: These are signals that communicate when it is time for a speaker to continue, stop, hurry up, or explain his or her words. Slow, regular nodding of the head indicates agreement with what is being said. Quicker nodding means, "Hurry up and finish."

Physical characteristics: These are characteristics that do not change during the course of a conversation—body shape, size, attractiveness, odors, and the like.

Touching behavior: What is the effect on a conversation if one of the participants touches the other's arm? His head? His neck?

Paralanguage: These are cues that relate to how words are spoken, including vocal qualities, voice *characterizers* (such as laughing, crying, yawning, clearing of the throat) and voice *segregates,* such as the verbal pauses of "uh-huh" and similar indicators. As an example of the paralinguistic effects of voice quality or intonation, consider the phrase "That's really smart." The intonation can show either appreciation or derision.

Proxemics: The use and abuse of personal space. How close do

---

*Many of these categories were identified by Mark L. Knapp of Purdue University in his book, *Essentials of Nonverbal Communication* (New York, Holt, Rinehart & Winston, 1980).

you stand or sit in a conversation? How does speaking from behind a lectern differ from speaking without one? When do you leave your desk to meet with colleagues in the more intimate surroundings of your sofa, upholstered chairs, and coffee table—your informal conference area? What messages does this transmit regarding your respect for those attending? Strongly positive ones, for sure.

Chronemics: This has to do with communication through use of time. What is the meaning of silence or pauses in conversation? What is communicated by a speaker who arrives half an hour late for an engagement? By a speaker who delivers a five-minute presentation? A two-hour monologue? Chronemics communicates how organized you are as well as how busy and considerate you are. If you keep a person waiting thirty minutes for a scheduled appointment, what messages are you sending about yourself and allowing him to infer about himself?

COMMON NEGATIVE CUES

I've detected the following negative nonverbal cues from many speakers in the seminars conducted by my firm and in actual speeches and media appearances we analyze. Most reflect anxiety and lack of confidence. You may not be conscious of these behaviors as you speak; learn to recognize and avoid them.

Cue	Possible Message
Hands holding tightly onto lectern	Anxiety, lack of confidence
Absence of eye contact, gesture, or facial expression	Same
Playing with speech notes, paper clip, microphone cord	Same
Repeatedly removing and replacing eyeglasses	Same

Cue	Possible Message
Drinking water repeatedly	Same
Speaking too rapidly, too softly, or too monotonously	Same
Head tilted upward	Aloofness, arrogance
Arms folded across chest	Defensiveness
Biting lip or clenching jaw while listening to a question	Defensiveness, anger, or expected inability to answer

IT'S ALL IN THE EYES

It has long been said that "the eyes are the windows to the soul." They are also essential to you in establishing and maintaining credibility. ("Look me in the eye and say that," we say when we attempt to determine a speaker's honesty.) An audience is more likely to believe a speaker who makes eye contact with its members. Moreover, the audience is more likely to believe that the words uttered are the speaker's own and to sense his or her genuine conviction.

Many speakers have been advised to stare over the heads of the audience at some mystical spot on the back wall of the auditorium. Not only does this ruin your chances of communicating to your listeners with your eyes, but it also prevents you from reading their responses. The impact of eye contact and the feedback it yields are strong arguments in favor of extemporaneous speaking for situations in which you need not rely too heavily on notes or a manuscript.

Speakers are occasionally advised to pick someone in the audience to speak to. This is better than staring at the back wall, but you run the risk of turning your presentation into a limited engagement.

The Scan Plan

My scan plan can help you make the most effective use of eye contact. This approach involves your self-imposed obligation to make direct eye contact with as many audience members as possible. As you do, mentally divide your audience into approximately eight to fifteen sections and then address each section before moving on to the next. The size and shape of the section, the direction in which you move to address each, and the length of time you spend with each is your judgment call—one that will become more fine-tuned with experience. However, don't jerk your head from one section to another; your eye contact and head motion must be fluid as you acknowledge each section, making sure that no section feels deliberately ignored.

As you relate to each section of your audience, pick out the friendlier and more reassuring faces. Be prepared to return to them when you're not receiving the most positive feedback or are feeling anxious.

The scan plan has three distinct advantages:

1. It allows you to establish more direct communication with your audience.
2. It diminishes your sense of the vastness of the audience.
3. It allows you to adjust your message to audience feedback.

What's the best way to use eye contact before smaller audiences and during media engagements? When you're speaking to smaller audiences, divide your audience into smaller groups. In addition, be ready to look a target audience member straight in the eye when making a point related to his or her interest. During media engagements you should look directly at the person with whom you are communicating. Seldom should you look into the camera unless you are hosting the show, are on a talk show responding to a caller, or are presenting a prepared response to an editorial.

IN YOUR FACE

Have you ever watched a conversation across a room or through a window? Seen a movie on an airplane without listening through the earphones? You don't really need to hear what is being said to gain some idea of the emotions of the participants. ("I can read your face like a book," we tell people. Or we react to a look of contempt with the saying "If looks could kill. . . .")

Remember that when you are speaking, your audience is examining your facial expressions. Don't let the pressures of making a presentation turn your visage to stone or to a silly, nervous smirk. Relax and be yourself. Show your best face to the audience.

Research has shown that when a person's words and facial expressions or gestures are inconsistent with his or her speech, the listener gives less credence to the words. In other words, "Watch what I do, not what I say." When someone says, "I believe you," with a forehead knit tightly in a sign of puzzlement, we don't really trust the statement. And what kind of message is sent if someone says yes but shakes his head from side to side in the recognized emblem meaning no? Become conscious of your expression as you talk; make sure it enhances rather than contradicts your message.

HANDING THE AUDIENCE A LINE

"What in the world do I do with my hands?" That has to be one of the most common concerns of the inexperienced (or ineffective) speaker.

The answer is: Use your hands and your body in a natural and spontaneous manner as part of the delivery of your message. Have someone study the way you use your hands in everyday conversation as part of your preparation for a speaking engagement or media appearance. It's okay to talk with your hands. It's expressive and attention getting. Additionally, the more you focus on your ideas, the more likely it is that your hands and arms will move naturally in response to the energy transmitted by your belief in what you're saying. And remember, speakers are far more prone to be underanimated than they are to be overanimated. In fact, I can't remember the last overanimated executive I worked with.

In addition to the negative cues listed earlier, become aware of the following types of unnatural positions that can make you appear stiff, uncomfortable, or nervous:

- Leaning forward at the podium with your head supported on your arms.
- Standing bolt upright with your hands clasped tightly behind your back (called the reverse fig leaf) or with your arms folded tightly in front of your chest like a shield, or with your hands clasped tightly in front of your groin (yes, the infamous fig leaf).
- Pointing to a screen or easel with your body turned away from your audience.
- Stuffing your hands into your pockets and leaving them there, sometimes adding music by playing with keys or loose change.
- Using any repetitive gesture that blocks the audience's view of your face (especially problematic for televised appearances).

Natural positions require no definition. They are movements that do not draw attention to themselves but serve instead to illustrate or emphasize a message. They do not interfere with your delivery or make you appear or feel uncomfortable.

SPEAKING YOUR PIECE

Have you ever heard a talented speaker turn an indifferent text into a memorable presentation? Or a less-endowed speaker ruin a marvelous piece of writing with a hemmed, hawed, and slurred delivery? To a great extent the mode of your delivery affects the reception of your message. It is important, then, to think about your voice, a critical nonverbal element of presentation.

There are five general dimensions of voice: volume, rate, pitch, emphasis, and quality.

Volume

This refers to the intensity of the voice used by the speaker. "Loudness" is a subjective evaluation of that volume, as affected by distance, acoustics, and other noise. This is an area in which most persons have developed an automatic regulating ability. Nonetheless, some people at an intimate cocktail party seem determined to yell as if they were at a Times Square subway stop at rush hour with four trains pulling in. And, of course, some choose to whisper in a packed auditorium.

We need to reinforce our skills—to fine-tune our antennae—in order to estimate approximately how much volume we need to communicate in a particular setting.

It is important to add a few refinements to your volume-setting ability—the use of varying levels of volume to keep your voice interesting to your listeners and to emphasize words or phrases. It is a very common and problematic practice to allow one's voice to fade off at the end of sentences, particularly at the end of ideas and at the end of the presentation, almost as if the speaker were collapsing at the end of a race.

Achieving quality "volume control" is generally not difficult. Place cues in your speaking notes, such as underlining key words or writing "louder" in the margin. Tape-record your practice sessions and listen to your volume plus your other vocal qualities. If you do not have a good ear, seek open, reliable feedback from trusted colleagues. When speaking, consider relying on a "third-base coach" in the audience to signal you subtly regarding volume as well as rate.

Microphones can also create "volume control" problems. We often find it difficult to hear a speaker when he or she turns toward a slide or flip chart to make a point. Here a microphone attached to your tie, blouse, or lapel can be far more helpful than the traditional lectern-based microphone. If your microphone is fixed to the lectern or table in front of you, practice the coordination of your visual aids and speech well in advance so that you won't commit the cardinal sin of turning away from the microphone as you speak.

Rate

Rate is another area of difficulty for many speakers. In addition to the ability to enunciate clearly, the most common speech problems are speaking more slowly than necessary and too quickly toward the latter one-third of a prepared presentation. A typical recommended rate of speed is between 140 and 170 words per minute. Tape-record one of your practice sessions and check a section against a watch. Experts say that the mind of the listener can typically accept three to four times as many words per minute as a speaker can deliver, but that doesn't mean you should be racing your speech to the finish line.

The pace of your delivery should vary depending upon the nature of your message; it should also vary within the presentation in order to offer variety to the listener. Generally you should deliver serious material a bit more slowly, humor a bit more quickly. A formal setting, or one before a very large gathering with a great deal of distance between you and the audience, would probably justify a slower, more deliberative presentation; a small, informal circle might require a quicker pace.

Pitch

This is the measurement of "highness" or "lowness" of voice. As with volume and rate, pitch is something you should learn to vary for emphasis and meaning.

We often assign greater authority to a speaker—male or female—who uses a low to moderate range of voice. For examples, look to the professional news readers on television.

Because pitch is to a large part determined by the tension or relaxation of the vocal cords, many speakers find their voices at a higher pitch when under pressure—for example, when making a presentation. Relaxation is the cure, and that is something that comes with practice and experience. It should not be your goal to alter your voice—particularly not to lower it artificially—but you should strive to achieve a normal, relaxed tone.

Emphasis

Emphasis is a significant element of our nonverbal communication. A change in emphasis greatly alters meaning. Read the following sentence aloud, emphasizing the italicized words:

What do you want me to do? (anger)
What *do* you want me to do? (querulousness)
What do *you* want me to do? (as opposed to what *he* wants you to do)
What do you *want* me to do? (what you *really* want)
What do you want *me* to do? (as opposed to *him*)
What do you want me to *do*? (a plaintive plea)

Quality

Quality of voice is a subjective matter, as determined by the listener. This includes elements such as breathiness, hoarseness, nasality, and other qualities. Again, listen to a good-quality tape recording of your voice. Seek open feedback from others. If the problem persists, seek the advice of a communication consultant who specializes in voice and articulation.

The quality of your voice is also measured by the presence of some "speech defects," including slurring of words, problems with particular speech sounds, and chronic mispronunciation of certain common words—"revelant" for *relevant,* "li-berry" for *library,* "ag-cul-ture" for *agriculture,* and perhaps the most common one I come across in our seminars, "nu-cu-lar" for *nuclear.* You may find you have a habit of adding sounds ("judg-ah-ment") or dropping sounds ("goin'," "doin'").

THE PAUSES THAT REFLECT

Pauses are a crucial and often overlooked aspect of our nonverbal communication. They can aid the audience's comprehension of your message and give added emphasis to your ideas. They can also heighten your sense of control and command. Put another way, speakers who don't pause often project the sense that they are not in control of either their message or themselves—or both.

Despite these obvious benefits of pauses, speakers normally overreact to the temporary silence associated with them; the pauses seem longer to them than to their audience, a perception undoubtedly fed by anxiety.

Anxiety also feeds our tendency to utter so-called vocalized pauses—"ah," "uh," "you know," and "like" (the teenager's favorite). We use these because of our irrational discomfort with temporary silence. In fact, since the vocalized pause is such a widespread malady, the Toastmasters, an organization dedicated to developing the speaking skills of its members, appoints "Ah Counters" to tally the number of *ah*s surfacing in each member's speech.

*Ah*counting may help you too. However, a few vocalized pauses here and there shouldn't do you any—ah—harm. Rather, they can help convey your sense of deliberation and counter the perception that you are too smooth or glib.

The best way to cultivate the effective use of the pause (as well as your other vocal qualities) is to rely on feedback from trusted advisors and to practice with an audiotape recorder.

Chapter 13

PRACTICING AND PRESENTING: THE MARTEL METHOD

How do you get to center stage? Practice!
How do you earn a standing ovation? Practice!
How do you win rave reviews? Practice!

You know everything you need to know about your audience, the setting, and the occasion; you've prepared your speech. Now comes the time for rehearsal.

Don't begin rehearsing until you are reasonably pleased with your speech. Otherwise, your sense of discomfort or conflict about it will reflect in your delivery. This is another reason why you should not leave the completion of your speech until the last moment. Try to give yourself at least a week to practice for a major engagement.

THE PRACTICE ENVIRONMENT

Practicing your presentation involves a systematic process of replacing the fear of the unknown with familiarity. Familiarity with your audience, the setting, the occasion, your message, and, yes, familiarity with your own style of delivery. There are several ways of breeding that sense of familiarity during the practice session.

Don't practice sitting behind your desk or floating in your

bathtub—unless that is the setting you will use for the actual engagement. If possible, when you're rehearsing for major engagements, go to the very room where you'll be delivering your speech. If that is not feasible, arrange for a reasonable simulation. If you expect to use a podium, have one in the practice room. If you'll be using a microphone and amplifier for your presentation, include them in your practice sessions.

Try to replicate the lighting conditions of the speech site. If you plan to use visual aids, include them in your rehearsal. Practice your script with the projectionist, if you will be using one, to make sure he or she understands your cues.

THE MARTEL METHOD

The Martel Method is a surefire, step-by-step approach to improving your delivery. It consists of four phases: verbal, vocal, physical, and the complete dry run. You need to master each phase before you address the next one. This allows you to stay focused on one aspect of your delivery at a time. Otherwise, if you are too conscious about too many aspects of your delivery at once, your anxiety quotient can shoot through the roof. Here's how the method works:

I. Verbal Phase

Focus first and exclusively on the basic fluency of your outline. Identify the words and phrases that come slowly to you, cause you to trip over your tongue, or promote breathing problems. Chances are, unless you address these problems, they will surface during your engagement.

Once the flow is relatively smooth, focus next on embellishment, elaboration and transitions, internal summaries, and lead sentences. Do you need to add adjectives or adverbs to make your ideas stronger or more visual? Do you need to develop your thoughts further? Is the flow from one idea to the next sufficiently smooth? Are you launching each new idea with a sufficiently interesting or compelling lead sentence? For example:

Version One:
    The studio needs a newer look.
    The chairs are starting to look worn.
    The rug is nothing special.
    The use of space isn't well planned.

Version Two:
    The studio needs to be warmer and more inviting.
    We need comfortable, stylish chairs to add to the guests' sense of importance.
    We need a new rug to accent the overall feeling we are seeking to generate.
    We need to lay out the room so that it is intimate without being confining.

II. Vocal Phase

This phase is focused on volume, rate, pitch, emphasis, articulation, and overall tone. By using a tape recorder you can analyze your vocal image and decide which elements of it require the most attention. Or, if you, like most people, don't have a good ear, you may be better advised to work with a speech coach who specializes in voice and articulation.

III. Physical Phase

The major elements of this phase are eye contact, facial expression, gestures, and overall bodily movement.

Your gestures and movements should be communicative without being distracting. At one time, classical instruction in speech delivery included a set regimen of movements tied to certain specific ideas and phrases. For example, specific gestures, body positions, and facial expressions were associated with such emotions as worry, fear, resoluteness, indignation, indifference, and so on. The effect was like that of a ballet—and, as you know, not everyone can look graceful in such a rigidly choreographed dance. Instead, your gestures should arise naturally from delivery. The more you are in command of your ideas and willing to communicate, the more natural your gestures will be.

Videotaping your practice sessions is the very best basis for analyzing the physical phase. How did Demosthenes and the men and women of eloquence who followed him through the ages do without it? They used mirrors, and you, too, can benefit from using one to reinforce the physical dimension of your speech.

As you improve your physical delivery, seek to capture the essential features of your conversational style. Chances are, in conversation you gesture easily and smile spontaneously. You should be just as spontaneous with your delivery of a presentation or speech.

One frequently overlooked aspect of the physical dimension involves your various movements in using visual aids. The following advice should be helpful:

- Make sure you face the audience, not the aid.
- Do not block the aid with any part of your body.
- Motion toward each aid when it appears, but point only to details that cannot be easily found by the audience or those that definitely need to be accentuated.
- Do not play with the pointer. In fact, put it away when you don't need to use it.
- Practice before using a laser or flashlight pointer. Otherwise, your audience may ridicule your hand-eye coordination as you frantically search for the proper place.

IV. The Complete Dry Run

Practice your remarks first in segments, for example, introduction, body, and conclusion, then practice by delivering the entire message. Time yourself.

Consider inviting a group of reliable critics to provide feedback. Pay close attention to what they tell you and to what the videotapes reveal. It really doesn't matter if *you* think you are getting your points across—if your candid critics tell you otherwise, consider a different approach.

After that last fine-tuning, stop the changes. Too many last-minute changes will clutter your outline or manuscript as well as your mind. Your last rehearsal should be as close to the final presentation as you can make it.

HOW DO I PREPARE WHEN I AM GIVEN VERY SHORT NOTICE?

The basic answer is, "don't leave out any of the steps that you would rely on if you had weeks or months to prepare; just devote less time to each of them." Therefore, if you are given extremely short notice be sure to:

1. Define your net effects, substance, and image goals.
2. Analyze your audience.
3. Select and organize 3–5 key points to support your goals.
4. Select proof to clarify or support your points.
5. Prepare an introduction with an attention getter, need-to-know step ("carrot") and preview.
6. Prepare a conclusion to recap your main points and to direct your audience to action or leave them with a predefined feeling or impression.
7. Anticipate major questions.
8. Practice (if time permits).

THE SPEAKER AS PHOTOGRAPHER

As you move through your outline during your practice sessions and during the speech itself, think of your eyes as the shutter of an expensive camera. Photograph with your eyes the key words or sentences (highlighted by a marking pen or by underlining) in your outline; lift your eyes to your audience to deliver the idea with maximum impact, making sure that you don't lower them until the idea has been fully presented; drop your eyes to photograph the next key word or line—and so on. As long as you don't overreact to the momentary silence associated with the photography process, and if you practice this technique diligently, you will discover a whole new dimension to your speaking skills.

"TO SIT OR NOT TO SIT"

This is one of the more frequent questions asked during my seminars: "Is it okay to sit on the edge of the table while speaking?" While the answer depends on many factors related to the audience and the occasion, I normally respond by asking the speaker why he or she wants to sit. To mask his or her own speech anxiety (since sitting is normally more comfortable than standing)? To create a more informal atmosphere? To establish greater intimacy with the audience? Certainly, there are better ways to alleviate speech anxiety than sitting; hence sitting is far more justifiable if it is tied to a communicative purpose, such as changing the tone or intimacy level of the presentation. To be effective, your sitting down must be timed and choreographed carefully—and not be overdone.

Wired for Sound

If anything is likely to put Murphy's Law on full display, it is the sound system. Therefore, the setup for electronic amplification should be an important part of your regular advance work.

If you plan to speak without a podium, consider wearing a cordless lavaliere or tie-clip microphone to allow you freedom of movement. Or, if the microphone you'll be using has a cord, practice walking to avoid tripping on the wire.

A microphone on a stand or attached to a podium requires you to stay nearby—about a foot in back of the podium with the microphone six inches below the level of your mouth. The placement is important both to capture your words and to prevent the view of your face from being blocked.

Before you speak—preferably before the event begins—check out the microphone and amplification system. Determine how far away from it you can stand without sacrificing volume or vocal quality. During the event itself, avoid testing the sound system by tapping the microphone or going through the "testing one, two, three" routine. Audience feedback will be your most reliable test.

Don't handle a microphone mounted on a stand as you speak; it looks unprofessional; it can affect sound quality; and it inhibits free gestures. However, walking around the stage purposefully with an unmounted microphone can project stage presence.

Speak directly into the microphone. As you do, be yourself vocally, maintaining an even, natural tone of voice. Leave it to the sound technician to adjust the amplification level.

If, following the speech, you can field questions without the lectern, consider leaving it; that is, if you don't need a microphone or if your microphone is mobile. The audience will feel closer to you—and you will feel closer to them.

FIELDING QUESTIONS
DURING THE ADDRESS ITSELF

Normally a speaker should complete his or her address before fielding questions for three major reasons: first, interruptions can impede persuasive momentum; second, such questions are typically parochial, and, as a result, neither the question nor the answer adds much to the audience's understanding; third, the speaker often has difficulty knowing how to cut off questioning and return to the body of his or her presentation, regaining stride.

There are, however, three particular circumstances in which it may be necessary to allow for questions during the presentation: one, when a well-rooted norm has been established for this practice by an important body you are addressing, for example, a board of directors meeting; two, when a key member of the target audience is asking the question; and three, when your presentation is so long or technical that you might be well advised to break it into discrete ten-, fifteen-, or twenty-minute segments, each followed by a five- to ten-minute question-and-answer period with a general question-and-answer period to follow your presentation.

If you are not sure whether or not your presentation may be interrupted by questions and want to prevent them (without violating a well-rooted norm), you may

- Ask that questions be held to the end.
- Indicate that you will be speaking for only X minutes (implying that the audience should be able to wait until you finish).
- Speak with added force and cadence to make it more difficult for anyone to interrupt—but take care not to sound rushed or on the defensive.

MOUNTING THE PLATFORM

A speech of ten thousand words begins with a single step—from the wings to center stage.

You have found out in advance of the presentation, of course, what the setting will be—whether you'll be seated on stage to await your introduction, whether you'll wait offstage, whether you'll be called from the audience. You have examined the path you must take, seen whether there are any cables on the floor or steps you must climb.

You've chosen your clothing with care—not just an outfit that will show well while you're standing and speaking but clothing that fits you well while you're seated.

Don't fidget, adjust your clothing, or riffle through your papers while waiting for your turn to speak; it communicates a lack of respect or interest, or both, in the current speaker. Spend the time fine-tuning your analysis of the audience or the occasion. Listen carefully to the current speaker to see if there is any necessary adaptation you must make in your own presentation: Is he or she covering some of the same ground you have staked out? What kind of reaction is coming from the audience? Is this situation providing you with an opportunity to display your wit? (Some of the funniest lines are spawned just as the speech is to begin.)

UP AND OVER

Walk to center stage purposefully but calmly and with a sense of command—and don't hurry. When you arrive, take a deep breath. Arrange your papers on the podium if you're going to use one. If you want your suit jacket buttoned, do so before you walk across the stage. Look around at the audience to establish contact, comfort, and command—to signal to them that their attention is wanted. Greet them with a firm but friendly "Good morning," "Good afternoon," or "Good evening." This is part of the critical thirty seconds, a period during which your presence as a speaker is established.

Everything should have been set up before you stepped onto the stage, but if not, now is the time to adjust the lectern and check the microphone.

You must feel physically comfortable as you stand to deliver a speech; so, too, you should communicate through your stance an open and relaxed manner.

Your weight should be evenly distributed on both legs, with your right foot placed approximately five to seven inches in front of your left foot to avoid swaying back and forth. On occasion, you can put your hand into your pocket (if that is a natural gesture for you and if you can easily and unobtrusively change your position to allow you to gesture). Your hands and arms should not dangle loosely at your sides, nor be on your hips, clenched across your chest, locked behind your back, or draped heavily on the podium.

Wait for applause to end before you start. Acknowledge and thank your introducer, turning to him or her if convenient. Then, when all is ready, begin.

As you speak, you want each audience member to believe that you have prepared your remarks and come to the hall specifically to speak to him or her. Therefore your speech needs to convey a sense of freshness versus the "tonight Chicago, tomorrow Cleveland" feeling.

Again, maintain the aura of being in command. You should appear alert and aware of the audience and intimately involved in the ideas you are presenting. All of the verbal and nonverbal elements of presentation should be brought into play.

If the audience is sending you no message at all, they're possibly "asleep." Ordinarily the audience will "tell" you when you're right on target or when you're losing them.

Watch the faces of your listeners. Are they straining to hear you? Are they following your presentation? Are they restless and studying their watches? Are their expressions friendly, hostile, bored? If they are hostile, you may need to work harder to achieve common ground (see chapter 4). If they are bored, you may need to use more effective attention getters (see page 67) or common ground. You might need to choose more striking examples or speak more forcefully.

It is also possible that distractions will emanate from the audience or from outside of your shared environment—a crying baby, a wailing siren, a tray of dishes crashing to the floor. Don't compete! Wait for the situation to calm down before continuing. The audience is generally on your side—share the moment with them. It might even provide an opening for humor. For example, years ago I heard former Senator Birch Bayh (D., Ind.) address a group when a physician's beeper went off. Without a moment's hesitation and to the audience's obvious delight, Senator Bayh said, "Tell the president he'll have to wait."

YOU'RE FORGIVEN

You're going to make mistakes. You'll leave out an important fact, you'll misstate a critical premise, mispronounce a word or a name, you'll sneeze or cough, hesitate in search of an elusive word or phrase. More often than not, your audience will never know the difference, so don't point out the mistake. You will impress more audience members with a sense of poise than with a claim to perfection. If it is important that you communicate the idea you missed, don't be afraid to go back and restate it without apology.

You're now ready to capture the persuasive edge. Think positively; focus on your net-effects, substance, and image goals and on your ideas; look the audience members straight in the eye; and communicate in earnest to seize the opportunity your engagement represents and to earn the strongest reception they can offer.

Chapter 14

QUESTION-AND-ANSWER SESSIONS

You've completed your speech. Everything you've said was carefully planned, outlined, and presented to the best of your ability. Everything was under control.

But now, instead of walking back to your seat in relief, you are facing a sea of hands waving urgently to gain your attention to ask you questions.

First of all, it should come as no surprise. If you conducted proper advance work, you probably agreed to and even announced a question-and-answer period during your introduction. If you didn't want to answer questions, you should have informed your hosts in advance.

Why would you want to be exposed to questions?

- A question period is a second opportunity to reinforce your key messages. Research has shown that your last remarks are often most remembered.
- It is an opportunity to demonstrate your expertise and openness.
- Skillful responses allow you to defuse critics.

NOTE: Many of the concepts presented in this chapter are developed further in my book, *Mastering the Art of Q&A: A Survival Guide for Trick, Tough and Hostile Questions* (Homewood, Illinois: Dow Jones-Irwin, 1989).

- A question period stimulates a more direct sense of involve-ment with your audience. In fact, it is often perceived as more relevant than the presentation.
- It is an excellent way of finding out what is on the minds of your audience and how successfully you have communicated with them.
- For many speakers, as noted earlier, it is more comfortable to engage in the give-and-take of a question period than to deliver prepared remarks. Some speakers, as a matter of fact, will prefer giving a very short opening statement and then turning immediately to an extended question-and-answer period.

What are the possible disadvantages of a question-and-answer session?

- You may be exposed to questions on subjects for which you are not prepared.
- You may be giving the floor to an unfriendly adversary.
- If you completely lose control, you could end up being an unhappy observer at what had been your own presentation.

Note that I have listed these disadvantages as "possible." Your basic guiding principle must be to maintain command and con-trol of the situation.

(Note: Most of the suggestions contained in chapters 16 through 19 on conducting interviews with reporters are applica-ble here too.)

YOUR FIVE RESPONSE OPTIONS

Whenever someone asks you a question, you have five basic ways of responding:

1. To respond only
2. To insert only (i.e., to present your message, regardless of the question)

3. To respond and insert
4. To insert and respond
5. To ignore

Let's take the simple question, How strong was your firm's sales performance last year?

1. To respond only (with proof): "We had a terrific year last year; sales were up nine percent; and we experienced double-digit sales growth in each of our regions."
2. To insert only: "We maintained our leadership position last year." (Note: This is an insertion because it does not answer the question. Maintaining leadership position can involve an increase or decrease in sales.)
3. To respond and insert: "Our sales performance last year was our best in ten years [response]; we expect steady, strong growth for at least the next five years—and then a plateau [insert]."
4. To insert and respond: "Before I answer your question, let me comment on the remark Joe just made regarding the impact of imports on our sales performance." (Note: comment regarding imports is then followed by response.)
5. To ignore: "Our sales future is nothing but bright . . ."

Be tactical in selecting the appropriate response option.

If the question is of limited potential interest to your target audience and provides little or no latitude for you to advance one of your key messages (the respond-and-insert option), you should "respond only" briefly, but without appearing curt.

If the question is unclear or potentially embarrassing, you may wish to "insert" your own message without pointedly responding to the question.

If someone who has just spoken before you has made a point you need to react to before answering, for example, a potentially damaging attack, you should normally respond first to it (insert) and then respond to the question per se.

If the question is multifaceted, and one of the facets is of limited interest to your audience or potentially embarrassing if addressed, you may choose to ignore it as long as your target audience doesn't expect you to answer it.

HANDLING THE QUESTION-AND-ANSWER SESSION

Open the question-and-answer session by setting a positive, approachable tone (e.g., "And now I will be pleased to respond to your questions.").

To gain the persuasive edge, define and remain focused on your goals (see chapter 2). Look for openings to fit your substance and image goals into your responses, even if the connection seems remote initially.

Keep your target audience in mind as you answer. Remember, the questioner may not be a member of your target audience and may or may not represent their interests through his or her question.

Be prepared to place any boundaries on the questions, for example:

"I can't discuss that matter because it is in litigation."

"I don't feel I have to answer that question; it's too personal."

"For security reasons I cannot answer your question."

"I will be pleased to answer questions regarding X; I am not prepared to answer questions regarding Y because that is not my area of expertise."

"I prefer not to answer that question because we make it a practice not to criticize our competition."

"I can't answer that question because it would cause me to divulge confidential (proprietary) information."

Anticipate difficult questions. And remember, you have no guarantee that the questions will be directly related to your presentation.

Practice your answers to the questions you can anticipate—first for content, then for style.

Listen carefully to the question. Make certain it is appropriate and does not contain misinformation, misstatements, or incorrect assumptions. Don't be baited by offensive words or phrases from the questioner. If the statistics used are incorrect, say so without sounding too contentious. If you doubt the accuracy of a statement, politely request the questioner to identify his source. Any element left unchallenged may be assumed to be correct by the audience. Avoid interrupting the questioner unless you feel he's taking too much control of the floor.

Be sure your audience can hear the question. If necessary, repeat the question, carefully recasting it to remove any confusing or offensive language. Repeating a question is also a good device to earn you additional time to think before you respond. But don't repeat the question if almost everyone heard it, or you will probably make your stall all too transparent.

Pause reflectively before answering especially challenging questions. Jumping in without testing the water with your toe—without thinking first—can be a chilling experience.

Respond in headlines or lead sentences. Give the gist of your response at the very beginning. Otherwise, you could be perceived as either meandering, withholding information, or not knowing the answer. As a result, your credibility can suffer.

Stay cool. Try not to debate with the questioner. If he has a valid point, admit it. If he doesn't, consider stating your disagreement politely—demonstrating respect for another point of view. Or you may want to stress some shared basic agreement. For example, "While we seem to disagree about means, we do agree on goals." Follow that with a bridge back to one of your other points. The audience will appreciate your graciousness.

Be tactful. Don't tell or imply to a member of the audience that his question is "dumb"; don't tell him you already answered that question. You might instead wonder if your presentation was as clear and as comprehensive as you had hoped. And don't overuse "That's an excellent question" or "I'm glad you asked that question" (often more of a stall than a sincere compliment).

Be personable. In many situations it may be advisable to ask the questioner to mention his or her name and affiliation or hometown. Referring to this person by name during your response can project you as more engaging and may soften his or her contentiousness.

Don't hesitate to ask for clarification or to ask an audience member a question. This can help you formulate your thoughts better, prevent potentially embarrassing misinterpretations, and demonstrate genuine interest in the audience member's point of view.

Be compassionate. The questioner may be more interested in cathartic relief—airing a grievance or personal viewpoint—than in your answer, no matter how good it may be. Moreover, the audience may also be as interested in discerning your genuine feelings or sentiments as in learning the actual content of your message. If the questioner is expressing a grievance about your company, the government, or the world in general, be a therapist first, then an expert (e.g., "I understand how you must feel. I'm sorry you had to go through all that red tape. Let me outline some approaches we've found to be very helpful.").

Don't be afraid to say, "I don't know." In fact, the worst thing you can do is to fabricate an answer. No one expects you to know everything; you'll stay out of trouble and maintain your credibility by saying, "I don't know" (and explain nondefensively why), or "I'll find that out and get back to you." And keep that promise if made!

Monitor your body language. Don't turn your back on a questioner, unless it is to break contact. Don't fidget with your notes. And be sure to maintain eye contact with your questioner until you are ready to move on to someone else.

Monitor the length of your responses (see discussion below). And know when to end the session. Generally it's time to wind down when the hands begin to appear less frequently. Working out your exit ahead of time with the host can be most helpful. And try to end on a positive note.

LONG VERSUS SHORT

One of the major conclusions I've drawn from preparing business and political leaders for challenging question-and-answer sessions is that a wide variety of hidden messages and tactical implications are represented by the "shortness" or "longness" of a response. These are summarized in the following table:

The Long Response

Clarity and Interest-Value Implications

Positive
- The longer the response, the greater the opportunity to clarify and reinforce the point being made.

Negative
- The longer response can be boring, especially if unstructured, too redundant, too technical, and devoid of examples, illustrations, anecdotes, or interesting statistics.

Tactical Implications

Positive
- The long response gives you more thinking time (stalling time) to produce a complete answer.
- It increases the perception that at least a portion of the answer may appear responsive.
- It reduces the number of questions that can be asked (when you don't seek active questioning).
- It can widen the opening for bridging into a proactive theme.
- It reduces the exposure potentially available to the opponent, if any.

Negative
- It can open Pandora's Box, laying the groundwork for damaging follow-up questions.
- It increases the potential for misstatements and gaffes.
- It provides the audience or opponent with additional time to prepare a rebuttal.
- It reduces the likelihood of your being quoted (if being quoted is an objective).

Image Implications

Positive
- The longer response helps project your knowledgeability or expertise.
- You enhance your sense of cooperation, including your respect for the question, the questioner, and the audience.
- You appear more open.

Negative
- It can make you appear unaware of the answer.
- You may appear unwilling to provide an answer.
- You may lose credibility because of your diversionary approach.
- Some long-winded answers can sound too defensive.
- Your long-windedness can demonstrate insensitivity to the audience's level of interest or respect for time.
- Finally, a thin line often exists between long-windedness and preachiness.

The Short Response

Clarity and Interest-Value Implications

Positive
- The short response isn't burdened by unnecessary verbiage and is less likely to strain the audience's attention span.

Negative
- Without sufficient elaboration, the short response may be too abstract.

Tactical Implications

Positive
- The short response is less likely to create the traps for follow-up questions or rebuttal often produced by lengthier responses. It therefore also allows the respondent to drop a "hot potato" issue quickly.
- It allows more time for questions (if active questioning, including greater interaction with the audience, is desirable).
- It limits the audience's or the opponent's time to prepare a rebuttal.
- It increases the likelihood of being quoted (if being quoted is desirable).

Negative
- It gives the opponent more potential exposure.
- It allows more time for questions to be asked (if fewer are desirable).

Image Implications

The short response can communicate:
Positive
- Confidence
- Directness

Negative
- Authority
- Respect for the audience's time
- Too much of a "trust me" tone
- Caution
- Arrogance or aloofness
- Disinterest or indifference
- Defensiveness
- Lack of knowledge or depth
- Lack of cooperation

THE DIFFICULT QUESTION

Crucial to your ability to perform well during the question-and-answer session is your ability to listen to a question, understand what it means, know what type of question it is, and remember its elements. You must also, of course, have been adequately briefed on the issues related to the question and be able to answer it persuasively in a manner compatible with your substance and image goals. This is a difficult task, but the skills necessary to accomplish it can be cultivated.

Listening to a question, particularly in a heated session, is not as simple as it may seem. As the question is being asked, you may, for instance, be thinking about how you could have improved on an earlier response; about points unrelated to the question that you want to make during the next response opportunity; about how well you are doing so far, and so on. Compounding the difficulty may be the phrasing of the question itself. The questioner may becloud it with too much background information or may state an assumption or argument with which you disagree. This may cause you to tune the questioner out or to refute him internally while losing focus on the question itself. And to make matters worse, you may be hesitant to ask for clarification, fearful that the rephrased question may be even more difficult to answer or that your lack of understanding may project lack of intelligence.

Remembering the elements of the question can also be complicated for these same reasons. Although taking notes might help some speakers to cope with this problem, they are often reluctant to do so. This is either because (a) they do not want to sacrifice eye contact with the audience; (b) they are fearful that such behavior might communicate lack of intelligence; (c) they are confident that they can remember the elements of the question; or (d) they may not want to "remember" all the elements because one or more might be difficult or awkward to answer—or actually unanswerable.

"BANANA PEELS"

Crucial to your effectiveness in Q&A is your ability to handle questions that pose danger because of their phrasing. These questions, called banana peels because of a speaker's potential to "slip" on them, fall into twelve categories. Listed below are examples of each and your major options in responding to them. The basic premise of this approach is that your aptitude in answering questions will be strengthened by your ability to label the type of question being asked and to employ the appropriate tactical options associated with it.

TYPE	EXAMPLE	MAJOR OPTIONS
1. Hostile	"How do you expect more business with your *rotten* customer-service record?"	■ Maintain composure. ■ Display humor without being unduly sarcastic or strident (e.g., "With that question I can no longer include you in my will."). ■ Ignore or take exception to terms chosen—for example, *rotten*—without repeating the term.

TYPE	EXAMPLE	MAJOR OPTIONS
		■ Refute assumptions.
2. Speculative	"What do you expect sales to be next year?"	■ Answer if response is relatively risk-free. ■ If not risk-free, label question as speculative and note risk (e.g., "I don't make my crystal-ball gazing public anymore because I am tired of eating crushed glass.").
3. Hypothetical	"If sales increase within the next year, would you still propose cutting the advertising budget?"	■ Answer directly. ■ Point out hypothetical nature of question. ■ Challenge/question refutable assumptions.
4. Picayune/ Overspecific	"What has been the percentage of growth of the building/ maintenance budget since 1982?"	■ Answer directly. ■ Label question as overspecific. ■ If you don't know, say so. (Sometimes you may need to explain in a nondefensive manner why you don't know and offer to provide the answer later.)
5. Leading	"Bob has done a great job instilling new life into this company, hasn't he?"	■ Agree or disagree. ■ Note that the question is leading.

TYPE	EXAMPLE	MAJOR OPTIONS
		■ Challenge/Question the assumption(s).
6. Loaded	"Why can't your company attract more business with one of the best management teams in the nation?" This question carries three assumptions: 1. Your company is not attracting new business as it should. 2. Your company has one of the best management teams in the nation. 3. The management team should attract more business.	■ If you agree or disagree with any of these assumptions, let it be known and then respond.
7. Value	"Is American manufacturing becoming *better* because of foreign competition?"	■ Apply your definition of *better* without drawing attention to this term. ■ Point out the value term, define it, and then answer the question. ■ Ask questioner to define *better*; then respond.

TYPE	*EXAMPLE*	*MAJOR OPTIONS*
8. Multifaceted	"How many females do you employ? How has this level changed over the past four years? How does your firm's employment of females compare with that of competing firms? Why is there only one female on your board?"	■ If each facet can be remembered and answering all won't cause harm (assuming there is ample time), then answer fully. ■ If harm can be caused by answering a remembered facet, it is probably best to "forget" it and answer the others. ■ Don't hesitate to ask for a facet to be repeated if you are reasonably certain you forgot a "safe" one. ■ If the questions cannot be realistically answered within the time allotted, politely say so. ■ Sometimes it may be advisable not to respond in the order in which the facets were asked; for example, if the last facet is the most crucial, it may require your initial attention.

TYPE	EXAMPLE	MAJOR OPTIONS
9. Vague, Unfocused	"What are your company's plans for the future?"	■ Define the question the way you wish—consistent with your persuasive goals. ■ Ask the questioner to clarify his or her focus.
10. "Yes-No"	"Interest-rate fluctuations are the reason why your bank didn't do so well last year, yes or no?"	■ If *yes* or *no* is safe by itself, answer accordingly. ■ If risky, point out how the forced alternatives can interfere with a presentation of "the full truth." Then answer the question.
11. "Either-Or"	"Have your sales declined so dramatically because your sales team has lost morale or because your competition is underselling you?"	■ If assumption within first part of question is incorrect, refute it. ■ How accurate are the assumptions within the second part of the question? If not, refute them. ■ How correct is the causal connection between the sales decline and the morale and competitor assumptions? If it isn't, refute.

TYPE	EXAMPLE	MAJOR OPTIONS
		■ How complete an explanation is it? Are other factors—possibly more significant ones—involved? If so, explain, possibly labeling the question as "either-or."
		▣ If sales have indeed declined and you have a positive message to insert (e.g., "The situation is already turning around."), consider using it.
12. Nonquestion	"Unemployment is climbing, inflation is still spiraling, we are in a depression and ought to admit it."	■ Ask for a question, noting the nonquestion.
		■ Respond to the nonquestion in whole or in part, seeking an opening to reinforce your persuasive goals.

THE HOSTILE QUESTIONER

"How do I handle a hostile questioner?" is one of the most frequent questions posed to me during our seminars. The first and most obvious answer is to maintain your composure. Blowing your cool can be far more memorable than your most eloquent words. In fact, a hostile questioner properly handled may constitute a valuable opportunity—an opportunity for you to demonstrate grace under fire and to project the impression that you can perform well in your position under pressure.

A key factor in maintaining composure is your capacity to depersonalize the hostility as much as possible. Keep your ego out of the equation as you do your best to represent your organization and the point of view it represents. To help you to depersonalize the exchange, keep the following points in mind:

- The questioner's hostility may be more a function of his personality than a reflection of his feelings toward you.
- The questioner may be more upset with your organization than with you personally.
- Your target audience does not necessarily agree with the hostile questioner. In fact, if you handle yourself well, you may win additional support from them as they react negatively to the questioner.

In responding to the hostile questioner, consider the following advice:

- Avoid debates. This can degenerate into a disastrous loss of control.
- Don't feel you have to refute in detail every hostile assertion; sometimes flat denial can be more authoritative, especially if the accusation was not supported.
- Seek out and highlight areas of agreement without being patronizing or gratuitous.
- Unless the questioner is too long-winded, allow him the opportunity to vent his emotions.
- Avoid communicating derision, verbally or nonverbally (unless you are reasonably sure your target audience would regard your behavior as appropriate).
- Avoid asking the masochistic "Did I answer your question?"
- Find a way to bridge from your basic response to a broader point that allows you to establish eye contact with someone seated in another part of the audience.

THE MONOPOLIZER

Monopolizers are an even more common breed than hostile questioners. Many monopolizers lack sufficient self-awareness or interest in the audience's regard for themselves. As well, many assume the role of special pleader, using the forum to advance their own agendas. Although controlling a monopolizer can be difficult, especially if other audience members are not actively participating, the following advice can be helpful:

- Say, "Other people are raising their hands; let me take their questions and if time allows, I'll get back to you."
- Invite the person to discuss his or her concerns personally with you or someone designated by you.
- Be prepared to interrupt the long-winded monopolizer with a tactful line (e.g., "Excuse me, I think I understand the drift of your question.").
- As you field questions, try to ignore the monopolizer with your eyes.

The quintessential double whammy is the hostile monopolizer—an all-too-common species. Handle this person as you would both the hostile questioner and the monopolizer. As you do, remember that such a situation should be regarded far more as an opportunity than as a threat.

A TERRIBLE SILENCE

It won't happen often, but it is possible that you may ask for questions and receive none. Don't let it throw you; you may have covered the subject so well that you've left no question unanswered. More likely, no one in the audience has yet worked up the courage to be the first questioner.

- Try interviewing yourself. "You know, the last time I gave a presentation like this, there was a really excellent question about . . ." And then answer your own question.
- Try to raise some questions. "There are some areas I didn't get into in my presentation that might be of particular interest to you . . ." Or, you might have picked up an interesting question when you arrived early at the session. Restate it and answer it yourself—and, if you use a bit of embellishment or editing in rephrasing the question, no one will be the wiser.
- Conduct your own "survey" of the audience. Ask them some questions, get them involved and thereby break the ice for a two-way flow of communication.
- Many speakers make use of "planted" questions from a confederate or "shill" in the audience. If you choose this method, be careful. People have a way of disclosing—consciously or unconsciously—when they are working from a script. Indeed, your credibility could be severely harmed if the audience catches on.

Finally, if no questions come, thank the audience, consider making a few brief, polite closing remarks to reinforce your substance and image goals. Then decide whether or not you should mingle with the audience, remembering that the mingling may still be another opportunity to pursue your goals and to capture the persuasive edge.

Chapter 15

BECOMING A BETTER SPEAKER BY BECOMING A BETTER LISTENER

We admire people for their speaking ability and deftness in dealing with the media, but we tend to undervalue a person's ability to listen. How unfortunate, for one's inability to listen contributes significantly to misunderstanding and poor performance in conversation, media interviews, and question-and-answer sessions. Listening is, and will probably always be, the weakest link in the communication chain.

Why do we undervalue listening? One principal reason is that listening doesn't place on display potentially captivating overt behavior the way speaking, singing, or acting does. Good listening frequently involves silence, and in our society silence is hardly as golden as the tireless axiom implies.

Although we tend to undervalue listening, it is the primary communication activity in our lives. One highly respected research study concluded that 45 percent of our involvement in communication is devoted to listening, 30 percent to speaking, 16 percent to reading, and 9 percent to writing.

Our listening inefficiency is also supported by research. In one study, subjects were asked to listen to a ten-minute oral presentation and were tested immediately afterward. The average listener heard, understood, evaluated properly, and retained only about half of what was said. In tests made again after forty-eight hours, the listener could comprehend and remember only about one-fourth of what was said in that ten-minute presentation. Another study revealed that 80 percent of an original message is likely to be lost in three sequential downward transmissions. Remember the "telephone" or "whispering down the lane" games we played as kids?

POTHOLES AND PITFALLS

Several behaviors are largely responsible for poor listening. As you study these, ask yourself which ones apply particularly to you:*

The perceptual filter. This is the sum total of preconceptions, prejudices, attitudes, motivation, personality, and societal mores that can stand between the message you are sending and the one that is received. Do you really think someone dressed in blue jeans and a T-shirt could receive an unfiltered hearing at a formal business meeting? How about a senior colleague committed to the survival of polyester knit suits? Or a junior executive with a good mind but with a limited vocabulary and poor grammar?

Faking attention. Most people are aware that it is both rude and potentially damaging to their career to be perceived as "tuning out" a conversation. The unfortunate solution for many people, though, is to develop ways to appear attentive. Figuratively—and sometimes literally—they sleep with their eyes open. Of course, those who are less proficient at this art give themselves away with their glassy, unresponsive stare.

Giving way to distractions. Good listeners are able to tune out "noise" and other interruptions in order to concentrate on content. An example might be a reporter who *must* listen to get the story, no matter what the circumstances. The ability to listen when equipment is running, phones are ringing, and voices are shouting back and forth requires commitment to concentration.

Listening only for the facts. Or as deadpan Sergeant Joe Friday

---

*These listening pitfalls were first identified by R. G. Nichols and L. A. Stevens in *Are You Listening?* (New York: McGraw-Hill, 1957).

used to say on *Dragnet,* "Just the facts, ma'am." Tuning out ideas and conclusions can be a way of protecting yourself from overload. You teach yourself to learn just enough to answer the question on a test or the specific demands of a specific job. But you'll be equally confused when all you can see are the trees and not the forest. "Big-picture listening" is, therefore, the remedy.

Preparing your response. Also known as verbal battle, this is a habit born of argumentative situations. We've all been in situations where we've been concentrating so much on what we will say when we have the chance that we don't listen to what the speaker is saying.

Writing everything down. The words go direct from your ears to your hand, virtually bypassing your brain. The listener tunes out all but key words and ends up missing the ideas.

False security. We normally speak at a rate of 135 to 160 words a minute. However, the brain can usually comprehend approximately 400 words of nontechnical spoken English per minute. As a result, we often find our brains racing ahead of the speaker. This is not necessarily a bad tendency, but it can lead to misunderstandings.

ON TO QUALITY LISTENING

Quality listening involves three A's: Awareness, Attitude, and Ability: The *awareness* that you're perceived as a poor listener can undermine the willingness of others to share important information with you. As a result, it can undermine your overall image. An *attitude* that the person speaking may—or probably will—say something worthwhile will heighten the speaker's interest in you. The *ability* to keep your impatience in check and your listening focused, as well as the *ability* to signal the communicator in an appropriate manner if he or she is unclear, boring, speaking too loudly or softly, or saying something you don't agree with, also enhances the speaker's sense of your respect and interest.

YOUR LISTENING APPRAISAL

The best way to determine how good a listener you are is to rate yourself. Use the questions below as but a sample. Place the number that corresponds to the most accurate response beside each question, then total them at the end to see how much improvement you need.

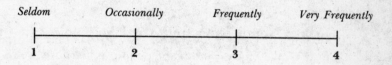

Seldom	Occasionally	Frequently	Very Frequently
1	2	3	4

1. ___ Make and maintain a commitment to listen and to understand what is being said.
2. ___ Commit yourself to being perceived as a good listener.
3. ___ Maintain eye contact with the speaker.
4. ___ Avoid playing with keys, pens, or other objects during a conversation.
5. ___ Maintain contact with the speaker instead of walking or turning away until the conversation has ended.
6. ___ Avoid excessive nodding or other body movements aimed at expediting the completion of a conversation.
7. ___ Create an environment free from unnecessary distractions and conducive to open communication.
8. ___ Avoid cutting the speaker off in midsentence.
9. ___ Transmit appropriate verbal or nonverbal cues to demonstrate understanding or misunderstanding.
10. ___ Take notes to aid listening patience and message retention.

Add the total number of points you assign to each item and rate your ability according to the following table:

40	Perfect
36–39	Excellent
33–35	Good/very good
30–32	Fair
30 and below	Take notice!

Based on your self-assessment, establish specific listening objectives for yourself. Then, at a later point, take the survey again to track your development as a quality listener.

Quality Note Taking and Mind Mapping

One of the reasons why we interrupt people is because we're afraid that we'll forget the point we want to make. Although this is a very human condition that might affect you on a regular basis, you need to ask yourself one pointed question: How often can you avoid interrupting the speaker by simply jotting down a key word to refer to later? *Key word* is the key word, because, as mentioned earlier, excessive note taking easily undermines effective listening.

One form of note taking that has gained enormous popularity within the last decade is mind mapping. A mind map is basically a note-taking method more in tune with the way in which our brain accesses and stores information. It is based on four principles:

1. The brain thrives on order and organization.
2. The higher the percentage of key words, the greater the recall.
3. The brain associates information better if words related to the same idea are clustered visually.
4. The brain more easily retains experiences and information that are visually interesting and outstanding.

Mind mapping is, therefore, a departure from conventional note taking. Rather than engaging in mindless linear transcription or copying, mind mapping allows you to create a highly personal set of notes in a less time-consuming manner.

How to Take Mind-Map Notes

- Put the main idea(s) in a circle at the center of the page.
- Print.
- Represent only one idea or concept per line.
- Use lines and arrows to link related concepts.
- Keep the mind map open-ended; leave room to add key words.
- Draw. A cartoon or diagram can give words a three-dimensional emphasis.
- Outline, circle, and shade groups of words to keep them together.
- Let your imagination reign free. Mind maps should be like your fingerprints—no one else's will be identical to yours.

The following is my mind map of our discussion so far.

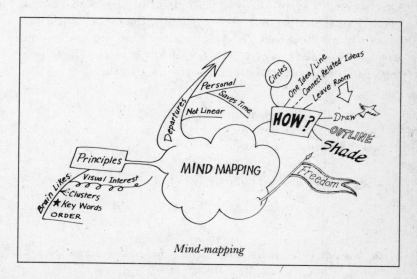

Mind-mapping

If you are mind mapping correctly:

- The main idea will be clear.
- The relative importance of ideas will be indicated by their

distance from the center or closeness to the edge of the paper.

- Relationships will be clear because of proximity and linking lines.
- Ideas should be easy to add without squeezing or erasing.
- Recall should be easier and more efficient.

Mind maps are not only for listening. You can use them to prepare an initial outline to your speech, to "work out" an action plan or decision, and to take notes while reading. In addition, drawing a simple, attractive mind map on a flip chart during a presentation can stimulate interest and understanding and facilitate recall.

Active Listening

One surefire way of becoming a better listener is to commit yourself to active listening. Active listening is a process involving one or more "feedback checks" to make sure you understand what is being said before you discuss the next point. The following example illustrates how active listening works:

CEO TO COMMITTEE CHAIR:

I want a full report from your committee regarding why our one-person kayak sales are down.

CHAIR:

Is the report supposed to be written or oral?

CEO:

Both.

CHAIR:

Do you want to receive the written report before the oral presentation?

CEO:

Yes, a week in advance.

CHAIR:

Should the report present solutions or just analyze causes?

CEO:

Deal first with the causes. We'll brainstorm regarding solutions after we discuss the causes.

Throughout this active-listening exercise, the chair was clarifying the meaning of the word *report*. Without such clarification he or she could have made one or more serious misassumptions regarding the form (written or oral), the timing, and the committee's scope of authority.

Yes, active listening requires concentration, patience, and intelligent questioning, but wouldn't you be willing to devote an extra measure of each to prevent the potential headaches that a simple "Yes, boss" in the example above might have produced?

Part III

THE
MEDIA

Chapter 16

MEDIA RELATIONS— YOUR SECRETARY CALLS

Your secretary calls you on the intercom. "It's that reporter, Randall, from *The Clarion Call*. He says he *must* speak with you right now. Something about our plans for the Valley Forge plant."

The Clarion Call—the local newspaper that ran a piece last week listing all the complaints of the union against your company's management; the paper that regularly features on its "environment page" poorly researched and often just plain wrong articles about pollution by some "expert" or another; the paper whose business editor lately seems interested only in running speculative and damaging articles about your company's proposed merger with Consolidated Corp.

And Randall, this freshly minted cub reporter assigned to the business desk, who doesn't appear to know the difference between a debenture and a denture, has somehow found a pipeline deep into your company providing all sorts of privileged information. And now he apparently has something on your "confidential" plans to close the Valley Forge plant and shift production to Taiwan.

Why should you even bother to talk to him? And if you do, wouldn't it be better—and easier—to simply deny any and all rumors about Valley Forge, although they're mainly true?

Before you do anything, consider a few facts of business life:

The media need you, no question about it. But you may need the media—sometimes to an even greater extent. As you make such an assessment, ask yourself the following questions:

- Can the media be helpful in calling into question an untrue rumor or in rectifying inaccuracies?
- Can the media be helpful in conveying to your target audiences positive key messages regarding your organization?
- Can the media, through its coverage, provide you with information you can't readily acquire elsewhere?

In short, does the interview provide your company with an opportunity that outweighs the risks associated with not responding?

To answer these questions, you need to understand the capacity of the various media to reach and to influence your target audience. Therefore, as with speeches and presentations, you must define your target audience as specifically as possible. For example, are you mainly interested in reaching your customers, employees, shareholders, suppliers, bankers, or the community at large?

As you define your target audience, keep in mind how your degree of cooperation with the media might influence your target audience's perceptions regarding the following five channels of credibility: (a) your corporation; (b) your division; (c) your industry; (d) you; (e) your ideas. Put another way, imagine what "stonewalling" or projecting a bunker mentality to *The Clarion Call* in the hypothetical example above would probably do to most of these channels.

WHEN AN INTERVIEW
MAY NOT BE ADVISABLE

Certain circumstances may make it inadvisable to meet directly with the media. For instance, if your company has done something significant in the "negative" news category, but not of crisis proportions (e.g., manufactured a defective product or dismissed a key executive), it may be more advisable to release a carefully worded statement about the situation in order to control the message as much as possible than to field tough questions.

Avoiding the face-to-face interview in such circumstances is especially advisable in dealing with the electronic media. The television or radio reporter or anchor can often represent your message more credibly than you under the duress of tough questioning.

GOALS AND KEY MESSAGES

Regardless of whether you've consented to a face-to-face interview, a telephone interview, or decided instead to release a statement to the media, you need to define your net-effects, substance, and image goals, and the key messages that will help you consummate them (see chapter 2). Your approach to the media, therefore, should be proactive, goal oriented, and control oriented. Examine your goals in turn:

- What are your net-effects goals? That is, what specifically do you want to happen or prevent from happening as a result of the media interview(s)? Are you seeking to influence certain attitudes or behaviors within your target audience—or both?
- What are your substance goals? What specific key messages need to be understood and believed by your target audience in order to increase the likelihood that your net-effects goals will be consummated? What do you need to do strategically or tactically to make the messages as convincing as possible?
- What are your image goals? What specific tone and traits do you intend to convey regarding your organization, division, industry, and yourself in order to reinforce your key messages? How can your words and body language help project the desired image?

Once you define your goals, *remember that your job during the interview, regardless of the questions asked, is to seek openings to insert or bridge to your key messages.* In so doing, you are capturing the essence of being a proactive (versus a reactive) communicator; you are on the right route to capturing the persuasive edge.

THE NATURE OF "BUSINESS NEWS"

The business pages of our newspapers and magazines and the business reports of radio and television have changed greatly in the past decade or so, reflecting the general shift in journalistic emphasis to "investigative reporting."

No longer are business stories confined to the "what"—a new plant, a new product, a new executive. There is much greater emphasis on the "why."

This does not mean that reporters are necessarily antibusiness. In fact, there is increasing specialization in business reporting among publications and the writers who work for them. Many reporters now take undergraduate and graduate courses in business administration, economics, and labor-management relations.

However, this doesn't mean that the business reporter is there to help you. The reporter is after a story and usually doesn't care if your stock will plummet or soar as a result.

The newspaper or television station is also a business and is interested in its own sales or ratings; you and your company are raw products for their industry.

The key, then, is to find the point of convergence of interests. The media need you for their business; if you find you need the media, as you almost certainly will, then you must find a way to work together.

Let's return to the example of the Valley Forge plant. The rumor about the plant closing is correct, but the company wasn't planning to announce the closing until all of the contracts with Taiwan were made final. Disclosing it now might foul up the deal and would certainly complicate negotiations with the union on the new contract.

But denying the rumor to the reporter would probably not prevent publication of the story. And you'd look like a fool—or a liar—when the plans are officially announced in a few weeks.

The fact is, as you are often too painfully aware, most reporters or publications get their information from many sources—not just from your official public relations department handouts. One of your most loyal executives may have let the word slip in an offhand remark to a reporter. Perhaps she merely mentioned it to her husband, who dropped the word at his bowling league to a buddy, who then told his neighbor, who just happened to be the newspaper's circulation manager.

Or maybe the reporter just happened to notice some unusual activity—surveyors or appraisers at the plant site or an unusual influx of Asian visitors (confirmed by the flight operations center of your local airport). Many a major story has surfaced through sheer coincidence. Reporters are paid to notice things.

And the fact is, much of your business operation is not secret anyway. A reporter can find out about your employment practices from state and federal equal employment opportunity agencies; about your safety records from OSHA and state labor departments; about some of your financial plans from state and federal commerce departments. If your company is publicly held, there are reams of documents on file with the Securities and Exchange Commission, most of them accessible to an industrious reporter. And if you really are pursuing foreign investment opportunities, there may be additional information available through federally guaranteed import-export loan programs.

What should you do, then, to engender good relations with the media?

First of all, as in every other area covered in this book, you should take the time to think *before* there is a crisis. Do you have a competent, well-informed public relations staff? Are you—or is any other likely company spokesperson—prepared for such a role? Do all the executives and managers understand your company's policy on responding to inquiries from the media? You do have a policy, don't you?

And most important—has your company established a good relationship with the media, a relationship based on trust? There are two sides to that equation: implicit in trust *by* the media is trust *of* the media. A paranoid feeling that the press is out to get you is usually due to a misunderstanding of their role.

UNDERSTANDING
THE ROLES AND THE PROCESS

Effective media relations require understanding the roles of the different persons involved in the genesis of the story—from the point of conception to that of readership. Frederick D. Buchstein, director of research for Dix & Eaton, a full-service communication firm based in Cleveland, pinpoints clearly (with sprinklings of humor), the key roles in the process of producing a printed news story and what can go wrong at each checkpoint.

JOB	*WHAT HE DOES*	*WHAT CAN GO WRONG*
Newsmaker	Makes news.	Refuses to talk to the reporter in search of facts.
		Purposively misleads reporter or gives only part of the story.
		Doesn't know how to explain what happened so any dummy can understand it.
Reporter	Gathers facts. Writes the story. Forwards it to the editor.	Fails to understand what the story means.
		Fails to get the facts right.
		Fails to put the story into context for the reader.

JOB	*WHAT HE DOES*	*WHAT CAN GO WRONG*
		Writes a dull story that no one reads. Is too dumb, lazy, busy or facing too tight a deadline to overcome the above. Is anti-business. Ignores the facts so he can tell a good yarn.
Business editor	Manages reporters to make sure the news is covered and features written. Fights with the sports, city, and other news editors for page one space. Must live with managing editor's policy decisions, whims and fancies. Tries to balance coverage of what readers want and need to know against space availability.	All of the above. Ignores reporter's advice and overplays or underplays a story. Like his reporters, he can fail to realize when he has a good story or is being bamboozled. Like his reporters, he bows to policies and whims of the publishers.
Copy editor	Edits the story for language, logic, accuracy. Writes the headline.	He's in a hurry or misunderstands the story and screws up the headline or rewrite. Readers can't yell at him because they don't know who he is.
Makeup editor	Oversees printers who physically produce the paper.	Trims the meat out of the story to make it fit in allotted space.

JOB	*WHAT HE DOES*	*WHAT CAN GO WRONG*
Paper boy	Delivers the paper.	Tosses the paper into a puddle or bush. Never delivers it when you want it. Wants a tip for delivering bad news to your doorstep.
Reader	Selectively reads the news.	Avoids business news when it's on the business page. Only reads the headlines. Is more interested in the sports page and funnies.
Newsmaker	Reads the story about himself.	I didn't say that. That stupid reporter got his facts wrong. Why didn't I say more? Why wasn't my story on page one? Why didn't I get more space? I'll never talk to a reporter again. Where's my p.r. man? I want my name in the paper again.

One of the key messages to be inferred from Buchstein's analysis is the importance of learning as much as possible in advance about both the publication and the reporter. If you are not familiar with the publication, secure copies of it, read it, and pay particular attention to articles written by the reporter who wants to interview you. Seek out other sources that can provide additional background to help you prepare for the interview.

THE TELEPHONE VERSUS
THE IN-PERSON INTERVIEW

Whether conducted by a print or radio reporter, these two types of interviews have unique differences. The telephone interview prevents you from witnessing the reporter's nonverbal reactions to your answers, including his or her note-taking behavior. Furthermore, if the interview is conducted by a reporter you have never met, you are frequently precluded from the luxury of the rapport-building period that often accompanies an in-person interview. However, the telephone interview can also be advantageous. It is usually more time-efficient (if saving time is important in this situation), and you can use notes containing key messages, outlined responses, important facts, and, yes, quotable quotes.

ADVICE FOR
THE TELEPHONE INTERVIEW:

1. Clear from your desk anything that might distract you during the interview.
2. Assume a comfortable sitting position. General discomfort can show up in your voice—something you clearly want to avoid, especially during a radio interview.
3. Although you should keep your key messages and choice quotes in front of you, take care not to make them sound read, particularly if you are being interviewed by a reporter from a radio station.
4. If you want to be quoted, don't refer specifically to the reporter's question within your response. During the editing process, the reporter may want to present your response more as an opinion than as a response to a specific question.

A MEDIA RESPONSE MANUAL

Your large corporation has a chairman of the board, a chief executive officer, an executive vice president, 10 vice presidents and division heads, including a director of public affairs, plus 125 senior managers.

But who does the reporter from *The Clarion Call* happen to reach when he calls for comment on a report that three workers have been injured in an accident on the loading dock? A high school kid working as a summer temporary who grabbed the phone in the shipping department as he walked by.

"Terrible accident," he says. "Looks like that frayed cable on the crane that all the men have been complaining about for weeks finally snapped. Got to run. 'Bye."

It's not the reporter's fault for calling your company, nor is he wrong in printing the comment—true or false—from your employee—identified or not.

Step back for a second and ask yourself this question again: Does your company have a well-thought-out policy for handling media inquiries? And is that plan made known to every employee, from loading-dock helper to chief executive?

Here's what one media response manual might look like:

At Amalgamated Industries, our good image as a corporate citizen is one of our most valuable and valued assets.

What we have to say to the people of Maple Grove can affect that image and all our jobs.

Therefore, it is critical that media inquiries be handled by a person with the *background* and *authority* to do so.

It will always be our policy to promote good relations with the media and, through it, with the public.

It is Amalgamated's policy to:

- Disclose as much newsworthy information as possible *without* violating employee, corporate, or customer confidentiality
- Respond as quickly as possible to all inquiries
- Present a truthful, consistent message to the media

The *only* employees authorized to respond on behalf of Amalgamated are members of the executive staff.

No other employee is authorized to give *any* information to a reporter without specific clearance from a member of the executive staff.

If you are *not* an authorized spokesperson and you receive a call from a reporter, you should

- Politely decline to answer *any* questions
- Explain to the reporter that you are not an authorized company spokesperson
- Take down the name, organization, and phone number of the reporter

Immediately call the Public Information Office, at 4-7343, and relay this information about the call. The phone is monitored twenty-four hours a day, seven days a week.

If you *are* authorized to respond on behalf of the company, you should determine

- The reporter's name and the organization he or she represents
- The nature of the information requested
- The nature of the reporter's assignment
- The deadline

Do you feel qualified to answer the reporter's questions? If not, explain that to the reporter and promise him or her a return call from an appropriate authorized spokesperson. Contact the Public Information Office immediately with the details.

If you feel you can answer the questions, don't be rushed. If you need to check some facts, or if you'd just like to take a few moments to compose your thoughts, arrange to call the reporter back in a few minutes. Keep your promise!

In any case, fill out a copy of the "Media Inquiry" form supplied with this memo and have it *hand-carried* to the Public Information Office so that the staff there will be aware of the reporter's interest.

If you have *any* questions about company policy or how to respond to the media, please contact the Public Information Office.

This is, of course, just a small sample of what could be contained in one company's manual. You might want to have two versions—one that simply warns all unauthorized employees to refer all calls to your public relations department and a second, detailed manual for authorized spokespersons.

You also might want to involve your personnel office or training unit and have them include a discussion of media policy as a regular part of the hiring and evaluation procedures for your company.

HOW TO ESTABLISH GOOD RELATIONS WITH THE MEDIA

- *Be truthful.*
- *Be cooperative.* Offer to help reporters in covering their beats by arranging informal tours of your plant, meetings with executives, and background sessions on technical subjects. Provide the media with photos and visual aids or video clips for use in illustrating stories about your company.
- *Employ a competent and responsive public relations department or firm.* It should include persons with media experience, understanding of your community, and full background on your company. The department or firm should be on call at all times—either with staff in the office or by telephone. Security personnel should be advised of the phone numbers of key personnel if an emergency occurs at an unusual hour.
- *Respond promptly to all inquiries.* A response after deadline is no response at all.
- *Have a media inquiry policy for your staff.* And it doesn't hurt to tell reporters of your policy. You should also provide direct phone numbers of those persons authorized to respond on behalf of the company.
- *Establish ground rules.* Don't try to put something "off the record" after you've begun to respond. (See box.) Don't answer questions and then ask that your name not be used.
- *Meet with editors and editorial boards* (see page 196). It enhances your position as a corporate citizen and your understanding of the local media.

GROUND RULES

1. You may limit the interview to a certain topic. Whenever possible, negotiate this in advance. Otherwise, notifying the reporter by surprise during the interview can strain your relations with him or her.

2. Know how to use the following:

   - *On the record:* Everything you say can be used by the reporter with you being quoted directly.

   - *Off the record:* The information cannot be used in print. Its sole purpose is to buttress the reporter's background understanding.

   - *Not for attribution* (also referred to as "On Background"): You can be quoted but not by name (e.g., as "an informed company source"). It is sometimes advisable to meet with a reporter first on this basis and then decide whether or not you want to go "on the record."

   - *On deep background:* Whatever information you share with the reporter cannot be in any way identified with you as the possible source. Rather, it must be referenced on the reporter's own authority.

When invoking any of these ground rules, be sure you and the reporter have full agreement when they are to begin and end. I've heard too many war stories about off-the-record stories landing up on page one because the interviewee and the reporter did not get their signals straight. I generally recommend that you decline to speak altogether rather than make off-the-record remarks; the risks are just too great.

HOW TO ESTABLISH POOR RELATIONS WITH THE MEDIA

- *By dishonesty.* If you are not frank, fair, and factual, you are no friend of the media. And remember—*they* are the ones with the printing presses and the television and radio transmitters, not you.

- *By being uncooperative.* A deadline is a brick wall for a daily newspaper or electronic medium. Failing to return a reporter's calls or responding with information after deadline is at best useless and at worst little different from the bright red flag of "no comment." If you feel yourself unable to comment for legal, proprietary, or other reasons, explain why nondefensively. Otherwise a solitary "no comment" can strongly imply guilt, especially on radio or television.

- *By trying to be an editor.* You have no right, under ordinary circumstances, to review any copy prepared by a reporter. You'll probably end up earning the story more attention than it would have drawn otherwise. And unless you have specific evidence that a story was misrepresented, it doesn't pay to complain when your ninety-minute interview gains only fifteen seconds on the air. What's done is done; think about a particular medium's definition of news the next time you seek coverage and see if your efforts can be targeted more precisely.
- *By playing favorites.* Giving a hot story to one reporter rarely helps. You might get good play in one newspaper or on one television show, but the other media may decide to ignore the story on general principle. And they may become very leery of future dealings.
- *By seeking to "kill" a story.* It almost never works and almost always results in frayed feelings. And the attempted "kill" can become the lead of the story.
- *By complaining about a particular reporter.* Most media organizations will react just the way you would to an attack on one of your corporate "stars." Whatever the truth of the matter, the public stance will almost certainly be a vigorous defense.*

THE EDITORIAL BOARD

Every newspaper has an editorial staff. It may consist of one person or of several persons who specialize in various areas, such

---

*Note: See chapter 14 for further reference and advice regarding the question-and-answer exchange between the interviewee and the reporter.

as local government, federal government, state government, the environment, and energy. Frequently an editorial writer wears many hats and is expected to have extensive knowledge in several diverse areas.

Some metropolitan radio and TV stations also have editorial staffs, but they are small compared with those on newspapers.

Editorial people are a totally different breed. Virtually all of them are former reporters who have decided to remove themselves from the hectic day-to-day activities of reporting to the more sedate world of the paper's "think tank." However, that does not mean that they have rejected their roles as newspersons. They are very much newspeople, but with a different approach.

Editorial writers have the opportunity to research a subject before writing about it. They read voraciously, and it is their obligation to keep abreast of all major developments in many areas of general interest.

The editorial-page editor may seek you out for an interview, or you may want to take the initiative to acquaint him or her with your company's policies and goals. An editor may be willing to meet you for lunch, but don't expect him or her to visit you at your office. You visit the editor's office.

Editorial writers are usually great conversationalists. Your meeting with them, unless you're dealing with a crisis situation, will most likely be very informal, chatty, and lengthy. While they are not looking necessarily for "hard" news that will go into the next edition, they are newspeople. Don't ever forget that.

Basically, though, editorial writers are seeking understanding and in-depth knowledge that can be used to bring their editorials into sharper focus. They are not easily swayed by current fads, and they seek to keep the impact of popular emotions on the issues to a minimum. Many editorial pages continued to support former President Richard Nixon long after the front pages were calling for his head.

To prepare, bone up on likely issues that might be raised. But don't be surprised if the editorial board members pop questions out of left field.

Honesty and candor remain your best attributes when dealing with members of the editorial board. They will appreciate it, and it will greatly enhance your chances of getting a fair shake when your corporation next encounters them.

SHOULD YOU ANSWER AN UNFAVORABLE OR INCORRECT STORY?

The evening paper hits the streets with a front-page headline trumpeting, THREE HURT IN AMALGAMATED ACCIDENT. The sub-head reads, "Worker Says Crane Cable Was Frayed."

Where did they get that information? You know that your public relations department had acted very quickly to release an official statement: that the accident was apparently caused "by the unexpected failure of a steel supporting rod which had been installed and inspected only last week by federal safety officials." Several of the reporters had asked about the huge crane on the other side of the loading-bay area. Moreover, they had been told it was not in use when the accident occurred.

Fuming, you turn on your television for the evening news. You know that the reporter for *Action News* had visited the plant and been given the company statement. And the station had been planning to use just that explanation—at least until the news director saw the first edition of *The Clarion Call* just half an hour before airtime. In the remaining few minutes the story was rewritten by a different reporter, based on the unconfirmed second-hand information in the newspaper story.

"Three Amalgamated workers were injured today," the newscaster solemnly pronounces. "*Action News* has learned that workers had complained about a frayed cable on the crane for several weeks. Company officials had no comment."

Wait! Before you react: How serious is the case?

There is very little to gain in pushing a complaint merely because you don't like the angle (newspapers call it the peg) taken by the reporter. If the story makes you unhappy but does you no long-term damage, it would probably be better to try to deal with the problem (if it is indeed a problem) over time.

In this case, though, there are several serious aspects to the story:

- Your legal department is sure to squawk about any un-refuted claim that Amalgamated was negligent in mainte-nance of a piece of equipment.
- If you don't respond quickly to the story, erroneous claims in the story will come back to haunt you time and again in coming days and weeks. Every newspaper and most broad-cast outlets maintain "morgues" of clippings or stories (often indexed by computer) that serve as background for future news reports. Years from now you might see a story that refers to "a previous accident at Amalgamated in which a frayed cable snapped, injuring three workers."
- Once again, make sure that your media response policy is in place and that all of your employees are aware of its provi-sions.

HOW TO ANSWER AN
UNFAVORABLE NEWSPAPER STORY

Don't question the newspaper's right to inquire into your affairs; there is no way to win that argument.

Don't complain about the reporter's technique in pursuing the story. Let editors draw their own conclusions when they see that the story is incorrect. Show some understanding of the pressures and difficulties of publishing a daily newspaper.

Don't threaten to pull your advertisements. By the perverse nature of the relationship between the advertising department and the newsroom of most papers, you could be almost guaran-teeing front-page coverage for all your dirty linen for some time to come if you choose such a tactic.

Your only defense is reasoned, specific rebuttal. Don't just say that the story is wrong—prove how it is wrong. Encourage the newspaper to go to the scene if possible. Allow access to witnesses. And, if necessary, authorize release of police or insurance investigator's reports.

In the case of the loading-dock accident, the story is likely to continue for several more days. The "correction" may appear as a story in later editions—if you really move fast—or in the next day's papers.

Don't be surprised if it takes a really close reading to recognize that the new story is really a correction of the first. The lead might say instead, "Investigators now say that the loading-dock accident at Amalgamated Industries on Thursday was caused by the unexpected failure of a new supporting rod and was not the result of company negligence, as first reported." Not exactly the ideal apology, but a clearing of your company name—at least for the record.

There are other ways to seek a redress of grievances in a newspaper:

- Some newspapers run a regular column of corrections. Unfortunately, the corrections are rarely presented with as much boldness, or as close to the reader's eye, as the original error.
- You can draft a letter to the editor. A few tips: Respond quickly, while the issue is still current. Study the letters printed in recent issues for an idea as to length, style, and tone. Be firm, clear, and direct without being argumentative or unduly emotional; although your letter is addressed to the editor, remember your target audience.
- Many newspapers and magazines have allowed "guest columnists" the use of a portion of the editorial page. The *New York Times,* for example, devotes a full page opposite its editorial page (called the Op-Ed page) for such responses to the newspaper's opinions and those of other writers. *Newsweek* runs a regular column called "My Turn." Again, study some recent examples of pieces that have run on these pages for style, tone, and length.

RESPONDING TO AN UNFAVORABLE TELEVISION OR RADIO STORY

Television and radio present different problems and solutions for addressing an unfavorable report. Though a few programs include a "letters" or "feedback" segment from time to time, generally your effort should be to find a way of getting your response or correction into the extremely limited time available in the news show.

Again, if it is merely a question of disagreement over the tone of a story or its implications, you can bring the matter to the attention of the reporter or the station's news director and hope that the situation will not be repeated.

The following, an actual letter sent to a major television station, states the party's grievance and request for a meeting quite directly.

Dear News Director:

I have been monitoring your news broadcasts and detected an "attitude" that generally prevails at your station in your news coverage of (name of company). It would almost seem that your reporters are programmed to believe that only negative stories on (name of company) are either newsworthy or appealing to your audience.

My understanding of journalism is that reporters are supposed to be unbiased when they report on issues. It seems that no matter what effort we make to explain our position, the news reports (or editorial comments, for that matter) will focus on the negative, effectively removing the viewers' chances of making their own judgments. I question whether there is any value in providing interviews with your staff if this attitude continues to prevail.

This is a serious issue and one that deserves discussion. I would like to meet with you to discuss these concerns. Please contact (name) of my staff to arrange a meeting.

                                        Sincerely,
                                        (name)

Important: These are strong words—perhaps too strong. Whatever words you choose, make sure that you have the necessary documentation and can make a strong case for unfair reporting. If all you have is opinion, you'll simply make a bad situation worse.

When meeting with the news director, also be prepared to offer some good "possibilities" for future reports. Be realistic; the media will not act as public relations agents for your company, but they may be open to human-interest stories or other ideas with broad appeal.

If there is a serious error of fact, most stations will include a correction. Whenever possible, try to reach the news director during the broadcast and have a correction made while the show is still on the air.

You do have some small additional clout with broadcast outlets because they, unlike print media, operate under a revocable federal license. Under Federal Communications Commission (FCC) law and regulations, there are two avenues open to you: the community-standards measurement and the Fairness Doctrine.

All broadcast license holders are required to maintain a file of letters commenting on the quality of their service to the community. This file must be made available for inspection by the public and by the FCC and is supposed to be taken into consideration at license-renewal time. Often your promise (not a threat) of a letter for this file is enough to gain the news director's attention.

The Fairness Doctrine does not apply to questions of accuracy as such; it is aimed at the broader question of the presentation of contrasting points of view on controversial issues. The Fairness Doctrine is the reason for the disclaimers you hear when a radio or television station broadcasts an editorial.

If you or your company is attacked by a broadcast editorial, you should contact the station immediately and ask for the opportunity to respond. Actually FCC regulations require that you be notified of such an editorial within twenty-four hours after broadcast and that you be provided with a tape or transcript of it and offered station facilities for a rebuttal.

If you are not the primary target of the editorial—if the opinion affects all widget makers and not just Amalgamated—respond quickly and forcefully. The station is given latitude to choose among those seeking equal time, so make your case a strong one.

IF ALL ELSE FAILS...

If your polite but firm attempts for correction of broadcast- or print-media news stories or editorials are to no avail, there are several further steps to consider.

You might think about the option exercised by Mobil Oil Company. Unhappy about editorial opinion regarding "Big Oil," Mobil chose several years ago to run its own commercials and air its opinion on television and in newspaper advertisements. In fact, its ads became a regular fixture of the Op-Ed page of the *New York Times*. To maximize their impact, Mobil bound and distributed collections of these printed ads as "public affairs" pieces.

You also have the option of legal action for slander or libel. Your legal department is sure to advise you that such cases can be extremely expensive, time-consuming, and difficult to prove. Even if the newspaper or broadcast medium in question has made a grievous error, it is necessary to prove that malicious intent was involved. Gross incompetence is not sufficient. Remember, both your company and the newspaper or station are likely to be there still when the dust settles, and your relations will be none too good.

A COMPELLING CASE HISTORY

Some years ago the Alabama Power Company decided it was not going to take it anymore and went very public with its protest of what it claimed were incorrect reporting, editorializing, and printing of letters in the *Alabama Journal* in Montgomery.

In one of a series of large ads, the utility responded to an editorial:

A LITTLE OFF THE MARK

On September 3, the editorial page editor of the *Alabama Journal* gave his opinion concerning the salaries of Chrysler Corporation executives compared with those of Alabama Power Company.

To set the record straight, we have reprinted the editorial as it appeared. And in the margin, we've included some of the facts that the writer failed to include.

[The ad concluded:] In order for you to understand Alabama Power, you need the facts—*all* of them—presented in a clear, objective manner. What you don't need are prejudiced editorials.*

The campaign was obviously not aimed at winning friends at the newspaper. But Stephen E. Bradley, then vice president for public information, said later,

> We don't even care so much if they [reporters] like us or not, although we have good relationships with most media representatives in our service area. We do, however, want them to respect us and to realize that if their stories contain errors or if they write slanted stories or editorials based on factual errors, we will respond, and respond loudly. The next news story is the important one. We want reporters to write their stories looking over their shoulders. We want them to hear our footsteps.

*Stephen Bradley, "Defusing Media Adversaries," *Reddy News,* January/February 1982, pp. 15–19. The point-by-point rebuttal appeared in Birmingham's *Alabama Journal* on September 3, 1981.

Chapter 17

USING THE ELECTRONIC MEDIA TO PERSUADE

"In the future everyone will be world-famous for fifteen minutes."
—ANDY WARHOL

I f Andy Warhol was correct, then television news is one of the best ways to make this happen. Television news is our principal source of information about the world around us; in the past twenty years its impact has virtually eclipsed that of newspapers and magazines. In fact, today, 60 to 75 percent of Americans get their news from television on what one writer calls a "fast-food-like diet": lots of color and visual appeal, short bites of information, and not much meat to the story.*

If fleeting or enduring fame via television awaits you as an authority figure, expert, witness, victim, or culprit, then you need to understand television news—its purpose, complexity, and standards—and how you can best use your initiative in order to use the electronic media to attain the persuasive edge.

---

*Communication Briefings, April 1983.

TELEVISION NEWS AS A BUSINESS

But what is television news? No one, not even the practitioners, can give you a hard-and-fast definition. Basically "news" is operationally defined by the editor—or, in the case of television, by the news director or the assignment editor.

In most instances television news is an event or announcement that promises to interest a large number of the viewers of a particular television station—specifically their target audience. If you are dealing with a television station that covers a medium-to-large population area, you are likely to find that the definition of *television news* excludes far more events and announcements than it includes. And, of course, the converse also applies; relatively minor items—hardly newsworthy in a more populated area—can be arresting features in less populated areas.

While the local pages or business section of a newspaper frequently have room for some of the most minor or highly specialized bits of "news," television stations are, of course, limited by time rather than by space. Moreover, in their headlong chase after "ratings," television stations are often guilty of limiting their coverage to the more sensational rather than to the more important.

Further, television news depends upon one more inherent trait of the medium, something often unrelated to substance: TV is in essence a visual medium. Reporters and editors have to find ways of telling their stories with pictures as well as with words. That is why the most common television news story is the spectacular fire or the multiple-car accident, rather than, for instance, the thoughtful analysis of municipal finance trends.

The demand for pictures also turns every quest for a story into a minor expedition. While a newspaper reporter can cover a story with a ten-cent pencil and a fifty-cent notebook, the television reporter goes on the road accompanied by a crew with tens of thousands of dollars' worth of electronic cameras, video recorders, microphones, lights, and sometimes even a helicopter. And while technology has brought great advances, including the ability to transmit live from "on location" to the main studio, these capabilities often result in increased reliance upon equipment.

Therefore, put yourself in the position of the corporation owning a television station: You have hundreds of thousands of dollars tied up in electronic devices, trucks to carry them about, and equipment to broadcast their signal. You have dozens of employees, including a stable of high-priced "stars." You have a sharply limited amount of time (twenty-two or so minutes in a half-hour news, sports, and weather broadcast). And you are competing with other stations on the basis of your ability to attract and hold viewers. Is it any wonder that most television stations feel they can't afford to waste time and effort on stories that don't help their business win and retain viewers?

Advance Work

How do you determine what constitutes "news" on your local station and whether you or your company might serve as a future feature? Assign a public relations professional to watch that station for a week with notebook and stopwatch in hand. Analyze the types of stories that survived the sifting process to showtime. What were the visual elements? What was the local appeal? How long were the features? And then ask, How can I sell my message in a way that matches the interests and techniques of the station I am aiming for?

One good way of gaining television time is to find a way to "follow" an ongoing story. If, for example, the station is running a series of stories about the American auto industry and your company is ready to announce a new program that will subsidize workers' purchase of domestic cars, you have a perfect peg to offer to the station. Perhaps you'll even want to move up the announcement to coincide with the present coverage. Think in terms of a picture: an announcement at a car dealership or at an assembly line presents a much more attractive lure than a "talking head" shot of you behind a desk.

The Assignment Editor

Let's say you've decided to try to get your company featured on TV. Your contact at the television station will ordinarily be someone with the title of "assignment editor." When speaking with this person, consider the following advice:

- Call early—7 A.M. is often the start of an editor's day.
- Keep the conversation short and to the point; the assignment editor's job is one of the most pressured positions at the station.
- Stress the "people" angle of your story.
- Suggest picture possibilities.
- Leave phone numbers where you or other contacts can be reached during the day.
- Leave open the possibility of alternate arrangements if today's story doesn't work into the schedule.
- Try to arrange for a live (versus taped) interview. It prevents editing, thereby providing you with more control of your message.

Editing-Booth Realities

Imagine yourself inside the editing booth of a television newsroom for a moment. The reporter has just returned from an interview at a local factory. She was on the scene for nearly an hour, the crew ran through nearly thirty minutes of tape—and she has one minute and ten seconds to fill on the *Six O'Clock Report*, which is only an hour away. Those numbers are not unusual; often the disparity between tape footage and the final segment is even greater.

The vice president she interviewed went on and on about the marvels of the new product the company was introducing, but the reporter has decided to summarize all of that in her fifteen-second introduction to the story. Instead, she runs the tape at high speed—the voices sounding like chipmunks—until she hears the segment she had marked with a great big red exclamation point in her notes.

It was a silver-plated gift. While the producer was moving around in the background adjusting a curtain that had flopped open, she and the vice president had chatted amiably. The talk had moved to production techniques, and the vice president had noted that the assembly line for the new product would be the first at Amalgamated to rely completely on robots. The reporter had signaled with her eyes to the cameraman, and he had nonchalantly turned on his recorder. "We won't have to add a single damned worker," the executive had said with some pride. "The machines won't join the union, either. And this is just the beginning," he had said with a broad wink.

The reporter had flashed her most gracious smile, too, and then had moved in for an unexpected kill. "How will this affect the tenor of your labor negotiations beginning next week?" she asked sweetly. "We . . . we're not going to announce it until next month," he had sputtered. "Hey, this is all off the record." The reporter continued to press, and this time the cameraman openly filmed the executive's reaction. Now all he would say was, "No comment." But she had everything on tape—from the wink to the dropping jaw. Great television!

Not exactly the best example of masterful use of the electronic medium by an executive, is it? But it does happen that way, and this hypothetical example illustrates two critical points: (a) the "dead mike" rule, which I'll explain later; and (b) the fact that your message—*as defined by the reporter*—will be plucked out of many minutes or even hours of conversation and edited down to "an electronic moment." Once you've gained the opportunity to use television to communicate your message, be sure that you use it to full advantage.

PREPARING YOUR
MESSAGE FOR TELEVISION

What should you do, then, to maximize the chances of getting your message across? I have two major pieces of advice:

First and foremost, you should know what you want to say and how you want to say it—down to the phrasing of quotable quotes (called sound bites by people from the electronic media). Second, deliver that message *early* and *often* in the course of an interview.

The same advice I've given throughout this book regarding net-effects, substance, and image goals applies to the electronic interview. In fact, since television is a visual medium that often emphasizes image over substance, you should be especially precise in defining the image goals to be projected by both your company and spokesperson and perhaps even your industry or profession. Based on my firm's experience, the following represent the more common positive and negative traits projected on television:

Positive	Negative
Confident	Nervous
Cooperative	Unduly cautious
Authoritative/Strong	Defensive
Commanding	Aloof/Distant
Engaging/Friendly	Arrogant
Sincere	Uninformed
Caring/Reassuring	Glib
Composed	Confused
Credible	Contentious
Competent	Shrill/Strident
Intelligent	Stiff

Structuring Your Response

As you present your responses to a television interviewer, be sure to *state your lead or headline—first.* *
Which delivers the quotable quote?

Q. *Is Amalgamated going to continue to grow here in Gardiner?*
A. Well, if we can find skilled workers and if we can continue to enjoy living in a small city that offers a nice place to live for our employees, our executives, and their families, and if the economy improves, then I guess Amalgamated will stay here. (15 seconds)

or:

Q. *Is Amalgamated going to continue to grow here in Gardiner?*
A. Yes. Amalgamated will grow and flourish in Gardiner. Gardiner has been good to our business and to our people. (6 seconds)

Practice stating your message in several different ways—as a flat-out statement, as a "therefore" conclusion, and in response to a question that seemingly has no relation to the subject. For example, let's say no one has asked you specifically about Amalgamated's future in Gardiner, yet that is an important message you'd like to send. Now you're asked:

Q. *Aren't widgets an outmoded and useless product, and won't Amalgamated have to make major changes in order to stay in business?*
A. No. There has been a temporary plateau in demand. Amalgamated will, therefore, remain in Gardiner and retain a leadership position in the widget industry. (7 or 8 seconds)

*Refer to chapter 14 for additional advice on fielding questions.

This approach is especially effective in live television or radio appearances, where you may have only seconds to get your message across. If you're asked about apples and you want to talk about oranges, keep coming back to oranges.

THE MECHANICS OF TV

If you have a scheduled television interview, your first notice of the approach of a TV crew may be the rumble of a van into the parking lot or the clatter of a hand truck in the hallway. But your planning for the crew's needs should have started long before. Checklist for the "technical side" of the interview:

1. Allow time for the setup of equipment and testing; plan on a minimum of twenty minutes.
2. Although modern videotape cameras, recorders, and television lights are battery powered, you should nevertheless be able to offer adequate electrical service if needed. Have your building electrician check outlets for sufficient amperage.
3. Leave the physical arrangements to the camera crew. Let them pick the most favorable location in your office for light and sound. They may want to open or close shades, lower or raise a picture on the wall, or even move some furniture. Don't try to play director—they know what they're doing. However, be certain to take a good, long look at the room when they have finished and before you start your interview. Make certain there's not suddenly an open copy of *Playboy* on the bookshelf over your shoulder, or a newspaper opened to an embarrassing headline or to a picture of a competitor's product sitting on your desk. Leave the technical aspects to the crew; keep the message design to yourself.
4. A technician will probably attach a microphone to you—usually a tiny "can" that will clip to your tie or jacket. He or she may want to string the cable from behind and out of sight, hiding the cord inside your jacket. The most professional

arrangement, used only infrequently, might call for running the microphone cable up a pants leg or under a skirt. The technician will probably ask you for a "voice check." Speak normally, in the tone you will use for the interview, until you are asked to stop. Don't say anything during the check you couldn't stand to hear on the air!

5. If you plan to sit, button your suit jacket, pull the two sides of your jacket together so that not too much of your shirt or blouse and collar show, and sit on the tails of your jacket to make sure the collar and shoulders of your coat look crisp.

6. If there is a light in your eyes or if something else makes you uncomfortable, tell the technician before the taping begins.

7. During the interview itself, *look directly at the reporter.* The cameraman may be moving around, the lights may be shifted, the reporter may be looking straight down at a notebook or a stopwatch. The technician or producer may be frantically flashing hand signals at the reporter. *Ignore everything but the subject at hand.* Keep your eyes focused on the spot at the level where the reporter's head is normally positioned.

8. After you've finished your interview, you'll probably be asked to remain in your seat while the cameraman changes his or her position to shoot over your shoulder at the reporter. This is called a cutaway or a reverse. The shot will be used in the editing process as a bridge between subjects. You may find yourself engaged in pleasant conversation about the weather while the shot is being made; again, remember not to say or do anything you wouldn't want to appear in the story.

9. You might also find that the reporter will repeat one or two questions directly to the camera. Listen in if you can and be sure that the question he or she says afterward is very close to the one you answered. Object politely but firmly if it is not. You'll have no chance to do this after the reporter leaves, so at least try to maintain control while he or she is in your office.

10. Remember the *three golden rules of microphones:* (a) there is no such thing as a dead mike; (b) dead mikes don't exist; and (c) remember the first two rules.

11. Remember the three golden rules of cameras. (Substitute the word *camera* for *mike.*)

NIGHTLINE AND OTHER "REMOTES"

A recent trend in television news coverage—part electronic advancement and part show business—is the move toward more and more "live" coverage. You may come across it in the form of an invitation to do a live interview on the set of a news show during the news; or technology may make your office or home into an instant television studio.

Live broadcasts generally use microwave or even satellite communications techniques. You need not be concerned with the details, but you'll find there is an even greater demand for setup time. The technical crew may have to find a way to beam a signal from your office down to a mobile transmitter in a truck—either by a short-range microwave broadcaster or by cable—or there may be other special requirements.

Perhaps your most difficult assignment will be to respond warmly to an interviewer who is not in the room with you. I faced this situation twice in the same day with an early appearance on the *CBS Morning Show* and another close to midnight on *Nightline with Ted Koppel.* Shortly before the morning show, I had a brief opportunity to chat amicably with the host, Harry Smith. However, there was no time to warm up before Ted Koppel fired his first question at me.

In neither instance was I able to see either Smith or Koppel, which compounded the challenge of performing well in front of a camera, including the obligation to maintain eye contact with the lens as the question was being asked and throughout my response.

If a monitor had been provided for me to see Smith or Koppel, I'm not sure how helpful it would have been. To look at it and then talk into the camera might have created awkward eye and head movements.

If you expect to find yourself in this situation, consider the following advice:

- Practice responding to the camera with your questioner out of your sight range.
- Practice looking into the camera while the person playing the reporter is providing the commentary, especially when you're not exactly sure when you'll be introduced.
- Secure feedback regarding how comfortable you look. It is easy to look stiff when you don't have anyone seated near you to relate to.
- Think friendly, relax your facial muscles and smile, especially if you are appearing as the expert and not as the accused.

DELIVERING THE MESSAGE

Regardless of the interview format, remember that although you are talking to a reporter, you are really speaking to the vast audience that will watch the news, and particularly to your target audience. Try to visualize someone (preferably a specific person you like and respect) sitting before the television screen in the privacy of his or her home. And then think of yourself as a guest in someone's living room; you don't want to shout at your host, you want to speak in a moderate tone—conversationally. You're being transmitted right into the room with these people. Therefore, your phrasing and actions should be intimate and friendly.

Body movements—appropriate gestures and nonverbal emphases—are a near-requirement of a speech in a large hall. On television, though, caution is necessary. You are being examined under a microscope at both transmitting and receiving ends. Passion is much better communicated by means of your tone of voice or look of determination than by a wave of the arm or a wallop to the podium. Natural, flowing hand motions—kept close to your body, however—are fine.

Remember also that you will probably have only a few precious seconds. Keep your message simple and direct and keep coming back to your key messages.

If you flub a line or if you deliver an unclear answer, don't hesitate to restate your answer more concisely if possible. The reporter would much rather have a good quote than a confusing, disjointed one.

As with any other encounter with a reporter, stay away from the "no comment" response at any cost, while being prepared to explain why you can't answer the question.

Clothing

When you're on television, you're going to be on physical display. Give some thought to your grooming and what it says about you.

Wear conservative, comfortable, and well-pressed clothing, making sure your outfit looks good whether you are standing or seated. Avoid patterns that might be distracting or that will "vibrate" on camera, such as polka dots and narrow stripes. Dress as you would for any important semiformal social occasion. Wear the color that looks best on you. There is no prohibition against ordinary business shades of gray or blue. A light blue or gray shirt is far more preferable than white (which can draw too much attention to itself). Make sure that your tie contrasts with your suit, but avoid yellow or silver (they create too much glare) and busy patterns. A deep maroon tie is preferable to a bright red one. And avoid distracting tie bars. If you know the colors of the background in advance, try to wear colors that will contrast sufficiently to avoid the "talking head" effect.

Be careful not to wear distracting jewelry. Large gold or crystal earrings or a pendant can catch the television lights and steal attention away from your message.

Makeup

Society's expectations—and those of television technicians—have changed over the years, and it is no longer mandatory to have all persons appearing on television covered with dense facial makeup. But if you have a shiny nose or forehead, deep shadows under the eyes, a heavy beard, or deeply veined hands, a light touch of pancake makeup can improve your appearance—and help retard any tendency to perspire.

Only the larger stations employ makeup artists, so a bit of advance planning and practice may be necessary if you want to tend to this yourself.

Regardless of who applies the makeup, check it on the TV monitor before going on the air. Even the most professional makeup artists can occasionally make mistakes.

A caveat for women: Avoid medium-to-bright red lipstick on television; it can draw too much attention to your mouth.

Eyeglasses

As in your choice of clothing, your glasses should not be so large or so unusual as to distract from you and your message. If you are comfortable without glasses, leave them off—it will definitely improve your eye contact. If you must wear them, avoid photosensitive lenses, for they tend to darken under the studio lights. The perfect answer to your needs may be the new, nonreflective glasses that allow your eyes to be seen despite the studio lights.

TELEVISION TALK SHOWS

Talk shows present some very different opportunities for interviews. For one thing, most are not chopped up and edited down into little bits. To capture the persuasive edge, consider the following advice:

Advance Work and Preparation

The first thing you should do for a talk show appearance is to find out everything you can about the ground rules and setting. If it is a regularly scheduled talk show, make it a point to watch several shows in advance and then practice.

1. *Study the format:*
   - How much time are you likely to have? (Sometimes the host or producer will tell you ahead of time how many total minutes you will have to convey your message.)
   - How and when will you be introduced?
   - Will other guests be on the set while you're being interviewed? If so, who?
   - Is there a studio audience? Do they become involved in the show? How are they selected? How active or vocal are they?
   - When do commercial breaks occur? How are they signaled?
   - Is there a telephone call-in segment? When does it occur? For how long?
   - Are clips from the talk show used on the news?

2. *Study the host:*
   - How well prepared is the host?
   - How would you characterize the host's style? Aggressive? Passive? Confrontational? Vacillating between two or more styles?
   - Is the host more a questioner than a talker or vice versa? Does he or she normally allow guests to finish what they're saying, or is he or she prone to interrupt?
   - What appear to be the host's goals?
   - Does the host show any particular political or ideological bent?
   - Does he or she seem to seek out conflict or controversy?
   - Which banana peels are typically placed in the guests' paths? Note: The show's producer might disclose in advance the topics or lines of questioning the host is likely to pursue, especially if you are the expert and not the accused. But don't bank on the host necessarily following through. When I appeared on *Nightline,* Ted Koppel did not pursue any of the lines of questioning the producer discussed with me four hours earlier.

3. *Set your goals:* What are your net-effects, substance, and image goals, vis-à-vis your target audience?

4. *Practice:* Should you simulate the talk show environment? How many practice sessions should be scheduled? When? Who should participate in each simulation and critique?

From the Studio Wings to the Set

Find out how you will get on the set. Will you take your place during a commercial break or will you be expected to walk to a seat while the camera is on? On many talk shows and interview programs you will be introduced while seated; the director or floor manager will ask you to "acknowledge" a particular camera. What he's asking for is a humble nod of the head after the host has introduced you. From that point on, look at the host and leave the camera work to the technicians!

If you expect to walk onto the set during the show, study the route you will be asked to take. Watch for camera stands and cables on the floor. You'll probably be summoned to a wing of the stage by a technician and held there until the proper moment. When you are signaled to go on, walk with authority but not hurriedly to your position.

A walk-on presents a few extra difficulties to the producer in terms of getting you a microphone. Find out in advance what the procedure will be. The simplest situation uses a boom microphone, which dangles from an arm over your head and just out of camera range. Try to ignore its presence; don't look at it. The microphone might also be placed on a desktop, as on the *Tonight Show* set. Or you may be handed a small clip microphone by the host when you arrive at your seat. Discuss with the technician in advance where and how you should attach it.

For some reason the chairs used on many talk shows seem to be designed to show you off at your worst; they're either too low and overstuffed, uncomfortably harsh, or swivel so easily that you could be continuously shifting direction during the show without even realizing it. Pay attention to the message you give with your posture. Sit forward on the chair to appear alert and interested, with your feet and arms in a comfortable position. In a seated position you may look best with your legs crossed. However, if you cross them knee over knee, don't allow your back to slump back in too casual a position. Don't wear a vest because it tends to darken your image (drawing too much attention to your midsection), giving you more of a "corporate look" than you probably want to project. In addition, vests often bunch up and retain body heat generated by the intense studio lights.

If you have the opportunity to select your seating and the engagement is clearly more of an opportunity than an obligation, try to sit next to the moderator; that's normally the power position.

Show Time

Be ready to be introduced. Too many talk show guests are caught staring off into space immediately before being introduced—hardly a desirable tone setter for one's appearance. You can be introduced in one of three principal ways by the host: (a) if you are merely introduced by name and title without a "Welcome to the show" directed at you, nod gently and pleasantly: (b) if the introduction and welcome are directed to you, say, "Thank you, (adding host's name)" or feel free to choose another suitable amenity: (c) if the introduction is a zinger to throw you on the defensive, be ready to display composure and strength without being unduly combative.

Refer to the moderator by name without sounding too pandering. Remember Dale Carnegie's saying (somewhat paraphrased) that the sweetest sound to any person's ears is the sound of his or her own name. By being personable, you may impede or soften the moderator's possible contentiousness.

Look at the moderator, unless one of the other guests is speaking. And again, don't try to upstage the host on his or her own show. Remember that many of the people who watch talk shows do so because they like and enjoy the host, not because you are the guest. Also bear in mind that not every local television show host is an Oprah Winfrey, Phil Donahue, or Johnny Carson, although many try to pattern themselves after one of the stars. Just be yourself and leave the host to his or her role.

Based on your analysis of the show and its moderator, work out in advance your expected lines of agreement and disagreement and think of ways to fulfill your net-effects, substance, and image goals without sounding too contentious. Otherwise, you will surely jeopardize your image and that of your company or organization.

Act as if the camera is focused on you at all times. Although someone else may be speaking, the director may call for a shot of your reaction or may show a wide-angle shot of the whole set. Don't watch the red "on" lights on the cameras; you should be watching the host, or the guest, or the participating member of the live audience—whoever is speaking—with interest. Besides, if the show is being taped for later broadcast, it is possible that the pictures from more than one camera are being recorded for later mixing.

Monitor your body language. Try to limit stretching, scratching, tie straightening, skirt tugging, and other distracting body motions to commercial breaks. And again, don't say anything during the commercial breaks or before or after the show that you couldn't stand to see broadcast or repeated.

Keep your goals, key messages, and target audience in mind. Remember, although your tone and manner should be suitable for a conversation with an acquaintance in a small room, your key messages are actually aimed at the vast audience (particularly your target audience) at the receiving end of the television signal.

If more than one representative of your company or group is on a panel with you, be sure to defer to that person or refer to his or her comments from time to time to communicate unity and, of course, to clarify your intended message. In fact, it is advisable to plan in advance how you might divide your labors. If an adversary or another guest is appearing simultaneously, be prepared to compete to be heard. This may involve being more aggressive than usual or developing your answers for longer than you might if you were to appear alone.

Be ready for the end of the show. The host's sign-off may contain a thank-you, or an earnest invitation to appear again on the show, or a quick parting shot. Following are a few suitable amenities:

"Thank you, Susan, for inviting me."
"It will be my pleasure" (to return to the show).
"I'll look forward to that, Susan" (to returning to the show).

If the parting shot is hostile (called a cliff-hanger), you may wish to shake your head in disagreement, flash a bemused smile, or, if the host is a bona fide agitator (e.g., Morton Downey, Jr.), you might choose to return fire.

READING A STATEMENT ON TELEVISION

With the increasing popularity of internal corporate TV news and the business world's reliance on videotape, you may be called upon to read a brief statement or make some major announcement from a television studio. This situation provides you with one advantage not ordinarily present when you're speaking in a conference room or auditorium—the use of a TelePrompTer or similar device.

The TelePrompTer projects an image of your statement directly in front of or just above or below the camera lens. In one system, a special television monitor is mounted on the television camera itself. The screen points up at a see-through mirror glass in front of the lens; you see the words, and the camera lens behind the glass sees you. This allows you to maintain eye contact with the camera while reading your statement.

If the device is available to you, find out about system requirements before you arrive at the studio and arrange for several practice sessions. Reading words off the TelePrompTer will still sound wooden if it's the first time you've worked with one. Make sure the operator of the prompter moves the words up the screen at the rate you normally speak.

Try to visualize the audience as you speak to the camera. It may help you to personalize your delivery if you have a friend or two stand next to the camera during your remarks. Or address your remarks to the camera operators. But don't allow your eye contact to wander from the lens.

Be careful not to become too reliant on using a prompter—a malady too many executives are developing; doing so may prevent you from becoming a natural television performer. Remember, the prompter won't be with you if an outside reporter is interviewing you with a minicam or if you're a guest on a local or national talk show. Key words, rather then full scripts, may in the long run be far more practical in many internal TV situations where a prompter is used.

DON'T OVERLOOK
OR UNDERESTIMATE RADIO

People *talk about* television and newspapers, but they *listen to* radio.

Radio wakes us up, accompanies us to work in our cars, plays in the background in our offices, and drives home with us. For millions, radio is a source of information and entertainment all through the day or night.

Radio's virtues include its immediacy; it is still the fastest with the news—as fast as the ability of a reporter to get to a telephone and call the newsroom.

Another strong point for radio is its command of the listener's attention while he or she is focused on other activities, such as driving or working.

Radio's phone-in talk shows may offer you both a good platform for your message and the ability to listen directly to the comments of your audience. Most cities have at least one call-in show; some radio stations are completely given over to the format; and several nationwide call-in shows are now on the air.

Appearing on a radio show gets you around many of the obstacles presented by television. You are likely to have more time to present your case; you are able to bring notes and documents with you. You don't have the awful electronic eye of the television camera staring you down. You can loosen your tie or your shoes and be far less self-conscious of your visual image.

Many radio shows, in fact, don't even require you to travel to the studio. You can be interviewed and answer listeners' questions over your own telephone in your office or at home. The price of this arrangement, though, may come in the tone the host takes toward you; face-to-face conversations are often more genial and less forced than telephone calls.

Radio is much more compact in its equipment needs than television, and studios are considerably less formal. A typical studio is a small room dominated by a control board with tape players and turntables. At larger stations the board and other equipment are operated by an engineer on the other side of a glass wall, with just you and your interviewer at a desk. At most stations, though, your host will serve as engineer, telephone operator, and interviewer. He or she will seem to pay very little attention to you from time to time, attending instead to technical needs. But don't let your attention wander; you may suddenly be on air.

As with television talk shows, the host's questioning can range from brilliant to banal and from benevolent to brutal. I have appeared on a dozen or so radio talk shows within the past few years, and I can state with feeling—impressive moderators are a rare commodity.

Before you appear on the show, remember to define your net-effects, substance, and image goals. In any radio situation, remember that the only way you have of communicating is through your voice. Deliver your messages in a way that is aurally attractive and clear. Think of the situation as a telephone conversation with a friend.

One show I appeared on sent me a list of "possible questions" two weeks in advance (a most unusual circumstance). On another, the host showed me her list of questions before we went on the air. Although talk show producers may occasionally want your input before the show, I don't recommend that you provide "suggested questions" unless they are specifically requested.

One of your goals in appearing on the show may be to promote your company's products or services. Yet the host might not mention the name of your firm or its location. Radio, unlike television, allows you to slip the host a friendly note asking that this information be conveyed, especially if you might appear too self-serving in conveying this information yourself.

Telephone call-in shows usually employ a system that delays the whole show by several seconds to allow the cutoff of an obscene word or inappropriate comment from a caller. The delay should be of no concern to you; you won't even know of its existence unless the host dives across the control board to hit the cancel button.

If you find yourself being harassed by a caller, you may find the host coming to your rescue. If not, treat the situation as you would a rough question-and-answer session and maintain your cool. Remember, the audience is most likely to be on your side when you're dealing with a hostile character.

Similarly, if you find yourself facing a hostile host (you should have known about this in advance), don't try to outargue him or her. It's most likely a battle where if you win, you lose. Don't, however, be intimidated by the host either. Feel free to use the "banana peel" approach described in chapter 14. As with television, be on the lookout for "cliff-hangers," potentially damaging statements the moderator slips in before the breaks for commercials, the news, or the end of the show. If you feel the statement is potentially damaging, refute it at the first opportunity—but be careful not to sound too defensive or you may be inviting an unwelcome debate.

THE MEDIA TOUR

Should you or one of your colleagues represent your company or your organization on a media tour? Or should you hire a well-respected celebrity who can be credibly identified with your service or product?

Surely, this PR approach has gained tremendous popularity—and why not? Effectively planned and executed, it can be a potentially powerful, yet inexpensive, form of communication.

If the media tour is a tempting proposition to you, what basic qualities should the spokesperson have?

- A sound understanding of the product or service
- A personable, confident manner
- The ability to handle the give-and-take of questions
- The ability to discuss the service or product without sounding too commercial

Once the spokesperson is selected and trained, key media markets must be chosen. In most instances, priority is given to major population centers, which, due to the overflow demand for exposure on their channels and stations, are the toughest to schedule.

After the key markets have been targeted, the person in charge of the tour must develop a list of media contacts to approach in each city, including a list of shows most appropriate for promoting the product or service. Several major reference works can greatly facilitate this process:

- *Broadcasting/Cablecasting Yearbook* (Washington, D.C.: Broadcasting Publications)
- *Radio Contacts* and *Television Contacts* (New York: Larami Publications)
- *National Radio Publicity Directory* (New York: Peter Glenn Publications)
- *Ayer Directory of Publications* (Philadelphia: N. W. Ayer)
- *Bacon's Publicity Checker* (Chicago: Bacon Publishing Co.)
- *TV Publicity Outlets Nationwide, Cable TV Publicity Outlets Nationwide*
- *New York Publicity Outlets* (Washington Depot, Conn.: Public Relations Plus)

Generating the attention and interest of local stations, newspapers, and magazines requires two major tools of the trade: first, a comprehensive, well-prepared media kit with relevant descrip-

tions, biographical materials, and photographs; and second, polite persistence by the person in charge of the tour—both in
writing (via a "sell" letter to the editor, program director, or
producer) and on the phone.

Jeff Close of Creamer, Dickson, Basford, a public relations
firm, offers seven additional tips for making the media tour successful:

1. Be prepared. Know the subject, the market, and, most of all,
   the media and their audiences.
2. Plan ahead and plan carefully. Remember Murphy's Law:
   "Anything that can go wrong, will."
3. Look for additional media outlets in each market. Often a
   relevant trade publication will be based in a tour city.
4. Keep in touch with the spokesperson and the media. Interviews do get canceled, and knowing about cancellations early
   enough may permit the scheduling of a substitute interview.
5. Follow up. Contact editors and broadcasters to thank them for
   interviewing the spokesperson and to purchase tapes of the
   broadcast interviews and copies of the print interviews when
   they appear.
6. Be persistent. Don't wait for the media to initiate contact.
   Remember, the competition is fierce for space and time. Don't
   be annoying, though.
7. Make sure the spokesperson is prepared, well rehearsed in
   communicating the message, and *enthusiastic.*

If you now have even the slightest notion that the media tour
may be an effective vehicle for you, your company, or your organization, consult with your major public relations advisor. You
may be able to take advantage of a platinum opportunity.

"FRONTING"

One of the more popular and apparently effective advertising
tactics to surface over the past several years involves the CEO

selling his or her company's product or service through television and radio commercials and printed advertisements. I call this tactic fronting.

Lee Iacocca is the premier "fronter," having brought the Chrysler Corporation from the brink of bankruptcy into the black within only five years. Other CEOs who have shared at least a fair percentage of the remaining limelight—and with apparent effectiveness—are Remington Shaver's Victor Kiam and Frank Perdue of chicken fame.

When "fronting" campaigns are successful, their results are largely due to the credibility the CEO is able to project to the public. That credibility is based mainly on the "safeness" and "competence" he or she communicates. Iacocca, for instance, projected himself as a strong, no-nonsense, sincere spokesperson who instilled confidence in the consumer—confidence that he had the requisite leadership qualities to keep Chrysler afloat and to stand behind his product.

While fronting may, at first blush, appear to be an imaginative tactic, it is actually a return to the past. Less than a century ago most businesses were identifiable by the shopkeeper as well as by his product. Our grandparents and great-grandparents could always rely on a specific person—a face—if their stove, furniture, or cloth goods proved defective. Today, in sharp contrast, corporations have become faceless giants. Fronting, therefore, gives these giants a face—someone specific to identify with in addition to the product or the name brand.

If you are thinking about fronting for your company or organization, consider the following questions:

- Is there room in your media market for another fronter?
- Do you project the image traits required for the campaign? Seek the most candid feedback you can.
- Can you perform—or learn to perform—superbly before the camera and under the lights?
- Are you totally comfortable with the overall design of the advertising campaign?
- Are you prepared to accept the glory as well as the inconveniences associated with "star" status?

- Do you have a persuasive response to accusations that you are seeking the limelight for personal gain or launching a veiled political campaign?
- Are you aware of, and ready to accept, the consequences if the campaign doesn't work?

Tough questions for most CEOs. But Iacocca's success is good reason to pause and reflect—*very carefully.*

Capturing the persuasive edge on television or radio is a formidable challenge for almost everyone. It requires a keen understanding of each medium, meticulous preparation, significant self-awareness, including self-assurance, plus the desire to do well. This chapter is but a primer; experience via trial and error will become your most influential teacher.

Chapter 18

THE NEWS CONFERENCE

The news conference is the quickest way of getting your message to the largest audience in a manner you can significantly control. However, despite its advantages, look before you leap—making sure that you are not calling one too quickly. For example, if you are responding to a negative story about your company or organization, will a news conference delayed a day or two allow the matter—and your emotions—to simmer down and help prevent the story from being extended any longer than necessary? Moreover, is the news conference the proper vehicle through which to air your views? Might a more informal media availability session be more appropriate? These are crucial questions, for as soon as you invite the media to any type of gathering, the credibility of you and your organization are at stake.

YOUR REASON
FOR THE CONFERENCE

The key question emerging from these questions is, When do you call a news conference? *When you have significant, timely news that will potentially have an impact on a large number of people.* Therefore, in calling one, you should feel reasonably confident that most of the invited media representatives will want your story.

Don't use the news conference to puff up a story that has limited appeal. A "no news" news conference can easily backfire. If a story is not readily apparent at your news conference, the reporters will fish for one (possibly with a hostile tone for being invited to a "no news" event). If a reporter returns to the newsroom with no story at all, his or her editor will be reluctant to assign a reporter to any future conferences you might schedule.

THE RIGHT DATE

Picking the right date for a news conference is part careful planning and part crapshooting. Select a date that will allow you sufficient time to prepare information and a message for the conference—and to notify the media and produce a news kit. Whenever possible, select a "slow" news day—one on which no major scheduled news event will conflict with your conference and, as a result, draw reporters, newspaper space, and broadcast time away from it.

There are a few bits of information you can gather to help select the proper day. Work backward from the immutable elements of your announcement. If you are committed to announcing a new contract on October 1, you have no choice as to date. If, however, you don't have such a strict deadline, think next about where you'd like to get your biggest play.

If the newspaper is your number-one target and if the paper has a large Sunday edition, you might want to schedule your conference for a Saturday morning. Saturday is also a very slow day for broadcast outlets—but bear in mind that most operations field only a skeleton staff on weekends. Other typically slow days are Mondays and the days immediately before and after holidays. Seek advice on proper timing from reporter friends.

THE RIGHT TIME

The next question is the time of day. Select your prime news target and aim to meet its requirements:

Morning newspaper. The paper on your doorstep or your desktop in the morning was written between about noon and midnight of the day before. An early-afternoon news conference will meet its needs as well as those of the nightly television shows.

Afternoon newspaper. "PM" papers are produced on a split schedule. Reporters typically work from dawn until midafternoon. Depending upon the size of the paper, its circulation area, and the number of editions published each day, the first deadline for copy may be as early as 9 A.M. Final deadline—for the papers delivered to commuter stations—may be as late as noon or 1 P.M. Feature stories and analytical coverage are usually done during the afternoon, after deadline.

Television stations. Crews and reporters typically report about midmorning and work into the evening. The best time for television coverage for the 6 P.M. nightly news is usually between about 11 A.M. and 2 P.M.

Radio stations. Radio is generally the fastest medium. News can make it on air in the time it takes a reporter to get from your conference to a telephone. The prime time for radio news, though, is the early morning and late afternoon—called drive time in metropolitan areas.

Two caveats: Despite these generalizations, be sure to check out the timetables and deadlines that apply to the various media representatives you plan to invite. Also, be aware that if a plane crashes or a building burns or some other major news event happens on the day of your scheduled conference, you need to be prepared to chalk it up to the breaks of the game. If there is enough time, you might consider rescheduling the conference; but be sure to quickly notify everyone you invited.

THE INVITATION

When announcing a news conference, try to let the news media know what the topic will be and who will make the announcement. This will give the news editors an opportunity to make an intelligent decision about sending a reporter or crew and will add to your credibility as a future source.

If you are announcing the conference through a release, here's a convenient form to follow:

DATE:	month/day/year
TIME:	AM/PM
PLACE:	company name
	location in the building
	street
	town
EVENT:	Announcement of details regarding last week's accident at the XYZ plant in which three employees were seriously injured. (Give enough detail to interest the editor but don't give away the story.) Statement to be given by name/title

LOCATION AND LOGISTICS

The best place to hold a news conference may be in your offices, especially if you have a room or auditorium large enough to accommodate the reporters and the television equipment. But before you make this decision, ask yourself whether or not the presence of reporters or crews might be too disruptive to normal business activities.

The quality of the conference depends significantly on your attention to logistical details regarding physical arrangements, acoustics, and lighting:

Physical arrangements. Do you have a table of sufficient size to hold a round-table news conference? Do you have an attractive rectangular table for a sit-down conference? Do you have a photogenic lectern or podium? Is your company logo available for use as a prop or backdrop? Are there easels or other devices to support graphics (prepared for TV) and displays? Following are several points to take into consideration:

- Make the news conference site available at least an hour before the scheduled starting time to allow crews to set up cameras and microphones.
- Make sure the room has sufficient electrical capacity and outlets.
- Make available rolls of gaffer's tape (wide cloth tape) for use in attaching equipment.
- Place the lectern against the proper backdrop—your logo or a neutral-colored wall.
- Don't speak in front of an undraped window; the light will blind the camera.
- Make sure there are no inappropriate or distracting pieces of art or wall hangings within camera range.
- Consider providing a newsbridge mixer or "mult-box" to prevent the lectern from being cluttered by the reporters' microphones and tape recorders.
- Provide ample and comfortable seating (unassigned).
- Make telephones available to reporters.
- Consider providing coffee, sodas, and light refreshments.
- Keep reporters confined to the conference area.

Acoustics. Will reporters be able to hear you? Will you need a microphone? Note: An amplifying system can present feedback complications; test it ahead of time.

Lighting. Do you have your own television lighting? Does it meet the current specifications of TV cameras?

PREPARING FOR THE CONFERENCE

To capture the persuasive edge and to maximize control of the conference, you'll probably want to draft some *brief* opening remarks. The reporters may not use the remarks in their stories; nonetheless, your purpose should be to paint a broad picture that sets the foundation for fulfilling substance and image goals, to preempt or provide a foundation for responding to any anticipated negative questioning, and to suggest areas for questions. The opening statement should also help calm your nerves. In essence it is a tone setter for the reporters—and for you.

Working with your public relations director or other executives, draw up a list of possible questions. Schedule practice sessions, preferably in the news conference room. Your communication consultant and associates should fire the toughest questions they can come up with. Get used to the room and its setup. Turn on the television lights if available. Analyze a videotape of your practice session.

Some of the best news conferences are undermined by leaks. Don't "scoop" yourself by allowing too many details of your announcement to get to the media in advance. Caution your staff against leaks from within the company. It is quite possible that a reporter may call and try to wheedle a story out of you. Resist— and don't go "off the record."

THE DAY OF THE CONFERENCE

Everything is ready. You have been fully briefed. Your public information officer has gone on ahead to the conference room to make sure that everything is in place and to greet and offer assistance to any early-arriving reporters.

Give yourself a few quiet moments alone. Calm yourself, attend to your personal appearance, go over your opening statement (which should not normally exceed four to five minutes), review your substance and image goals and your key messages (which you should have written on a single sheet of paper in front of you during the conference). Then proceed to the conference room a few moments ahead of starting time. You may want to shake hands with a few of the reporters—it helps make you more human in their eyes and vice versa. You're ready now to head for the lectern.

Relax. Deliver your prepared remarks clearly and with appropriate feeling; don't rush.

Now to the reason you are there: ask for questions. *Take control and keep it!* You can try to set the ground rules at this time—you can say that you'd like to stay away from a particular subject and you can ask that the reporters identify themselves. Be prepared, though, for none of your requests to be honored. And, in some instances, setting a particular subject off-limits is roughly equivalent to waving a bold red flag in the eyes of a bull. Be certain you have a reasonable—and quotable—explanation for your refusal ("in litigation" being the most common).

Whenever possible, respond to questions in short, declarative sentences. Don't forget to put forth your key messages early and firmly.

If you don't know the answer to a question and none of your colleagues can help, inform the reporter that you will get the information to him or her as soon as possible. Don't be afraid to admit there's something you don't know—or that it is not conveniently available. It's a lot better than being proven wrong.

Remain cool. Remember that your purpose is to communicate *through* the reporters at the news conference to their much larger audiences—*your target audience.*

Don't show impatience if you're asked a "dumb" question or a question you've already answered. It is very important that reporters understand you. It is also possible that a reporter may have arrived late. And finally, a radio or television reporter may want to record you answering "his" question and not the very similar one just asked by the reporter from the competing station. Or the television crew may simply have missed one of your answers; they rarely leave their cameras and recorders running throughout a whole session.

Don't say, "As I already said before," or offer any variation on this theme. It is condescending, serves no purpose, and it may ruin the value of your quote.

During the middle of a news conference the TV crews may suddenly turn their lights off. It's a shock! Because of the change in the intensity of the lights, it seems as if the room went dark and the news conference is over. But it isn't necessarily over, so don't feel let down. In fact, some of the best questions come after the "show biz" portion has ended. That's when the print reporters ask the more in-depth questions and the spokesperson has the best opportunity to strengthen his or her position. Moreover, an alert broadcast reporter will often piggyback on these comments.

You do need to know when to end the conference. Normally a news conference lasts twenty to thirty minutes, while an informal media-availability session takes ten to twenty minutes. Your public information officer will cue you and announce, "Last question," when the questioning starts to get repetitive, dies down, or when the reporters begin closing their notebooks.

After the Conference

You will probably be approached by one or more reporters after the conference for quick questions. There are two reasons for these "private" news conferences. Radio and television stations may want to make a tape—an on-scene report called an "actuality" in the trade—that showcases you and their reporter. A print reporter may approach you with a question because he or she doesn't want to share an "exclusive" angle with the other reporters in an open conference. Or perhaps his or her paper is on the other "cycle"; for example, if the morning paper will have the first crack at the story, the reporter for the afternoon paper will be searching for a different angle.

If you know a reporter by name or if the reporter identifies himself, use his or her name in your answer without overdoing it. This is particularly appropriate when dealing with television reporters; they are very much regarded as "personalities" by their employers and may be more likely to include in their report any comments that show them interacting directly with you.

THE MEDIA BRIEFING

The media briefing is another alternative to a full-blown news conference. The major purpose of this session is to "educate" the media regarding complex issues they are covering and to strengthen the organization's relationship with them. The briefing, therefore, usually lacks two criteria necessary for a news conference: timeliness and direct newsworthiness.

Public utilities and other companies that frequently find themselves under the media spotlight use media briefings extensively. These one to two-hour sessions, often conducted over breakfast or lunch, usually involve a series of carefully prepared presentations followed by Q&A.

THE ELECTRONIC NEWS CONFERENCE

When Johnson & Johnson announced its plans to reintroduce Tylenol capsules in 1982 following the tragic series of poisonings that seriously damaged the product's acceptance in the American marketplace, the company decided to seek both national and local press coverage to inform the public about the steps they were taking to prevent future tragedies.

Chairman James E. Burke conducted a news conference from New York that was sent by satellite to thirty American cities as he answered questions from reporters anywhere in the system.* This approach worked remarkably well; newspapers and television stations had their choice of a national wire service or network feed or a story by their own reporter, with any appropriate local angle.

Besides gaining entrance to a number of major markets at the same time, a tele-press conference also gains entry into smaller

*Several companies specialize in providing such multicity hookups.

communities that might otherwise be bypassed or covered in a very expensive and time-consuming manner.

If you take this route, you should provide full details on the technical arrangements for the conference to radio and television stations, including information on how they will be able to plug their equipment into the incoming video and audio signal to make their own recording. Some television stations may be able to receive the signals over their own satellite-reception dishes. In other instances, reporters will have to go to a motel, a company facility, or a special teleconference site in their area. You should also arrange a schedule for questioning—perhaps a preannounced order for all participants. Advance planning should also include distribution of packets and other materials to the tele-news conference site.

THE AFTERMATH

Once the conference is over, review in detail how well your organization and you or your spokesperson responded to it. Analyze the videotape, ask trusted reporters for feedback, encourage candor from every member of your team. And be sure to emphasize that although perfect news conferences are frequently hard to achieve, open feedback can make each succeeding one better.

Chapter 19

PREPARING FOR A CRISIS

On July 3, 1986, Tom Herskovits, president of the Kraft Dairy Group, was packing for a family trip to the Jersey shore when his phone rang. The news wasn't good. During an inspection of one of Kraft's plants, an unusual strain of bacteria had been found in a Polar Bar ice cream square, one of its major products. Herskovits quickly canceled his plans and caught a plane to the Kraft, Inc., headquarters outside Chicago to address the problem. After a detailed inspection of the plant, he and his colleagues decided to remove the product from the marketplace. Despite the expected loss of tens of millions of dollars, two principles dominated their thinking: "Protect the consumer and protect Kraft's reputation, including the reputation of the Polar Bar brand name."

We have all heard of numerous similar situations. But has the incidence of crises increased? Probably not. However, two trends seem clear. First, while product contamination is as old as mankind, product tampering is a relatively new type of crisis situation; second, the corporation's obligation to respond appropriately to a crisis has apparently increased since Johnson & Johnson's impressive handling of the Tylenol tampering incident in 1982.

Corporate vulnerability to crises, plus increased corporate accountability to respond appropriately, should prompt a widespread management mentality to "be prepared." But the evi-

dence indicates otherwise. A recent University of Southern California study found that only 38 percent of the nation's largest
industrial companies have a crisis team. A Western Union study
concluded that only 57 percent of the two hundred leading companies surveyed have a crisis communication plan.

Why do 62 percent of our nation's largest industrial companies
not have a crisis team? And why do 43 percent of our leading
companies not even have a plan? There are four major reasons:

1. *Classic denial.* Fundamentally, effective crisis planning requires
   replacing the "it can't happen to us" syndrome with "it can
   happen and we must be prepared." However, normal human
   behavior is filled with denial, the tendency to shun negative
   possibilities or probabilities because of the psychological burden that dealing with them often produces.
2. *Traditional management focuses on productivity and profits.* In any
   company, the executive's energies are harnessed by these
   business realities. Therefore, planning instead for seemingly
   improbable circumstances can be viewed as low-priority or as
   a waste of time.
3. *The inability to visualize what a proper response to a crisis requires.*
   The tendency to dismiss a crisis as improbable automatically
   reduces the likelihood that the executive has even attempted
   to develop a clear notion of what a crisis involves, including
   the pressures, the difficulty in locating key people immediately, and the complexity of the decisions required.
4. *The inability to understand how the media can influence public perception of the company, its executives, and its products and services.* CEOs
   are naturally accustomed to a relative sense of control over
   people and events. Some, especially those with limited prior
   exposure to the media, feel that their authority—even in a
   crisis situation—will be accepted by the media in much the
   same way it is accepted within the corporation. Yet nothing is
   more prone to marshal the media's proclivity for relentless
   pursuit of the facts than a crisis.

The media's pursuit of a crisis is often unmindful of corporate
protocol. Reporters will not be beholden to channels of commu-

nication as they search for the truth or for a good newsbite. Similarly, the deference the CEO enjoys in the boardroom is a far cry from the defiance, the skepticism, and the potential for personal and corporate embarrassment that often pervade a news conference about a crisis.

Companies can be perceived in one of two ways as a result of a crisis—as the victim or as the culprit. The company is perceived as a victim when a crisis develops despite the company's responsible efforts to create a safe environment, an effective and safe product or service, or a solid financial position. Product tampering is a perfect example of the company as victim, especially if it has taken reasonable steps to make its products tamper-resistant. The company is perceived as a culprit when the public senses that it has acted negligently.

The victim in a crisis situation must observe one fundamental caveat: while you may feel victimized, the media can quickly cultivate the perception that you are the culprit. Before the dust even begins to settle, angry fingers can be pointed directly at your company for a host of possible misfortunes for which it may feel innocently victimized: fires, explosions, industrial accidents, chemical or oil leaks or spills, product tampering, shootings, automobile accidents, robberies, food poisonings, product recalls, financial difficulty, labor unrest, and so on. The media will be ready to try the company's claims of diligent prevention and responsible reaction in the court of public opinion. And the jury is often tough, especially in reacting to crises involving issues of health and safety.

Three crucial pieces of advice emerge from any thoughtful discussion of crisis communication: (a) create a crisis management team; (b) develop a crisis communication plan; and (c) select a capable, credible spokesperson.

THE CRISIS MANAGEMENT TEAM

Although the nature of the corporation's business influences the composition of the team, normally the following positions are represented:

  The CEO
  The chief financial officer
  The head of personnel (human resources)
  The head of public information
  The general counsel
  The heads of manufacturing
  The medical director and head of security

The CEO's presence or representation is crucial since he or she must ultimately implement and quarterback the plan. The chief financial officer is best positioned to assess the economic impact of various options springing from the crisis deliberations. In addition, his or her role is indispensable if the crisis is financially related, such as in the case of hostile takeovers, plant closedowns, layoffs, or bankruptcy. The head of public information is the key link between the corporation and the public. The head of human resources or personnel is the principal contact between the executives and the employees and can have a crucial role in responding to an internal crisis. The heads of manufacturing and distribution are best positioned to deal with the logistics surrounding a product recall. The medical director and head of security can be especially helpful in preventing and responding to internal crisis situations related to security, health, and injury.

THE CRISIS COMMUNICATION PLAN

Two major questions serve as the foundation for a crisis communication plan. First, what types of crisis situations could occur?

Second, how should they be responded to? The first question can be most effectively addressed via a brainstorming session during which the crisis management team develops a "nightmare list" of possible crises. The second question includes preparing a list of logistical issues related to the following five-step framework:

1. Anticipate possible and probable crisis scenarios.
2. Alleviate the real crisis.
3. Investigate the causes.
4. Cooperate with the media.
5. Evaluate your overall response to the crisis.

Any crisis communication plan should include a detailed notification system. Who within your company needs to be notified? If the crisis occurs within the workplace, are employees properly advised how to respond? Who should be notified outside the company—the media, public safety agencies, the health department, public officials? Has a system been developed to make sure that crisis management team members or their alternates and key media contacts can be easily reached, day or night and on weekends?

Rumor control is a major communication challenge facing a company during a crisis. Rumors particularly about deaths, the cause or perpetrator, and other highlights of the crisis can spread like wildfire. To combat them, the corporation needs timely, credible interaction with the media and possibly an 800 toll-free number, an option selected by Kraft during the Polar Bar crisis. In addition, Western Union's Mailgram is an efficient vehicle for contacting specific persons, for example, investors, car owners, distributors, and dealers.

Crisis drills are an increasingly popular activity at chemical plants, oil refineries, and nuclear power facilities. In addition, banks stage mock robberies and airlines and public transportation systems stage simulated emergencies to increase the likelihood that personnel will react properly.

One drill conducted by our firm at one of the world's larger nuclear power plants instantly proved its worth. During a simulated crisis news conference the corporate spokesperson said that the town surrounding the plant should not be evacuated, whereas the technical expert, speaking to another group of reporters, said that it should be. Meanwhile, only the governor had the authority to comment publicly on the advisability of an evacuation.

THE SPOKESPERSON

Should the CEO be the spokesperson during a crisis? A fair amount of controversy surrounds this question. Those in favor argue that the CEO's credibility in such a serious situation is crucial to defusing the crisis and to reinstilling or reinforcing public confidence. This position has merit. However, if the crisis itself is commanding the energies of the CEO, designating another spokesperson is a more advisable choice. Once the crisis is under control and a plan to address the specific crisis at hand has been developed, then may be the right time for the CEO to step forward. It was therefore appropriate and highly effective for James Burke, Johnson & Johnson's CEO, to address the public once the Tylenol response plan had been developed.

Assigning Tasks

If possible, your principal spokesperson should stay in one place, near the pressroom. Other staffers should be responsible for going out into the field; the crisis communication person will have to handle the entire gamut of decisions and questions, and no time should be wasted in finding him or her.

Someone should be stationed at the building or plant entrance to direct media to the pressroom and relatives and friends to some other quiet, segregated area. *Keep members of the media separate from families and visitors.*

The media spokesperson should be available at the pressroom and have authority to answer questions fully and frankly within predetermined limits and be able to make on-the-spot decisions and arrangements necessary for news coverage.

A competent public relations professional should also be stationed in the room to which visitors and relatives have been directed, with instructions to answer questions as positively as possible and with appropriate discretion.

Assign a "floater" to tour all posts and other vital areas to check on how things are being handled. The floater should report to the principal spokesperson regularly with comments and suggestions.

A Crisis Checklist

- *Telephone service:* Do you have the capability to handle the extra load of incoming and outgoing calls without delays? Does your plan include instructions to employees and to switchboard operators to withhold personal and nonessential calls during emergencies?
- *Pressroom:* Is there a central location that can be given over to the press? It should be easily accessible to reporters, preferably near your public relations department. Consider purchasing a newsbridge mixer or "multbox" to avoid the confusion of microphones on the lectern. It should also have available telephones, sufficient chairs and desks, typewriters, paper, and other supplies. You should be prepared to offer coffee and food.
- *Radio communications:* Do you have a shortwave, citizens band, or other radio system that could be used if power or telephone service is lost? Arrangements to monitor the radio should be made with other offices or plants and with police and fire departments. Top executives and spokespersons should have portable radios of their own.
- *Electronic bullhorns:* Keep at least one bullhorn or portable public address system in your public relations office or with emergency equipment.
- *Central communications:* Members of your staff should be assigned to central locations and serve as relays for messages.

The Crisis Interview

The reporter needs you for his or her story. As you cooperate, your three guidelines should be credibility, composure, and control.

- Prepare a brief, clear, and reasonably candid opening statement to reflect your goals and to create a context for answering the more predictable questions. If time permits, practice delivering it.
- Be certain that the flow of information to top officers of your company is not lagging behind the flow going to the media.
- As in any interview, define your company's and your own net-effects, substance, and image goals and then work your key messages into your answers *early* and *often* (see chapter 2).
- Try to respond in headlines and quotable quotes. Get your main points up front in every answer (see chapters 14 and 17).
- Keep your target audience in mind as you answer each question.
- Don't permit a reporter to shove a microphone an inch or two from your mouth. Simply take your hand and gently move the microphone away or back. The reporter will soon get the message.
- Be prepared to close an interview should it begin to run too long. Stick to the facts and don't "wing it." If you don't know an answer, say so and offer to get back with details. Don't evade a question and never say, "No comment."
- Don't let a reporter reinterpret what you've said in a subsequent question. Correct the question before you attempt an answer. Similarly, don't use a reporter's words unless they are accurate and appropriate.
- If a factual question puts you in a negative light, acknowledge this and then move immediately to a discussion of how you are correcting the situation.
- Be fully prepared for "banana peels" (see chapter 14).

- Don't fall victim to a "speed-up" technique in which a reporter shoves a microphone back and forth rapidly between you. Comment on the microphone's movements lightly or take hold of the reporter's hand to steady the mike.
- Watch out for a "stall" technique, in which the reporter leaves the microphone in your face after you answer, hoping that you will say more. Say what you want to say and no more.
- Don't feel you have to rush into a response; pausing to take a sip of water or some other delaying device can be helpful.
- Don't interrupt a reporter's question unless it is absolutely necessary. You may be stealing your own thinking time. If a reporter interrupts your response, tell him or her politely but firmly that you want to finish.
- Try to spread the interviews around to all of the reporters. Don't play favorites—it could easily backfire.
- At the end of the interview, be prepared to restate your key points.

The Media Corps Tour

The media corps will probably ask to visit the site of the incident. Plan in advance, taking into serious consideration the following questions:

- Is there any personal danger—hot embers, escaping gas fumes, the possibility of collapse?
- Might a visitor inadvertently disturb evidence that would hamper official investigations by police, fire, safety, and insurance officials?
- If the tour is advisable, is a company official available to escort the press personally?
- Might there be an alternative to a tour, such as photographic blowups, videotapes, or floor-plan sketches? Should you offer a helicopter ride over the site?
- Can you assemble people who performed heroic acts so that the press can interview them? Make certain that any person

speaking to the press is fully briefed on the latest status of the crisis to avoid any discrepancies.

THE ETHICS OF CRISIS COMMUNICATION

No event capturing the media's and the public's attention is more prone than a crisis situation to bring out a desire by the victim or culprit to cover up the truth. Yet the risks associated with a cover-up are astronomical. If a distortion, lie, or piece of crucial information is willfully withheld, chances are "the truth will out" as a result of the media's pursuit or a legal action emanating from the crisis. Certainly the corporate spokesperson is not obligated to "tell all," but what is told must be fully truthful. Moreover, if the media are likely to learn from another source what the spokesperson is initially reluctant to disclose, it is generally best to cooperate. To do so can enhance your relationship with the media and your company's credibility.

After the Crisis

Analyze your performance. Examine logs kept during the crisis. Check the information your company gave out and compare it hour by hour to media coverage. How well did the plan work? Could it have worked better?

Inform the press about your efforts to restore operations and to care for anyone who was injured.

Finally, distribute "thank you" notes to the media, to the emergency workers, and to your own staff; that step reflects your overall effort to show your company's class.

IN FULLER PERSPECTIVE

The Chinese symbol for crisis consists of two characters: one represents danger; the other, hidden opportunity. Crisis situations, properly handled through a well-selected team, a well-defined plan, and a well-trained spokesperson, can result in hidden opportunity—the opportunity to enhance the public's confidence in your corporation.

Part IV

SPECIAL SITUATIONS

Chapter 20

"PLEASE SAY A FEW WORDS"

With increasing frequency, business, community, and political leaders are called upon "to say a few words" in a wide variety of special occasions, such as introducing a guest speaker, presenting or accepting an award, paying tribute to some person or group, opening or closing a conference, conveying a message of greeting from a prominent personality who could not attend, or placing someone's name in nomination.

Finding the "right" words is not necessarily easy. Most business leaders are not accustomed to speaking in the softer or more feeling-oriented tones required by most special occasions. In addition, this type of speaking places a greater premium on creativity and eloquence than reflected in most business-oriented messages.

Although speaking at special occasions may be challenging, it also provides you with valuable opportunities. Take, for example, a speech of tribute at a company retirement dinner for a loyal, productive, and well-respected employee. A few *choice* words from you allow the audience to witness your more human side and sense firsthand your respect for the values exemplified by the employee being honored. A well-composed and well-delivered speech during a special occasion can convey a touch of class better than in almost any other setting.

Before I offer specific advice regarding each of the special occasions discussed below, I encourage you to follow the following principles based on my experience in preparing business and political leaders for all types of special occasions, including inaugural addresses, eulogies of prominent figures, and inductions into halls of fame:

- Before you begin to prepare, make sure you understand what "a few words" means. I've seen a few words quickly become an eight- to ten-minute speech (1200–1500 words).
- Don't translate a request to "say a few words" into "that means I won't have to spend much time preparing." Chances are your preparation time may be greater for "a few words" than for many.
- Analyze the audience and occasion thoroughly, especially since many special occasions involve several speakers. Therefore know—or negotiate for—your position on the program; know who the other speakers will be; try to determine what their "slant" will be. This will help keep your remarks from becoming perceived as "refried beans."
- Define precisely your net-effects, substance, and image goals. Focus particularly on how you want the audience to feel when you are finished—about you, themselves, the event, the person being honored, and so on.
- Unless speaking on special occasions comes easy to you, write out your remarks verbatim. Then decide whether you wish to read, memorize, or deliver them via an extemporaneous outline. (Note: The extemporaneous approach is generally preferable because it better conveys the genuine feeling behind your remarks.)
- Don't be afraid to express or demonstrate your emotions. Don't be concerned that you may get choked up while paying tribute to someone you genuinely respect and care for, provided you have the inner confidence that you won't become too emotional. Your true feelings help make your words—and you—all the more genuine. Moreover, remember that in so many instances, your emotions merely mirror those of your audience. By expressing yours, you are helping them express theirs.

SPEECHES OF INTRODUCTION

We've all seen too many instances in which a speaker is introduced by a host who simply—but awkwardly—reads the speaker's biographical statement or résumé. No feeling, no originality—just an obligatory exercise that does little for the audience and perhaps even less for the speaker.

As you prepare a speech of introduction, allow the following questions to influence your goal-setting process:

- To what extent does the speaker's credibility need to be "sold" to the audience before he or she speaks?
- What facts about the speaker are most relevant to the audience and the occasion?
- Should the audience be oriented to his or her topic before he speaks?
- Should the audience be introduced to the speaker—their backgrounds and interest?
- Should the speaker be told about the audience's level of excitement or enthusiasm in having him or her on the program?
- To what extent does a high-quality introduction further motivate the speaker to give a high-quality speech?
- To what extent does a high-quality introduction reflect well on you and your organization?

These questions highlight one important reality: the introduction is an important tone setter affecting the audience, the speaker, the overall event, and you, the introducer.

Specific Advice for the Introducer

- Gather and read as much as you can about the speaker ahead of time. This investment will allow you to internalize what you are saying rather than merely recite lines.
- Think about the personal qualities the speaker exemplifies and build your remarks around them. Some of the more

popular touchstones: business acumen, results achieved, management know-how, problem-solving ability, determination, imagination, dedication, and so on. An apt quote can launch your discussion of the trait(s).

- Be brief. Except in rare instances, going beyond two to three minutes is flirting with danger.
- Add a personal touch. If you know something unusual, interesting, and relevant about the speaker, consider using it.
- Avoid allowing your ego to "run interference." Too many introducers use the introduction to showcase their personal friendship with the speaker (e.g., "When Senator Gates and I were fishing off the coast of Newfoundland last summer . . .").

Such references, by the way, can also embarrass the speaker.

- Don't make the frosting too thick. An introduction containing too many superlatives and flowery epithets or "schmaltzy" phrases can lack credibility and be downright embarrassing to the speaker.
- Close with a line that invites an overt audience welcome: "Let's give a warm Ballantine Books greeting to one of our newest authors, _____."

Special Advice for the Speaker

- Ask your staff to send to the host in advance a "suggested introduction" tailored to the specific topic or event. Include with it background information regarding you, your company, and your topic.
- Ask your communications staff member or assistant to speak with the introducer a few days ahead of time to make sure the materials have been received and to answer any questions.
- Carry an extra introduction with you. Despite your good efforts, introducers frequently "leave home without them."

PRESENTING AN AWARD

Most of us would agree that recognition is great sustenance for one's self-esteem and ultimately a key factor in enhancing one's morale, motivation, and effectiveness. This basic psychological insight has given rise to the hundreds of thousands of trophies, plaques, certificates, scholarships, and other types of awards given to people each year for achievements related to sales, athletics, the arts, community service, safety compliance, heroism, *ad infinitum*. As the presenter, you may or may not have influenced the original effort that resulted in the award, but you can influence the quality of the event and the memories it generates. Presenting an award is, therefore, an opportunity to capture the persuasive edge by highlighting the values the award symbolizes and the recipient embodies—values important to you and your organization.

Special Advice for the Presenter

- Before presenting the award, help the audience appreciate the award itself. If the audience does not know its history, briefly give it. Consider referring to prior recipients.
- Explain how the recipient meets the award's criteria.
- Avoid too much "frosting."
- If the award involved competition, display graciousness to the losers in a manner that is neither defensive, gratuitous, apologetic, nor likely to be perceived as a "left-handed compliment."
- Consider holding the audience in suspense until the end of the speech before you disclose who the recipient is. However, if they know ahead of time, this technique can smack of phoniness.

Special Advice for the Recipient

- A genuine "thank you" may be enough. But don't be too sure. Discuss with the host what is expected from you. Past events are often the best basis for making such judgments.
- Be prepared to "share" the award. Thank by name or category those who were most instrumental to you. Avoid the tediously long litanies that typify the Oscar, Emmy, Tony, and Grammy events.
- Display emotion appropriate for the occasion. Crying may or may not be appropriate for a newly crowned Miss America, but is it appropriate for winning your company's regional sales award? Jumping for joy may or may not be appropriate if you've just won the Academy Award for best actor, but is it appropriate if you're being cited for offering the best suggestion for streamlining the company's production cycle? You be the judge.
- Offer your personal thoughts about the import of the award. What does the award symbolize to you? To your colleagues? Here your openness, appropriately and skillfully expressed, can be most impressive.
- Thank the audience for attending, indicating that their attendance also symbolizes their identification with the values represented by the award.
- Value brevity, especially if several awards have been or are to be given. Again, exceeding two or three minutes may take you into the danger zone unless your acceptance speech is expected to be the keynote address. (Awards are frequently used to induce a well-respected personality or celebrity to accept a speaking engagement requiring a keynote address.)

SPEECHES OF TRIBUTE

A speech of tribute may embody the essential features of an award presentation or it may veer in a different direction by honoring some person or some group who may not necessarily be present or even living. Lincoln's Gettysburg Address and Reagan's remarks following the *Challenger* disaster are outstanding examples of speeches of tribute.

Speeches of tribute often become coping mechanisms that help us to deal emotionally with momentous events ranging from triumph to tragedy. The speaker chosen to deliver a speech of tribute becomes, in essence, our surrogate, with the opportunity to capture sensitively and eloquently the depths of our feelings.

Advice:

- Take an interpretive approach rather than merely reciting facts. The following list of questions prepared by Dr. Carolyn Keefe of our consulting firm should help stimulate your interpretive thinking:

  What traits of the person or organization being honored are most worthy of tribute?

  What factors contributed to their development?

  How have the traits found expression?

  What events are the most significant?

  How has culture exerted an influence?

  What set of values has governed behavior or shaped the public attitudes?

  What dimensions of religious experience have come into play?

  How have interlocking relationships affected persons and events?

  What good has resulted from this life, this movement, this place, this symbol?

- Value brevity and succinctness. Remember that Lincoln's Gettysburg Address was only 267 words long. Although you need not be confined to this length, remember that brevity and succinctness help communicate confidence, authority, and strength, as well as prevent the intrusion of boredom, which can seriously interfere with the emotions you are seeking to touch.

THE GRADUATION SPEECH

The graduation speech is no longer the exclusive property of politicians, authors, artists, or scholars. Increasingly, business leaders are invited to present graduates with practical insights and advice and to challenge them to respond in a manner conducive to personal achievement and to the betterment of society.

Advice:
- Shoot for a fresh approach; try to break the mold from which boring, condescending, and simplistic graduation speeches have been cast.
- Strive to reach the graduates and their families. Don't strive to impress the scholars.
- Establish genuine common ground via shared experiences, attitudes, or humor. The humorous touch, which offers good advice for other graduation speakers, was ably demonstrated by Arthur Levitt, Jr., chairman of the American Stock Exchange, when he began his address before the 1988 graduating class of the University of Connecticut: "When I told my daughter I'd be addressing you today, she advised me, 'Don't talk about how it was when you were in college; don't lecture them, and be very, very brief.' So in conclusion . . ." (laughter).
- Avoid graduation clichés:
  "You can make a difference."
  "Commencement means not an end, but a beginning."
  "The path may not be smooth, but the journey will be worth it."
  "Your destiny is in your own hands."
- Avoid trite expressions:
  "dedicated professors"
  "lasting friendships"
  "supportive parents"
  "Good luck!"
- Value brevity and succinctness. Yes, students do want to be inspired by your remarks, but they also want to celebrate

with their families and friends. Be aware of their emotions and the other factors affecting their patience, including the June sun, crowded seating, and warm graduation gowns.

SPEECHES TO ENTERTAIN

We all admire the after-dinner speaker who can effortlessly deliver a collection of jokes, lines, and anecdotes woven around the theme of the event. In fact, this type of speaking is often the most challenging, for in addition to all the normal speaking skills, it requires an added dimension of creativity or cleverness, including a highly effective use of humor.

Speeches to entertain have three objectives: to have fun, to poke fun, or to make a point. Any or all of these objectives can be reflected in the same speech. The key point here is to define your objectives carefully in relation to your audience and the occasion.

Advice:

- Try to be as free from your notes as possible. For the speech to work, the audience must sense your genuine personality through your facial expression, vocal tones, gestures, and so on.
- Don't go running to the joke books. If you do not have the ability to create humor yourself or don't have a good writer who can, chances are that what you hone from a joke book can make you the brunt of the audience's humor. In short, they don't deserve "rewarmed corn."

HOW LONG
IS LONG ENOUGH?

There are no hard-and-fast rules. Are you the principal speaker, the main attraction? Or are you part of a whole evening's program? What time of day is it? Has the audience just eaten? Is the audience waiting for dinner?

The principal speaker could legitimately lay claim to fifteen to twenty-five minutes. So, too, could a speaker before a college class or a seminar.

An after-dinner speech should be light in weight and short in length, otherwise it falls on sleepy ears. While an ordinary presentation might be twenty minutes or more, you might find twelve to fifteen minutes to be the top limit for a postprandial presentation.

An after-lunch speaker should be aware of the plans of the audience. Are they expecting to get back to their businesses for an afternoon of work? Are other events planned? Are the participants hoping to leave before the evening rush hour?

When in doubt, *it is better to be too short than too long.* You'll earn the gratitude of your host and your audience if you take slightly less than your allotted time.

_____ Chapter 21 _____

MEETINGS AND TELECONFERENCES

ARE YOU BEING "MEETINGED" TO DEATH?

On average, executives spend between 50 and 80 percent of their time in meetings. How well that time is spent is another matter. The experience of my company indicates that, increasingly, executives are taking a close, hard look at the necessity and quality of their meetings.

And they should, for meetings can be extremely expensive. Take a few moments and calculate the cost of your last meeting.

a. Executive meeting time (based on hourly rate calculated as annual salary divided by 2,000 hours) $ _____
b. Executive preparation time   _____
c. Room usage (based on monthly square-foot rental)   _____
d. Executive travel time   _____
e. Visual aids   _____
f. Secretarial support for preparation   _____
g. Photocopying expenses   _____
h. Telephone and courier expenses   _____
i. Other   _____

                                                          Total: $ _____

Are you surprised?

While scores of books, manuals, and seminars address this subject, few treat well the nitty-gritty problems that make too many meetings forums for frustration rather than for fruitful discussion and decision making. The advice that follows should be helpful in strengthening standing committees, ad hoc meetings, and teleconferences.

First, how carefully have you defined the purpose of your meeting? Is the major purpose to:

- Share information?
- Gather information?
- Make recommendations?
- Solve problems?
- Cultivate an attitude?
- Provide instruction?
- Advance a hidden agenda (e.g., showcasing your abilities or someone else's, testing the competence of one or more participants, etc.)?

Think about this question carefully, for when I pose it to executives, they often react with a pregnant pause followed by an admission that they haven't thought enough about their meeting goals. Look at each of the purposes listed above (of course, there may be other purposes not noted here) and decide which apply to your meetings. Then evaluate the intrinsic value of each purpose on a 1-to-5 scale. This assessment process will help you to establish priorities and plan your meeting with a more precise set of goals.

Once I help executives relate to this process, they soon learn—often to their dismay—that other regular meeting attendees have different—even conflicting—perceptions regarding the purpose of the same meeting. For this reason, I often advise clients to formulate and then circulate a statement articulating the purpose of a meeting.

Next, ask yourself, "How successfully is each purpose being

accomplished? Is the meeting the only way—or the best way—to accomplish it?"

Crucial to accomplishing each purpose is the ability of the leader to maintain enthusiasm. The following eleven factors can curb enthusiasm:*

1. The leader is not prepared.
2. The meeting does not start on time.
3. The leader gets the meeting off to a slow start.
4. The objectives seem unimportant to the participants.
5. The objectives are unclear to the participants.
6. The leader reads too much material.
7. The meeting gets out of control.
8. The leader dominates the meeting.
9. The meeting runs too long without a break.
10. There is no variety or change of pace.
11. The leader lacks personal enthusiasm.

Keep this list in front of you so that you're aware of these factors and can take steps to prevent them from surfacing.

THE LINEUP AND THE BATTING ORDER

If you've decided that the regular meeting is destined for survival, then you must ask yourself, "Is it properly composed?" "Do I need my best and my brightest?" "Are there too many or too few committee members?" Again, answering these questions is no easy task, especially in a large organization where being selected to attend or not transmits all kinds of personal political messages—particularly regarding each executive's perceived value to the meeting chairperson.

*These criteria were first elaborated by Donald Kirkpatrick, *How to Plan and Conduct Business Meetings* (Chicago: Dartnell, 1976), pp. 86–87.

How large the committee should be depends on several factors, including the purpose of the meeting, the extent to which various divisions of the corporation need to be represented, and the hard political reality of preventing bruised egos. If the committee's principal purpose is to arrive at major recommendations or to make major decisions not discussed in other settings, nine members is probably the upper limit, with five to seven being the ideal. However, if the committee is established primarily for reporting and general sharing, it can afford to be larger.

In selecting individuals to serve on standing committees, ask yourself, "Does this person understand what this committee means to me personally?" "Is my accountability in chairing this committee clearly perceived by the committee members?" In so many corporations, an executive's destiny is significantly tied to his ability to extract from the meetings ideas that can impress his superiors. If you have any doubt about how clearly your accountability is being perceived, using the appropriate degree of finesse, make it known to the committee as a whole or to the members individually.

THE AGENDA
AND THE ENVIRONMENT

Successful meetings normally require careful planning. Crucial to the planning process is the preparation of an agenda. Consider the following questions as part of your preparation process:

1. Should an agenda be prepared in advance?
2. If so, should agenda items be invited from the meeting participants?
3. When should the items be invited? By whom? (You, your secretary, the meeting secretary?)
4. How explicitly should the items be stated? Note: I often recommend that the items be phrased as objective questions—issues—accompanied by a short statement of justification for

inclusion on the agenda. For example: "Should we redecorate our studio? It was last redecorated in 1984 and is beginning to show wear from a rapidly increasing pattern of use."

5. Who should be responsible for each agenda item?
6. How far in advance of the meeting should the agenda be circulated?

The importance of the meeting environment must not be underestimated. How conducive is it to quality communication? Is the room large enough—but not too large? Is the table shaped to allow the participants to see each other easily? Are chairs comfortable? Should coffee, tea, or soft drinks be available? Is the room conducive to stand-up presentations, including the use of visual aids?

What norms apply to the meeting? How long should it be? Is the length reasonable? How is the length of a presentation decided? What types of visual aids are usually chosen? Do norms govern seating arrangements?

Who sits where in relation to you, the leader, is often a power game. You must decide whether or not you want to control the game. Do you want your closest and most trusted advisors next to you, or doesn't it make any difference? Phrased another way, if you don't take control, do you mind if the person most capable of giving you ulcers is seated next to you?

If you decide to take control, you may be issuing a potentially strong implicit statement about the status of each committee member. Do you want to be—or need you be—concerned with the implications of this control on their egos? Round tables alleviate many problems related to this issue, but the hard reality is that few boardrooms feature round tables.

YOUR LEADERSHIP STYLE

What kind of tone do you establish when you enter the meeting room? Do you strike the right balance between being sociable and being task oriented? And do you set the proper example by arriving on time?

Leadership styles have been traditionally placed in three categories: autocratic, democratic, and laissez-faire. Normally the autocratic leader demands almost absolute control of the discussion, the delegating, and the decisions. The democratic leader has a sharing orientation, regularly soliciting counsel regarding direction and decision making. The laissez-faire leader (an uncommon commodity in the corporate environment) calls the meeting to order and "goes with the flow," exercising little if any authority.

Usually a combination autocratic-democratic approach works best. Often, the leader may be more autocratic about the process of moving the meeting along, but democratic in soliciting the views of others, particularly if his or her respect for them is high.

One of the more frequent stumbling blocks facing leaders of meetings is their inability to differentiate between being a traffic cop and being a resource person. That is, they tend to inject their points of view into the discussion prematurely, rather than first soliciting and listening carefully to the views of others. Moreover, this tendency often manifests itself more as pontification or condescension rather than as high-quality policy input. The net result—a meeting climate crippled by defensiveness and gripped by self-protection to prevent self-destruction.

SYSTEMATIC DISCUSSION AND DECISION MAKING

When addressing a policy question (e.g., "Should we decentralize our computer operation?"), consider the value of conducting a problem-solving analysis, a methodical step-by-step format for ferreting out the crucial issues and for facilitating a more rational and coherent approach:

Problem Analysis:
Addresses who or what is being or might be harmed or affected and to what extent. This includes defining and assessing the risk of lost opportunity. If no problem can be defined, there may be no need for further discussion or adoption of any solution being proposed.

Is there a problem with our centralized computer system? If so, what are its effects and how serious are they:
- From a time/cost standpoint?
- From a morale standpoint?

Causal Analysis:
Focuses on why the harm or potential for harm is occurring or could occur.

Is centralization definitely causing or contributing to the problem? If so, what aspects of centralization are contributing most to the problem? To what degree?

Solution Analysis:
Addresses the means by which the problem can be addressed effectively and economically.

Can adjustments be made to prevent the necessity of decentralizing? How easily? What is their potential effectiveness? Cost?
If we cannot make adjustments, what type of decentralizing design should we consider? To what extent does this resolve the problems addressed earlier? To what extent might it invite additional headaches? Or provide unexpected benefits?

While the example above is but a shorthand version of the many issues that could be raised in contemplating decentralization of a computer system, the main point is this: sound decision making normally dictates that we define a problem and its causes before we even consider a solution.

As you move through your agenda, you should address each issue and item in a logical progression:

1. As you proceed through the decision-making process, check for consensus: "Do we all agree that we have a serious problem with computer centralization and that the problem is . . . ?"

2. Take care to allow each person's idea to be discussed to its logical conclusion. Many meetings are collections of randomized thoughts searching desperately for a unifying comment.

3. From time to time, take a few moments to summarize the meeting's progress. It reinforces the quality of the meeting, helps keep everyone on track, and ensures a better set of minutes (which, normally, should be taken for standing-committee meetings by someone who volunteers or is designated by the leader).

4. If you have a tendency to assert your ideas prematurely or your dominance unduly, try converting your assertions into questions.

   Version 1: "I think we should hire an outside consultant to evaluate our computer capability."
   Version 2: "Should we hire an outside consultant to evaluate our computer capability?"

   Usually, the results are remarkable—a freer, more positive flow of ideas.

5. If you decide to establish a task force composed of selected meeting attendees, consider conducting the selection process in the privacy of your office. Conducting this process during the meeting itself can only embarrass the rejected members who wanted to be chosen. In addition, prepare a written "mission statement" for the task force, indicating deadlines and reporting times. Indeed, too many task forces die because of ill definition and poor follow-through by the executive who created them.

Two of the more frequent obstacles to an effective meeting are the monopolizer and the reluctant participant. In handling the monopolizer, consider the following options:

1. Interrupt him midflow to indicate politely that everyone understands what he is saying.

2. Interrupt him midflow with a question that can be addressed to someone else.
3. Establish less frequent eye contact with him.
4. As a last resort, speak with him privately, or ask someone else to—someone who may have his ear and who may be less prone to bruise his ego.

For the reluctant participant:

1. Call on him directly to participate, particularly regarding his expertise.
2. Reward his significant contributions with genuine positive reinforcement.
3. Go around the table for comments, thereby "forcing" his turn.
4. Speak with him privately—or ask someone else to.

Dealing with Impasse and Conflict

Effective leadership requires being able to resolve impasse and conflict. More often than not these problems are related to unclear use of language or misassumptions. For example, one person's conception of the word *competent* may be far different from another's. The effective leader persists in making sure that terms are defined and assumptions clarified. The effective leader is also aware of the dangers of being too consensus oriented. Unless he or she takes a properly timed firm stand, the climate of consensus can quickly turn to chaos.

If the conflict mounts, the leader may need to stress the common goals of the conflicting parties and then move from the less contested points to the more contested, hoping to build on a climate of trust and agreement. If this fails, then the parties may need another leader to resolve these differences. This approach does not necessarily compromise the leader's position. In fact, in certain situations, removing oneself from the fray can help preserve one's leadership position.

Concluding the Meeting

Every meeting needs a sense of closure and possible future direction. Therefore, instead of allowing a discussion of the last issue to "eat the clock," take charge of concluding the meeting:

- Restate the meeting objective.
- Summarize the meeting.
- Express appreciation.
- Present assignments and provide time for clarification.
- Announce the next meeting.

As a final word of advice, I recommend that executives solicit input regarding the quality of their meetings through an occasional "meeting about the meeting," individual meetings with participants, or a survey. The amount of time executives spend in meetings requires this all-too-ignored process of self-study to prevent them from being "meetinged to death."

THE ELECTRONIC MEETING

There was a time when most business was conducted by letter. Meetings were much too expensive because of the time and effort involved in gathering people together.

Then came the rapid growth of our modern economy and the simultaneous development of the airline industry, and it became possible to hold meetings almost anywhere in the nation and bring people in and out in one day.

But now the costs of doing business have caught up with many companies. The cost of travel and the value of time spent in getting from place to place—even on a jetliner—have caused many companies to rethink their priorities.

Technology has begun to offer a solution for many businesses—teleconferencing.

The sophistication of teleconferencing can vary from an extended telephone conference call to a color-and-sound private television broadcast. Your company can use this technology for board meetings, staff meetings, or addresses to employees. Your public relations department can use a teleconference to hold simultaneous news conferences across the nation.

Preparing for the Teleconference

What exactly is a teleconference? Present technology now makes many options possible:

- Multistation telephone conference calls using ordinary phones or sophisticated amplifiers and microphones that greatly increase audio quality
- Slide shows, videotapes, and other visual aids, which, shipped in advance to meeting sites, can complement an audio teleconference
- Transmission of facsimiles of documents via telecopier; hard-copy printouts of images from television screens at each conference site; and direct computer-to-computer electronic mail so that papers can be sent to participants before, during, or after a meeting
- "Electronic blackboards," which can transmit drawings as they are made from one location to another
- Links to dozens of locations around the country and the world through color television and sound

The above list is ordered by level of complexity, although technology is advancing so rapidly in this area that the full video conference—already in limited use—should be easily available to any company soon.

You should investigate the services of one of the many consultants already working in this field. Many will assume all the details of setting up a conference, including the temporary or permanent installation of necessary equipment and rental of rooms in remote locations. Some major national motel chains have begun to offer video conferences that employ the same satellite-dish technology used to bring in pay television movies to their guests.

Setting Up a Teleconference

Setting the time for a teleconference can involve a massive juggling act. You must find a time convenient to all the participants, bearing in mind that 9 A.M. in New York is 6 A.M. in Los Angeles, 3 P.M. in Paris, and 11 P.M. in Tokyo.

As the leader, you should prepare a clear agenda that includes a specific list of objectives for the meeting and send it to all participants in advance, along with any written materials and a list of all the participants, their titles, and their locations.

You should give some thought to the psychology of the teleconference. For example, teleconferences that discuss facts, ideas, or schedules, or engage in problem solving are generally more successful than those that involve negotiations, bargaining, or conflict resolution. People simply tend to be less comfortable dealing with these latter situations without the benefit of the many cues and factors extant in face-to-face interaction.

Conferences are usually more successful if the participants have previously met face to face. If not, circulating photographs of each participant in advance can establish a sense of familiarity.

Of course, the missing elements in a teleconference are eye contact and the visual elements of audience feedback. Some of this can be transmitted via a video conference.

Consider appointing a leader for each site to be linked to the conference. This person should be responsible for contacting participants, ordering visuals, arranging for refreshments, introducing participants, and encouraging participation.

Participants are often unsure of their social or political position in the teleconference, which includes their ability to interrupt and their range of freedom.

The chairperson should remain neutral, acting as a "host" and encouraging each participant to share equally in the meeting. One way of overcoming "mike fright" is for the chairperson to encourage a brief period of personal conversation back and forth at the start of the conference. This allows the participants to relax, just as they would at the convening of an ordinary face-to-face session.

During the opening discussions the teleconference operator can work to solve any technical problems.

This process of "assembly" also gives each participant a chance to associate a voice with a name.

The Teleconference Is Underway

At the assigned starting time, the conference chairperson or secretary should call the roll to assure that all the participants are on the line. After that, the leader should identify himself or herself and introduce each of the participants.

If an electronic blackboard is available at each location, it is often valuable to have each participant "sign in" or check off his or her name on a preprepared listing. If the conference is using television facilities, a listing of participants can be broadcast, and the speakers' names and locations can be superimposed on the screen as they speak.

All visual aids should be clearly marked with an identifying number and name. If slides are to be used, the chairperson should announce to all participants, as an example, "The next portion of the meeting will refer to the slide presentations I sent you. Please turn on your projectors and advance to slide number one."

The chairperson should always attempt to address each participant by name; it helps to reduce the artificial barrier and identifies the speaker to the other participants.

The conference should have a specified duration. If the conference must go on for several hours, breaks should be scheduled so that participants can talk informally or leave the room and return when the meeting starts again.

Participant Protocol*

- Be on time. You should be in your seat and ready for introductions at the appointed starting time.

*From Protocol for Video Teleconferencing Participants, Bell Atlantic Companies.

- Be prepared. Have your agenda and all appropriate materials handy.
- Be yourself—act and speak naturally. It is not unusual to experience a few initial jitters, but you'll lose them as your meeting progresses and you become more relaxed.
- Call other participants by name. This prompts individual reactions.
- Pause occasionally so that others may comment.
- Turn your head away from the microphone if you must cough or sneeze. Don't try to cover the microphone with your hand.
- Courtesy counts. If you want to make a point, wait for a lull, identify yourself, and begin to speak.
- If you are a presenter, plan carefully and be mindful of the time allotted to you.
- Stick to the agenda and save nonrelated discussion for a future meeting or teleconference.

Conclusion and Follow-up

At the conclusion of the meeting, the chairperson should summarize all the main elements in the conference and reiterate any decisions made. After a formal end to the meeting, the lines should be kept open for a while to allow informal discussion— just as people tend to talk to each other about a meeting as they walk out the door.

Now the time for follow-up has arrived. This may include, but not necessarily be limited to: distributing minutes, confirming assignments and action items, contacting participants who need additional information or who can provide further input, circulating decisions and action plans, and analyzing the effectiveness of the teleconference itself.

Before you jump on a plane for a meeting in Chicago, Dallas, Los Angeles, or wherever, ask yourself, "Can I capture the persuasive edge just as well via a teleconference?" If "the personal touch" is not a major reason for your trip, then a teleconference may save you time, money, and, given the nature of today's airline travel, a lot of anxiety.

Chapter 22

PANELS AND
DEBATES

You are asked to participate in a panel discussion or a debate. Where do you begin?

Step one (assuming you are available) is to determine whether or not the engagement is worthwhile to you and your organization. Can participation

- Enhance your company's profile or image?
- Enhance your industry's profile or image?
- Enhance your profile or image?
- Attract new recruits to your company?
- Potentially enhance sales?
- Defuse critics?
- Enlarge your support base?

Put another way, could your failure to participate hurt your company, industry, or you in some manner, by generating bad feelings for example, or even negative publicity? Again, I recommend that you keenly define what net-effects goals (positive and preventive, overt and covert) you might or might not attain by responding "count me in" to an invitation to participate on a panel or in a debate.

In making such an assessment, ask yourself whether sharing the limelight with others might dilute the audience's attention on you, especially if the panel or debate climate becomes highly competitive. This concern explains why I frequently advise my clients to try to secure a sole position on a program before agreeing to participate on a panel or in a debate.

THE FORMAT

Once you've defined your net-effects goals, you're not quite ready to decide whether or not to participate. You first need to understand fully the format and the cast of characters:

- What is the specific topic for the program?
- Who will moderate the program?
- How good a job do you expect him or her to do?
- Can you expect fair treatment from this person?
- Who else is participating?
- What are their goals?
- Are their points of view compatible or in conflict with yours?
- Are you and they on the same status level? (E.g., CEOs don't want to appear on the same panel with vice presidents).
- What do you know—or can you learn—about the other participants' speaking or debating skills?

Next, you'll need to find out what the ground rules are:

- Will there be opening remarks?
- How long will they be?
- Will participants be presented from a standing or seated position?
- How will the Q&A take place?
- Will panelists be allowed to question one another?
- When and how will audience questions be fielded? By spontaneous participation? By written questions being submitted in advance?
- How long will the question-and-answer segment last?

- Will time limits be placed on Q&A? Do these limits provide sufficient time—or are they excessive?
- How will the sequencing of speakers be established? How strictly will it be enforced?

What is the nature of the staging?

- Who will sit where?
- What will be the nature and color of the backdrop?
- Where will lecterns be placed?
- How will the participants take the stage?

Who will attend and what ground rules will apply to them?

- Will the audience be balanced or will it be stacked for or against you?
- Will new audience members be admitted once the program begins?
- What will be their seating arrangement?
- Will a "no applause until the end" rule be put into effect?
- Are provisions made for handling disruptive audience members?

The questions listed above are but a sampling of the hundreds posed and often hotly debated during format negotiations for televised political debates. And when the candidates can't come to terms, the debates don't occur.

Regardless of whether you're invited to participate on a panel or in a political or nonpolitical debate, you, too, should not necessarily accept a proposed format lock, stock, and barrel. If you feel that the format should somehow be adjusted, say so. In fact, if the format is decidedly problematic (e.g., you're not being given enough time to express your position), you may need to gently, or not so gently, offer an ultimatum: "Give me more time or I will not participate."

GETTING READY

Once you've resolved the preliminaries related to your decision to participate and to the format, you're ready to begin the preparation process. This involves defining your target audience as precisely as possible; setting your substance goals (including your key messages); setting your image goals; studying; and practicing.

Once you're ready to practice, establish a clear set of criteria for analyzing your performance. I regularly use the following checklist to prepare candidates and executives for debates and panels. Be sure you're satisfied with your performance level for each of these criteria:

- Fluency and clarity
- Ability to memorize themes and arguments
- Ability to memorize statistical and numerical information
- Ability to deliver both opening and closing addresses clearly and confidently under time constraints
- Ability to listen carefully to and dissect panelists' questions
- Ability to listen carefully to and dissect opponents' responses
- Ability to produce clear, coherent, concise, and cogent initial responses and rebuttals in a given period of time
- Ability to produce concrete illustrations and examples
- Ability to produce appeals linking your positions with your audience's values, needs, and attitudes
- General comfort level in a nontelevised audience setting
- General comfort level in a television studio, with or without an audience
- Ability to control nonverbal reactions, such as eye contact, facial expressions, gestures, and tone of voice.

As you prepare, keep in mind your six response options and the accompanying advice:

1. *To sell or advocate a position, action, or record.* Normally you should "sell" more than attack. Otherwise you could be branded as too negative. Select your "sell" points based on what will most likely impress your target audience.

2. *To defend or refute.* Defending or refuting is especially appropriate if your opponent has possibly undermined your target audience's regard for you. The key is to avoid appearing too defensive, a formidable challenge if you are becoming a bigger issue than any of your positions.

3. *To attack.* Keep your target audience in mind when selecting a line of attack. Avoid stridency; it normally results in a backlash effect that rebounds to your opponent's favor.

4. *To counterattack.* Pointed counterattack can be enormously effective, particularly if it is a turning-the-tables ploy that implies that the opponent is hypocritical (e.g., "How dare you criticize me for X when your record regarding X is deplorable?"). When advancing a counterattack, ask yourself if your target audience might be more interested in a refutation or defense. If so, a combination of defense/counterattack may be the perfect move.

5. *To agree.* Agreeing with your opponent can project your likability or statesmanlike demeanor. However, make sure you are *not* conceding an important point or inviting the accusation that you were too "me-too" in the debate.

6. *To ignore.* Ignoring your opponent verbally and visually can be a viable option when he or she is obviously trying to goad you or when an attack has been leveled that your target audience is likely to perceive as not credible. This is frequently a difficult decision, but an important one if you are committed to sticking to your game plan and not to attacking your opponents.

TACTICS

To fulfill your substance and image goals, there are three ways in which you relate to the audience: *physical* (actual movements), *forensic* (argumentative behaviors or ploys), and *tonal* (attitude or tone projected through physical and vocal cues).*

Physical Tactics

Getting on stage. Should you take the stage first or wait to make a grand entrance? The first participant can project his or her confidence and eagerness to do battle. However, he or she could be left anxiously onstage waiting for his or her opponent. The late-comer can create an air of expectation, which, upon his arrival, allows him or her to take command of the stage. This was the decision made by Ronald Reagan in his 1980 debate with President Jimmy Carter. (I was Reagan's personal debate adviser.) Reagan heightened his command by walking across the stage to shake President Carter's hand. This not only projected Reagan's image of command and friendliness, but it caught Carter by surprise and diminished him before 120 million television viewers.

Eye contact. If you are on television, the camera affords the audience a much closer view of your gaze than that received by persons in the room with you. Think about what your eye contact might communicate. Sometimes you might not want to watch your opponent when he is speaking for fear that you will communicate too much interest in what he is saying. Or you may choose to ignore visually and orally a minor opponent in order to prevent giving him unwarranted legitimacy. There is a fine line, though, between these tactical considerations and the appearance of arrogance or inappropriate disrespect.

During preparations for the 1980 presidential debates, we ad-

*For a more detailed discussion regarding debate strategy and tactics see my book, *Political Campaign Debates: Images, Strategies and Tactics* (New York: Longman, 1983, pp. 57–115.)

vised Reagan to look at Carter when expressing righteous indignation. ("There you go again," was Reagan's famous phrase.) He was also advised against looking downward, a tendency he had shown in an earlier debate with presidential candidate John Anderson—a look that suggested a lack of confidence, indecisiveness, or lack of preparation.

Note taking can complement your eye-contact tactics. In 1976, President Gerald Ford was advised to take notes in his debates with Governor Jimmy Carter, not only to help him remember points he wanted to make but also to distract his audience from his expression when Carter was saying something with which he disagreed.

A debater may decide to stare down an opponent or even point a finger at him to communicate willingness to confront him. This tactic is often effective, but can backfire if it is too obvious or showy. In John Anderson's 1980 Illinois Republican primary debate against George Bush, Anderson called Bush on this behavior: "George, you don't have to point your finger at me. Really, don't get so excited."

Seated or standing? During the negotiations that led to the 1976 debates between President Ford and Governor Carter, much controversy involved whether the candidates should stand or sit. Carter's aides wanted their candidate to sit on stage in order to communicate his informal style. Ford's advisors wanted him to stand, a more "presidential" demeanor. The compromise allowed for stools behind the lecterns.

The proper smile. There is little doubt that the public is impressed with the "nice guy." Looking too serious can communicate a lack of confidence and a feeling of tension. In 1980, Reagan's engaging smile contrasted strongly with Anderson's taut, professorial face and with Carter's edgy, self-conscious appearance. But be careful: a fine line exists between a friendly smile and a disrespectful smirk.

Forensic Tactics

Forewarning. If you can anticipate your opponent's attacks, you might find it useful to forewarn the audience of them and answer them in advance.

The shotgun blast or the laundry list. A forceful combination of accusations or questions can leave your opponent with too many points to answer effectively or force him or her to go on the offensive ill prepared. The risks are that your opponent will be able to answer your points or mount a strong offense of his or her own.

Turning the table. Redirecting an opponent's attack back at him or her can often be successful (e.g., "You have called into question my record on environmental protection. Let's take a look at the legislation you've approved that has resulted in an increase in acid rain and toxic chemical dumping.").

Flat denial. Assuming you are dead certain of your facts, a flat denial is a very strong argumentative statement. You can say, "That is not true," or you can combine a denial with an unspoken message, as in Reagan's "There you go again" to Carter. Flat denial, therefore, can carry a ring of confidence and authority stronger than the most sophisticated, developed argument.

Tossing a bouquet. In certain instances it may be advisable to compliment your opponent on conduct in office or business. This projects an image of fair-mindedness, diminishes the impression that you are overly contentious, and may make it more difficult for your opponent to direct a strong attack against you.

Timing. How you use time has numerous implications. If exposure is important to you, then you will need to compete for as much time as possible—perhaps aggressively. The more you can keep your opponent "off the tube," the more you will both limit his or her attacks and increase your visibility and opportunity to capture the persuasive edge.

Tonal Tactics

Controlling backlash. Backlash, generated when we are perceived as too harsh or negative, is one of the more serious risks facing a debater. The more prepared the debater is to "sell" or to advocate a position *strongly* and *positively,* the less the potential for backlash.

Avoiding defensiveness. Righteous indignation is the happy medium between too much anger and too much defensiveness. By projecting this trait or tone the debater appeals to the audience's sense of fair play and diminishes the potential for backlash.

Chapter 23

EXECUTIVE TESTIMONY

Presenting testimony before a regulatory or legislative body offers a highly structured—and legally predefined—forum for a persuasive presentation.

Testimony is the presentation of facts, opinions, or, in some cases, arguments to influence the decision of a judicial, administrative, or legislative body.

If you are called to testify in a civil or criminal court, some of the discussion about behavior in the witness chair may be of value to you, but this chapter is not meant to serve as instruction on appearances in a court of law.

Clearly, testimony is a form of communication, and your ability to capture the persuasive edge as a witness depends upon many of the same factors discussed in the earlier chapters on speech presentation and question-and-answer sessions. There are, however, some aspects of testimony that require special attention:

- Testimony is generally given under oath, and witnesses are subject to the laws of perjury governing the jurisdiction involved.
- It is usually presented in a true adversarial setting, in which other participants have a direct, financial interest in the proceedings.

- It is generally subject to "rules of evidence," a sometimes peculiar body of rules governing style and content.
- A witness is usually subject to a unique—and sometimes difficult—form of structured questioning and testing referred to as cross-examination.
- The success or failure of testimony can often be measured by tangible results; whether or not the position is accepted or rejected. To put it another way, a corporation or government agency may be more forgiving of an ineffective presentation in which the consequence is a few days of bad press than of one in which the consequence is the loss of tens of millions of dollars.

In quasi-judicial settings, such as utility-rate case hearings, testimony is very much dependent upon the cooperation of the witness and his or her attorney; its effectiveness is almost directly proportional to the extent to which the skills of the witness and the lawyer are coordinated.

Think back on the lessons of the chapter on listening: The stress of being on the stand is considerable, and in large part your ability to listen effectively will determine the level of success you will have in delivering your message.

A PRIMER FOR WITNESS AND LAWYER

The Lawyer's Role

The lawyer is ultimately responsible for the outcome of the case. It is his or her job to determine the legal requirements necessary to bring about a desired result, to communicate those to the witness, to try to make certain that the witness's evidence meets those requirements, to assist the witness in direct and cross-examination, to use the witness in cross-examining opposing experts, and to defend or attack a decision in an appeal.

The lawyer and the witness, obviously, must function together as a team:

- The lawyer must alert the witness to the specific requirements of a regulatory hearing, legislative session, or court. There must be adequate time left to prepare and to rehearse.
- You should expect instruction in how to handle peculiar rules of evidence. Is hearsay a problem? If so, it is up to the lawyer to propose a solution. Are the witness's working papers and draft reports "discoverable" by the opposition? If so, you should be instructed to be careful about committing preliminary conclusions to paper.
- The lawyer should know the opposition and alert the witness to any unusual events that may occur. Is the opposing attorney the type given to histrionics? Will he or she yell and scream? If so, practice being calm. Is the opposing attorney not likely to follow up a question? If so, practice giving short, direct answers.
- Finally, you should expect information on the various rules of interrogation. For example, what (if anything) can be done to protect you when you are being cross-examined? Can you expect your attorney to object when the going gets rough, or will he or she stand back so as not to give too much of a tip-off? One helpful technique is to ask for consultation with your attorney; if you start this early and often, it may become accepted and not be regarded as a sign of weakness at difficult moments.

The Witness's Role

The witness bears the ultimate responsibility of persuading the decision makers to adopt his or her position.

This is the most difficult task, and it involves more than a detailed mastery of the subject. It also requires an ability to marshal all available facts to back up each and every opinion, plus the skill to present the material in an understandable and convincing manner.

- You must teach the lawyer the subject matter and point out pitfalls and weak spots in his or her case.
- As a witness, you must help to examine the opponent's case and assist the lawyer in analyzing it and in cross-examining opposing experts.
- You must take great care to be consistent with any prior public statements on the issue. Lawyers will try to turn up past testimony or publications and use any inconsistencies or contradictions to impeach your credibility. You must let your lawyer know of any prior work you've done on the subject and alert him or her to any mine fields.
- Finally you must assist the lawyer in preparing legal briefs. Has the lawyer included all available facts in support of the argument? If a critical fact is missing from the record, are there any accepted reference materials that could be cited?

Presentation of testimony has two phases—the first "opportunity," and the second "protective." The ultimate success of a witness's efforts will depend upon the extent to which he or she has taken advantage of the opportunity to present the company's case in the best possible light and the extent to which he or she avoided the pitfalls presented by the opposition.

DIRECT TESTIMONY— THE FIRST OPPORTUNITY

This is the time to put forth facts or supported opinions without interruption or interference. Depending upon the forum, you may prepare your statement in advance and present it in writing (if you're appearing before administrative and regulatory agencies) or present it orally from the witness stand (if you're appearing in a court of law).

Preparation

Know your case. In most cases you will be just one of several witnesses presented by your side. It is essential that you understand your role as part of the team. Your testimony must be part of an overall strategy.

Know your adversary's case. Don't contribute to the opposition when you've got the floor to yourself. If you know what your adversary is trying to prove, you can attempt to avoid giving him or her a helping hand during your own direct presentation.

Know your forum. Who are the decision makers? What are the rules? Generally, administrative agencies present far more permissive forums than do courts. Rules of evidence and procedure are not applied as strictly. In particular, an administrative or regulatory setting may give you the opportunity to offer "expert" opinions in your testimony for which a court of law might find you unqualified.

Identify your net-effects, substance, and image goals. What are the most important goals you need to accomplish? What key messages or themes can best help you achieve these goals? Tailor your message to reinforce them.

Know what you want to say. The most obvious element of preparation is to know thoroughly the facts or opinions you will present in your direct testimony. If you are being questioned by your own attorney and you are aware of an important issue or fact that has not been raised, you have the responsibility to do so. While your answer may appear to be out of place, all that really matters is that the fact or opinion become part of the record of the proceeding; it does not matter how it got there.

Presentation

Be clear. Direct testimony has only one purpose—to communicate facts or opinions favorable to your side. No matter how well prepared a witness is and no matter how thorough the witness is in presentation, the entire process is meaningless unless the decision maker understands the facts and the message.

Avoid technical jargon, presenting too many concepts in one sentence, as well as oversimplification. You should assume that your audience is mature and intelligent but knows little or nothing about the subject matter of your testimony.

Be yourself. Don't put on a role that isn't natural for you. Your purpose is to present material facts and opinions; it is not to showcase your knowledgeability beyond the issues at hand. And it is *not* to entertain.

Don't vary the script. You and your attorney should have rehearsed your appearance, particularly for oral testimony presented from the witness stand. Don't make changes in the heat of the moment.

Be fully truthful!

CROSS-EXAMINATION:
THE SECOND OPPORTUNITY

Your primary assignment when under cross-examination is to avoid undoing all the positive and productive accomplishments of your direct testimony. Beyond that, you may be presented with or stumble across an opportunity to repeat and reinforce portions of your direct testimony. Be prepared to take advantage of these opportunities.

It is important to understand the purposes of cross-examination: first, to reduce the effect or to impeach the credibility of your direct testimony in the eyes of the decision maker by attacks on you or your testimony; and second, to try to get you to agree with some element of the overall theory of your adversary's case.

Almost every attorney has been taught two basic rules of cross-examination: (a) that a lawyer should never ask a question to which he does not already know the answer; and (b) that all questions should be leading questions—that is, they should suggest a particular answer (see chapter 14 re: "banana peels").

As with direct examination, you should know the overall theory of your side's case so that you can recognize attempts to impeach any aspect of it. These attempts can be indirect. For example, you might be asked a question that appears to have no bearing on your own testimony, but it may in effect impeach the testimony of another witness for your side.

Preparation

Review the past. You must assume that anything you've ever said or committed to print can and will be used against you by an effective cross-examiner. Review previous testimony for contradictions or for changes in fact or policy. Be sure to advise your own attorney of your history.

Anticipate the questioning. Almost every case contains some weaknesses, and your opposition will seek to exploit them during cross-examination. If the weaknesses are obvious, one tactic is to discuss them in the most favorable light in your direct presentation. If the weaknesses are more subtle, you must assume that the opposition will recognize them and attempt to use them. You should anticipate the most damaging possible questions and come up with answers to neutralize them.

Once you've formulated an appropriate answer, make notes of the points you want to use. But don't memorize the exact phrases. At best, a memorized answer may make you appear programmed; at worst, if your memory fails, you could look as though you've had a mental power failure.

Your attorney should work with you in practice sessions, simulating your appearance on the witness stand. One practice that has become increasingly popular is to select a speech communication expert and an additional attorney as consultants. Preferably, the attorney should be someone who has represented opposing interests in the specific administrative jurisdiction involved. You should guard against the reality and the appearance of conflict of interest. In addition, you should also seek an agreement with this attorney that he or she will not turn around and face your company in a future proceeding.

PRACTICE SESSIONS

Your practice session should be as close a simulation of the real setting as possible. Set up the tables and chairs in a conference room to simulate the positions of the hearing officer and opposing counsel. If television crews are expected to appear, use high-intensity lighting in the room. If your company has video equipment, record the session for review.

Go through your presentation. Your counsel should offer the same type of assistance he or she will be able to give at the actual hearing—no more and no less. Your "outside" legal consultant should play the role of opposing attorney and be as realistic and as demanding as possible.

Under Cross-Examination

Of course you're nervous. Who wouldn't be? In fact, if you're not nervous, that may be a danger signal. Tension is a sign and a product of the ability to think. The nervousness will not last. As the questions are fired at you in cross-examination, you will quickly begin thinking about the subject rather than about yourself.

Trust yourself. You know who you are and that your abilities have brought you to the position you hold. And you know you have been called to answer questions because you know the answers. Do your job!

Here are some suggestions for your behavior on the stand:

Don't be disarmed. Many witnesses are thrown for a loop when confronted by a cross-examining attorney who adopts the style of a favorite relative or a naive and stumbling rube. He or she may well be one or the other, but remember, no matter how nice, charming, or helpless a cross-examiner may appear, he or she is paid to tear your case apart—and you with it if necessary.

Don't be intimidated. Remember that you will be facing leading questions and loaded questions. If you believe a simple yes or no answer is misleading or inadequate, don't hesitate to offer further explanation, no matter how hard the cross-examiner tries to prevent that explanation.

Don't punish yourself. Almost inevitably you're going to make some type of mistake. Don't dwell on it. Cross-examination can proceed at a very rapid pace, and you will only make the problem worse if you allow guilt or remorse to distract you. Look instead for an opportunity to rehabilitate yourself.

Don't argue. Regardless of the provocation, don't engage in an argument. Keep your cool. Even the most inflammatory question should be addressed with composure ("Yes, my wife is a bookie. But she reports all of her income faithfully on her federal tax form."). Let the questioner lose his or her composure—you'll look the better for it.

Don't emote. This is not your chance to display your contempt for lawyers or the judicial process, nor to show your fine wit or discuss your pet peeves. Answer all questions soberly and with dignity.

Listen very carefully to the opposition's questions. Of all the skills you will bring to the witness stand, perhaps the most important is your ability to listen. Trick questions ("Are you still beating your wife?") are rarely put forth deliberately. However, lawyers do pose ambiguous questions by accident. If you are asked an unclear question and you answer it, your reply will also very likely be unclear. And be assured that at the end of the case, the lawyer for the opposition will argue for his or her interpretation of what you meant, not yours. If the question is not clear, simply throw it back. Say, "I don't understand your question. Can you put it another way?" or "Do you mean . . ." and then say what you think the attorney meant.

Listen very carefully to your own attorney. In particular, pay attention if your attorney makes an objection to the question posed to you. Often your attorney will make such an objection with no real expectation that the judge will agree. Instead it was meant as a signal to you to be particularly careful in responding.

Think before you answer a question. Despite the impression you may have gained from television portrayals of courtroom procedure, a witness is entitled to take a reasonable amount of time to think through an answer. In fact, pausing before answering every question is a very good tactic. You may not need much time to answer the question "How long have you worked for the company?" But if you consistently pause before answering a question, you will buy yourself some free time to think when the going gets rough—without appearing to be stalling or searching for an answer.

Don't guess at an answer. If you don't know, say so: "I don't know," or "I'll have to look it up and answer later," or defer to an upcoming witness. That's a much better position to be in than to guess wrongly and give the impression that you're a dunce—or worse, destroy your credibility.

Don't volunteer unasked-for information. Remember the setting you're in; don't lapse into ordinary social conversation. The opposing attorney may ask, "When did you last hire an industrial engineer?" Going well overboard, you might answer, "That was Joe Doakes. We hired him last November at a starting salary of thirty thousand dollars a year, but of course he got a raise along with all the other nonunion personnel when the strike was over. We always try to adjust the nonunion scale when the union rates change." This unnecessary gabbiness is likely to invite the opposing lawyer to ask about the strike, about management personnel policy—perhaps even to demand a ten-year accounting to show whether and to what extent *every* nonunion employee was given a raise after each union contract. Is that what you want?

By the way, the correct answer to that question was, "Last November."

And remember again,
Always tell the truth!

LEGALITIES YOU SHOULD KNOW

Laws differ in each state and locality and in each administrative or legislative setting. However, here are some broadly stated general principles you should know:

The burden of proof. In general, if your company is seeking a particular regulatory position—as an example, a utility seeking a rate change—the burden of proof is with your side. The previously approved position, rate, or rule is presumed to be reasonable. Therefore, any party seeking to adjust the existing position cannot simply suggest that a change be made. Instead, they will usually have the legal burden of persuading the decision-making body that an adjustment is necessary.

The record. In quasi-judicial hearings the decision-making body is normally supposed to limit its consideration to those elements contained in the record of the proceeding. This means that all factual matters necessary to meet the burden of proof must be included. Your side must make a careful analysis of each logical step in your case to make certain that every point is supported by acceptable evidence. If you forget to get a key fact into the record of a regulatory hearing, it is possible to reopen the proceeding for the limited purpose of hearing the omitted evidence; or an affidavit can be submitted setting forth the missing material.

Rules of evidence. The rules of evidence used in courtrooms are almost impossibly complex. However, the rules used in administrative settings have been greatly simplified. As a general matter, any evidence can be admitted if it is of the type that "responsible persons are accustomed to rely upon in the conduct of serious affairs." Under this test, hearsay evidence is usually accepted, unless it seems too remote. (Hearsay can be briefly defined as "an out-of-court statement by a person not a witness in the proceeding.")

CONGRESSIONAL AND LEGISLATIVE TESTIMONY

A legislative hearing is usually more in the arena of politics than matters of fact, but your needs as a persuasive speaker are no less real.

- First of all, define your net-effects, substance, and image goals vis-à-vis your target audience.
- Determine who is on the committee and what their particular

goals (including their "hidden agenda") and interests might be. How do they perceive you, your company, your position?

- Attend a hearing conducted by the committee, analyze a hearing transcript—or both. What kinds of questions are asked? Who seems particularly interested in which issues or types of issues? What is the committee's tendency to use "banana peels"? Who else has spoken or will speak on the issue? What have they said or will they say? How does your position in the "batting order" influence what you need to say?

- Determine in advance the layout of the room.

- Find out as much as you can about the norms of the committee or subcommittee. For instance, a written statement is almost always requested for the record, but during your appearance it might be common practice to speak extemporaneously on a subject. (If the extemporaneous presentation is permissible, I strongly recommend it.) What are the time limits? How strictly are they enforced? What types of exhibits are allowable and potentially effective?

- Decide whether you need to be accompanied by counsel. What will be his or her specific role during the hearing?

- If you are going to be making a joint appearance, work out a scheme in advance to separate subject matter and to defer questions.

- Don't be afraid to ask the members of the panel a question, whether in search of clarification or merely to indicate your interest in their perceptions. It can draw the committee or subcommittee into your presentation.

- Deliver the prepared or extemporaneously prepared testimony with feeling, applying many of the principles discussed in chapters 11 through 13. In fact, a friend of mine who served for three terms as a congressman told me that the most painful part of his job on Capitol Hill was attending hearings; there, he complained, he had to subject himself to seemingly interminable sessions marked by lifeless, boring testimony.

- Finally, engage in a simulated hearing. It will sharpen your presentation, your answers, and your confidence.

Chapter 24

SPECIAL ISSUES

HOW DO WE PREPARE
FOR A TEAM PRESENTATION?

Capturing the persuasive edge is often a collective effort involving a team of presenters. Among the more popular settings for team presentations in the business world are meetings before financial analysts, annual shareholder meetings, sales conferences, and perhaps the most popular of all, the team presentation before a prospective client.

The four interrelated criteria governing an effective team presentation are unity, smoothness, consistency, and overall professionalism. Unity involves the impression that the entire team presentation coheres as a single unit. Smoothness refers to the logic of the overall program, including the quality of flow from one presentation to the next. Consistency pertains to the capacity of the presenters to present messages that do not conflict in content or tone. Overall professionalism connotes the net impression of the entire program, including each presentation within it.

The following advice should help you meet these criteria:

1. Designate a team leader.

2. Select the presentation team carefully. What should be the size of the team? What criteria should govern the selection process (e.g., expertise, presentation skills, political considerations)? How should each criterion be weighed?

3. Define the net-effects, substance, and image goals for the overall team presentation and for each individual presentation vis-à-vis your target audience(s). Make sure each presentation helps fulfill the team presentation goals.

4. Select a theme for the overall presentation that can be reinforced by each individual presentation.

5. Encourage cross-references to other presentations to help promote the perception of unity.

6. Work out seating and overall team choreography in advance to ensure smoothness.

7. Decide how each presenter is to be introduced. By the leader or by the chair? By the preceding speaker? Make sure that the introductions accentuate both the person's credentials and the program theme.

8. Conduct at least one dry run. To prevent last-minute changes, schedule it sufficiently in advance of the actual presentation.

9. Decide in advance how questions will be fielded. Do you need to assign certain topic areas to certain presenters? Work out a pattern for interjections.

10. When the presentation is over, conduct a debriefing. (I dislike the term *postmortem;* its literal translation is too morbid—and unrealistic if you faithfully follow the advice presented above.) Analyze the strengths and weaknesses and carry over your insights into future team presentations.

SHOULD YOU
HIRE A SPEECH WRITER?

You have an attorney to handle your legal affairs. You have an accountant to take care of the books. You have an appointments secretary to keep track of your schedule. If you speak frequently, you may need to hire a speech writer.

How do you choose a speech writer? You are, in effect, selecting a partner and confidant, a person who will be privy to some of your secrets. You want someone who will not be afraid to tell you when you are not at your best or afraid to make suggestions.

You also want someone who knows the business: how to conduct research, the meaning of a deadline, and the way business operates. Not just any writer will do either: he or she must have an ear for oral speech and, perhaps most important, the ability to adapt his or her writing to your tone and style.

You and Your Speech Writer

Making the relationship between you and your writer work requires your willingness to invest in the relationship, particularly to provide reasonable access. If you simply tell the writer (possibly through his or her boss) that you need a speech for a certain engagement, chances are great that your writer will not hit the mark squarely. However, if you meet directly with the writer to discuss the engagement, the likelihood of receiving a satisfactory draft increases greatly.

Advice for the Executive:

- Before you meet, collect and, if time permits, write down your initial thoughts.
- When you meet with the writer, make sure that you have collected sufficient background information regarding the audience, occasion, and setting.
- Thoroughly discuss net-effects, substance, and image goals.

- Allow the writer to tape-record your conversation.
- Consider asking the writer to present you with a sentence or theme outline before the writing process begins.
- Return drafts and outlines promptly.
- If the writer is new, be open in providing feedback regarding your stylistic preferences. For example, do you like to avoid or use certain terms? Do you enjoy using quotes, illustrations, anecdotes, rhetorical questions, lists, and so on?
- Provide feedback regarding the exact format in which the manuscript is to appear.
- Allow the writer to see you speak and then invite an open feedback discussion.

Advice for the Writer:

- Try to learn the subject of your meeting in advance. Any reading you can do on the topic of the speech beforehand can make the meeting more effective. If you've read anything the executive might also benefit from reading, be prepared to offer him or her a copy.
- Prepare in advance the questions you need to ask. Plan to press hard to define goals precisely.
- If your writing or thinking is criticized—even mildly—keep your ego, pride, and defensiveness in check. Remember that the executive needs to "own" as much of the speech as possible (see chapter 10).
- Offer to provide support beyond the writing itself, for example, analysis of the audience, occasion, and setting.
- Following the engagement, encourage open feedback regarding what appeared to work and what didn't. Whenever possible, review audio and video tapes.

HOW SHOULD YOU
CHOOSE A GUEST SPEAKER?

Choosing a guest speaker to reinforce the tone or theme of a major business conference is frequently a challenging decision, for the risk of selecting someone who might bomb is very real. The following advice, based on years of both helping organizations select speakers and helping speakers select organizations should prove helpful:

- Define your specific goals in selecting a guest speaker. Are you seeking to boost attendance? Influence the sense of prestige of the event? Create a specific tone?
- Decide which is more important, the speaker's name or the message. Although many speakers have both, some with names don't have a quality message or a distinguished speaking style. However, many less-known speakers do have important messages and the requisite talent to deliver them.
- Decide how much you want to pay. Top speaking talent in the "star" category is commanding between $10,000 and $35,000 per engagement, plus expenses.
- If you choose a "star," are you in effect committing yourself to selecting one year after year? If so, the selection process and the costs can become onerous.
- Consider using a speaker's bureau. Some bureaus have exclusive arrangements with speakers. Others serve mainly as brokers. If you work through an agent or broker, you may be able to book two or more superior speakers for the same amount you would pay a star. But again, your meeting goals should influence this decision.
- Working with the broker rather than approaching the agent directly may result in a double commission. This doesn't mean you shouldn't work with a broker, just make sure you understand the basis for the fee.
- Check with your trade organization to determine if it offers a list of recommended speakers. However, do have a backup

plan worked out. Here the speaker's bureau can be most helpful.

- Learn as much as possible about the proposed speaker ahead of time. The speaker or speaker's bureau should provide videotapes of the speaker appearing before a live audience plus a list of organizations addressed.
- If you find it difficult to afford a proposed speaker's fee, consider negotiating, especially if the audience is small or your organization is civic or charitable. However, don't be surprised if you are turned down. Speakers in demand have many engagements from which to choose. Moreover, they don't want to develop a reputation for giving one organization preferential treatment over another.
- It's not very likely that a speaker will cancel on you because of illness, a work-related emergency, or for some other reason. However, do prepare a backup plan. Here, a speaker's bureau can be most helpful.

Arranging for a Guest Speaker

- Confirm all arrangements in writing, including the date, time, location, and topic. Include background information regarding your organization as well as the specific program schedule and the introducer. Clarify audience expectations. Are they looking for fresh insight, motivation, humor, or some other quality? How formal will the session be? Will spouses be invited? Is your speaker expected to answer questions? Attend special functions? Will any media be represented?
- Outline in writing answers to all the questions you should ask yourself before making a major presentation.
- Appoint a contact person for the speaker and the bureau.
- Ask the speaker or agent to provide biographical information, photographs, advance texts, and so on.
- Try to meet with the speaker or talk with him or her by telephone at least a few weeks ahead of time. Determine his or her willingness to tailor the speech to your audience. Be prepared to offer specific advice.

- Arrange a rehearsal period if requested.
- Extend your organization's hospitality fully.
- Do your best to ensure that your program allows the speaker to be on schedule.
- Make sure that the speaker is well introduced.

WHERE TO FIND QUALITY SPEAKERS

American Program Bureau Inc.
Riverbend Office Park
Nine Galen Street
Watertown, Massachusetts
02172
(800) 225-4575; (617) 926-0600

Celebrity Speakers
1042 Second Street, Suite 3
Santa Monica, California 90403
(818) 887-5066

Chicago Speakers Bureau
414 N. Orleans # 606
Chicago, Illinois 60610
(312) 661-0616

Cosby Bureau International Inc.
2162 Wisconsin Avenue NW
Washington, D.C. 20007
(202) 833-2344

The Leigh Bureau
100 Herrontown Road
Princeton, New Jersey 08540
(609) 921-6141

National Speakers Association
4747 North Seventh Street
Phoenix, Arizona 85014-4506
(602) 265-1001

Nat'l Speakers Bureau, Inc.
222 Wisconsin Avenue
Lake Forest, Illinois 60045
(312) 295-1122; (800) 323-9442

National Speakers Forum
1629 K Street NW, Suite 700
Washington, D.C. 20006
(202) 293-5508

Harry Walker Agency Inc.
1 Penn Plaza, Suite 2400
New York, New York 10119
(212) 563-0700

Washington Speakers Bureau
310 South Henry Street
Alexandria, Virginia 22314
(703) 684-0555

SHOULD YOU RETAIN A COMMUNICATION CONSULTANT?

You're standing at the front of a room squinting into the glare of television lamps. A bouquet of microphones is arranged on the podium. Before you—some standing, some seated, some politely extending an index finger, others violently waving arms or note-books—are a dozen reporters.

They all begin yelling at the same moment:

"What are you going to do about . . . ?"

"When did you first learn . . . ?"

"Will you call for an evacuation . . . ?"

"Why did your company allow this to happen . . . ?"

"How could this sort of gross negligence occur . . . ?"

You choose one of the questions to answer, but you are inter-rupted—first by a technician who walks in front of you and holds a light meter in your face, next by a late-arriving radio reporter who tries to tape his microphone to your notebook, and finally by an impatient television "star" reporter at the back who insists that you answer his question now.

Is this every spokesperson's worst dream? Quite possibly. But in this instance, you're paying for the privilege of the abuse. The "reporters" in this scene are trained consultants; the "television crews" are filming you to allow you to see your reactions to stress and to help you learn; the "disaster" script you're working from comes from the real possibilities inherent in your own company. The scene comes from a training session of one of the profes-sional communication consultants available to executives.

In addition to the press conference simulation (and it feels like no simulation at all to the participant), a communication consul-tant can lead you through demonstrations of talk shows, one-on-one interviews with a reporter, telephone interviews, and crisis training. The speech-presentation program includes speeches from notes and from outlines, fielding questions, plus other situations. All work is videotaped and critiqued, and participating companies can obtain copies of the tapes for further use after the seminar.

Do you need to engage the services of a professional consul-tant? You regarded the subject of executive communication im-portant enough to read this book. A program or retainer offered by the consultant may provide the perfect postgraduate course.

Consider the following criteria when you decide to engage a consultant:

- A professional background in speaking, the electronic media, or print journalism
- A strong client list, including positive recommendations from them
- The right chemistry with the people to be advised
- Sufficient accessibility to you
- Understanding of your business or profession and its issues
- Actual speaking or media experience
- Successful experience with situations related to those you are facing or expect to face
- Impressive written contributions to his or her field
- Facilities for speech or media interview training
- Reasonable fees

How Can You Advise an Executive That He or She Could Benefit From Communication Counsel?

Some executives are reluctant to seek or listen to feedback regarding their messages, delivery style, or image. They sense that such feedback, especially negative feedback, can injure their pride or ego. For this reason, their staff members are often reluctant to provide the feedback or recommend a professional who can.

If you face such a situation, or know someone who might, consider this advice:

- Compliment the executive genuinely on his or her ability to communicate, stressing the potential to become even more effective as a result of high-quality counsel.
- Explain how such counsel is not merely speech coaching per se. Rather, it is an in-depth examination of how to capture the persuasive edge. Clarify how the counsel focuses on such factors as goal setting, idea selection, word choice and organization, and audience psychology.
- For media interview counsel, explain the importance of a positive television or radio performance from two standpoints: the executive's image and that of the company. Also

be prepared to emphasize how important it is for the executive to understand the complexity of a media appearance, including what works and what doesn't work.

- If you want to avoid singling an executive out, it may be wise to select a group of executives for a presentation or media seminar. Being chosen is usually regarded as a compliment—as an executive perquisite.

- Sell the consultant's approach and potential for "good chemistry" with your executives. Since some executives are wary of working with a communication consultant because of horror stories regarding how a consultant "brutalized" an executive, you may need to reassure your executives that the consultant you have in mind is "safe."

- Sell the consulting firm itself. If members of the firm have helped prominent business or political leaders, their successful experience with the consultant may help him or her realize that "if one executive decided to use a communication consultant and found him or her helpful, then perhaps I should."

THE ETHICS OF EXECUTIVE COMMUNICATION

The English poet and critic Alexander Pope once said, "He who tells a lie is not sensible how great a task he undertakes; for he must be forced to invent twenty more to maintain that one."

Wise and timeless advice for sure. Yet pressures facing today's executives can often blur the distinction between truth and falsehood. When push comes to shove, can a white lie told by an executive to an audience, reporter, or government panel help preserve the corporation's image and his or her own career path? Possibly, but the risks are, as Pope stated, entirely too great.

In reviewing our ethical standards as communicators, we must draw a clear line between truthfulness and openness. Truthfulness means that whatever we say is, to the best of our knowledge, factual and free from distortion. Openness implies the extent to which the faucet of factual and interpretive information should be opened. Therefore, as communicators, we should be absolutely truthful, while our openness should be relative or situational.

In establishing a personal set of standards for ethical communication, we should adhere to the following advice:

- Be secure enough to say "I don't know" rather than feign knowledge—and possibly expose your charade unwittingly, thereby compromising your credibility.

- Combat any tendency to distort reality through the selective use of language, examples, numbers, or statistics.
- Scrutinize your logic for any tendency to engage in fallacious reasoning.
- Double- or triple-check your sources for accuracy, proper context, reputation, and recency.
- Check the methodology behind any studies on which your case depends.
- Avoid any temptation to fabricate examples or other data when your case seems deficient.
- Be prepared to acknowledge persons who deserve credit for the good ideas or expressions you are using.

When setting our standards for ethical communication, we can derive added insight and guidance from the well-chosen words of William Penn: "Truth often suffers more by the heat of its defenders than from the arguments of its opposers."

RECOMMENDED RESOURCES

Anecdotes

Boller, Jr., Paul F. *Presidential Anecdotes.* New York: Oxford University Press, 1981.

Fadiman, Clifton, ed. *The Little, Brown Book of Anecdotes.* Boston: Little, Brown and Company, 1985.

Fuller, Edmund, ed. *2,500 Anecdotes for All Occasions.* New York: Avenel Books, 1980.

Humes, James. *Speaker's Treasury of Anecdotes About the Famous.* New York: Harper & Row, Publishers, 1985.

Quotations

Bartlett, John. *Familiar Quotations.* Boston: Little, Brown and Company, 1968.

Brussell, Eugene, ed. *Dictionary of Quotable Definitions.* Englewood Cliffs, N.J.: Prentice-Hall, Inc., 1970.

Davidoff, Henry, ed. *The Pocket Book of Quotations.* New York: Pocket Books, 1952.

The Forbes Scrapbook of Thoughts on the Business of Life. New York: Forbes, Inc., 1976.

Frost, Elizabeth, ed. *The Bully Pulpit: Quotations from America's Presidents.* New York: Facts on File, 1988.

Lieberman, Gerald F. *3500 Good Quotes for Speakers.* Garden City, New York: Doubleday & Company, Inc., 1985.

The Oxford University Press. *Dictionary of Quotations.* New York: Crescent Books, 1953.

Humor

Braude, Jacob M. *Braude's Treasury of Wit and Humor.* Englewood Cliffs, N.J.: Prentice-Hall, 1964.
Humes, James C. *Podium Humor.* New York: Harper & Row, Publishers, 1975.
Meiers, Mildred and Knapp, Jack. *5600 Jokes for All Occasions.* New York: Avenel Books, 1980.
Moger, Art. *Complete Pun Book.* Secaucus, N.J.: Castle Books, 1979.
Orben, Robert. *The Ad-Libber's Handbook.* New York: Gramercy Publishing Company, 1978.

Language

Berrey, Lester V., ed. *Roget's International Thesaurus.* New York: Thomas Crowell, 1962.
Rogers, James. *The Dictionary of Clichés.* New York: Ballantine Books, 1985.
Urdang, Laurence. *The Basic Book of Synonyms and Antonyms.* Bergenfield, N.J.: Signet, New American Library, 1978.
Webster's Rhyming Dictionary. Secaucus, N.J.: Castle Books, 1980.
Why Do We Say It? The Stories Behind the Words, Expressions and Clichés We Use. Secaucus, N.J.: Castle Books, 1985.
Wilstach, Frank J. *A Dictionary of Similes.* Detroit: Gale Research Company, 1924.

General Reference

Berkman, Robert I. *Find It Fast.* New York: Harper & Row, 1987.
Burnam, Tom. *The Dictionary of MisInformation.* New York: Perennial Library, Harper & Row, Publishers, 1975.
Glass, Lillian. *Talk to Win.* New York: Perigee Books, The Putnam Publishing Group, 1987.
Levy, Judith and Greenhall, Agnes, eds. *The Concise Columbia Encyclopedia.* New York: Avon Books, 1983.
McCormick, Mona. *The New York Times Guide to Reference Materials.* New York: Dorset Press, 1985.

Scribner Desk Dictionary of American History. New York: Charles Scribner's Sons, 1984.

The World Almanac & Books of Facts (Year). New York: Newspaper Enterprise Association, Inc.

Anthologies

Copeland, Lewis and Lamm, Lawrence W., eds. *The World's Great Speeches.* New York: Dover Publications Inc., 1973.

Dickson, Paul. *Toasts.* New York: Dell Publishing Company, 1981.

Pendleton, Winston K. *Speaker's Handbook of Successful Openers and Closers.* Englewood Cliffs, N.J.: Prentice-Hall, Inc., 1984.

Spinrad, Leonard and Thelma. *Speaker's Lifetime Library.* West Nyack, N.Y.: Parker Publishing Company, Inc., 1983.

INDEX

About the Author

Myles Martel, Ph.D., president of Martel & Associates (Villanova, Pennsylvania), is one of America's premier executive communication consultants. He has advised and trained hundreds of the nation's corporate and political leaders (including twenty-six United States Senators) for speeches, presentations, and media appearances. He achieved national prominence in 1980 by serving as Ronald Reagan's personal debate advisor.

Dr. Martel has appeared on numerous radio and TV programs, including the *CBS Morning Show, ABC Nightly News* and *Nightline with Ted Koppel.* His work has been featured in several national publications, including the *Wall Street Journal, Harpers,* and *U.S. News & World Report.* He is the author of two other books: *Mastering the Art of Q&A: A Survival Guide for Tough, Trick, and Hostile Questions* and *Political Campaign Debates: Images, Strategies and Tactics.* He received his Ph.D. and M.A. in Speech Communication from Temple University and his B.A. from the University of Connecticut. He resides in Radnor, Pennsylvania, with his wife and son.

FOR FURTHER INFORMATION

If you wish to receive either or both of the following items, please send a self-addressed stamped envelope and your business card to:

MARTEL & ASSOCIATES
One Aldwyn Center
Villanova, PA 19085

☐ Periodic Executive Communication
Memoranda

☐ Additional Information Regarding the
Services of Martel & Associates

NOTE: Please use two or more 25-cent stamps if you select both items.